App Accomplished

Strategies for App Development Success

Carl Brown

Addison-Wesley

Upper Saddle River, NJ • Boston • Indianapolis • San Francisco
New York • Toronto • Montreal • London • Munich • Paris • Madrid
Cape Town • Sydney • Tokyo • Singapore • Mexico City

QA
76.76
.A65
BT6
2015

Many of the designations used by manufacturers and sellers to distinguish their products are claimed as trademarks. Where those designations appear in this book, and the publisher was aware of a trademark claim, the designations have been printed with initial capital letters or in all capitals.

The author and publisher have taken care in the preparation of this book, but make no expressed or implied warranty of any kind and assume no responsibility for errors or omissions. No liability is assumed for incidental or consequential damages in connection with or arising out of the use of the information or programs contained herein.

For information about buying this title in bulk quantities, or for special sales opportunities (which may include electronic versions; custom cover designs; and content particular to your business, training goals, marketing focus, or branding interests), please contact our corporate sales department at corpsales@pearsoned.com or (800) 382-3419.

For government sales inquiries, please contact governmentsales@pearsoned.com.

For questions about sales outside the U.S., please contact international@pearsoned.com.

Visit us on the Web: informit.com/aw

Library of Congress Control Number: 2014938789

ISBN-13: 978-0-321-96178-5
ISBN-10: 0-321-96178-1

Text printed in the United States on recycled paper at RR Donnelley in Crawfordsville, Indiana.

First printing: July 2014

Editor-in-Chief
Mark Taub

Senior Acquisitions Editor
Trina MacDonald

Development Editor
Sheri Cain

Managing Editor
Kristy Hart

Senior Project Editor
Betsy Gratner

Copy Editor
Kitty Wilson

Senior Indexer
Cheryl Lenser

Proofreader
Kathy Ruiz

Technical Reviewers
Mark Kolb
Wes Miller
Bob Wesson

Editorial Assistant
Olivia Basegio

Cover Designer
Alan Clements

Compositor
Nonie Ratcliff

This book is dedicated to the app creators, entrepreneurs, CEOs, and managers who have an idea for a mobile app and bother to find the money, take the time, and expend the effort to get the app built. You have fueled an impressive ecosystem the past few years, and I am proud to be a member of it. I hope this book will help you to get better apps for your money and effort.

Table of Contents

Foreword

Mobile apps have become big news and even bigger business in recent years. There are shockingly few people who haven't had the "next great app" idea. With frequent news of overnight millionaires and multibillion dollar buyouts, who can blame them for wanting to explore app development? What prevents most of these people from making their mark in the emerging app market is failing to understand the process of creating the app itself. A great idea with poor execution isn't worth anything, but even the most modest idea with fantastic execution can be a valuable product.

Despite all the popularity and buzz surrounding mobile applications, there hasn't been a publication focused on how to successfully plan and build a mobile app—until now. *App Accomplished* fills the same demand that pick-and-shovel salesmen did for nineteenth-century gold miners. Without a proper plan, the right tools, and resources, no app project can be successful, and certainly not on time and on budget.

Carl Brown has been a fixture within the app consulting world for many years. His views are from the trenches and are battle hardened. The current world of mobile development for hire is fraught with peril, from less-than-reputable development companies to outright scams. The release of the iPhone Software Development Kit (SDK) in 2008 was said to usher in a new gold rush era for developers. The landscape quickly shifted from a small community of just a few thousand registered developers to well over a million in just a few short years. With the influx of developers came a lot of fantastic talent as well as a small minority looking to take advantage of those seeking to mine gold. Carl's unabashed and realistically candid look at the current state of mobile development will help even the most novice entrepreneur get a leg up on the competition.

In an industry that is still very much in its infancy, Carl has more than a decade of experience working with some of the most demanding and challenging projects conceived. Development is often described as having to break down a complex task into thousands or even millions of very small problems. Building a mobile app, whether as a developer, designer, or entrepreneur, follows the same pattern. It is all about knowing how to see each step and how to resolve it properly. Carl's experience with software consulting stretches back more than 20 years, and he has solved countless app development problems. *App Accomplished* provides guidelines, advice, and recommendations to handle the potential pitfalls that you will encounter along your journey. For the first time in history, the knowledge from more than a decade of mobile experience fueled by hundreds of projects is available in an easy-to-follow reference.

From understanding the project and development life cycle to finding the perfect developer for your project, from conception to marketplace, *App Accomplished* will walk you through the entire app development process. Communicating with developers and designers can often be more challenging than building the business strategy of a project. If you cannot properly convey your intentions and feedback to your partners and team, time and money will be wasted before you can bring your true vision to life.

As someone who has overseen teams that have shipped more than a thousand mobile apps since the release of the iPhone, I wish that every one of our clients would first read *App Accomplished* before hiring us. The information presented, from the author's warnings of potential pitfalls and beyond, provides the reader with the knowledge needed to understand the development process. Those aspiring mobile entrepreneurs who have a rich understanding of the process will encounter fewer disputes, speed bumps, costly change orders, and overall frustration. Thoroughly understanding the topics discussed on the following pages can easily save a not insignificant portion on the cost of development and design by repeating the history of those who have come before you.

—**Kyle Richter**

Kyle Richter is Chief Executive Officer of MartianCraft, a leading mobile development studio. He is the coauthor of *iOS Components and Frameworks: Understanding the Advanced Features of the iOS SDK* (Addison-Wesley, 2013) and author of *Beginning iOS Social Games* (Apress, 2013) and *Beginning iOS Game Center and Game Kit: For iPhone, iPad, and iPod touch* (Apress, 2011).

Preface

You have an idea for a mobile app. You want to build it, but you don't have the expertise or the time to build it yourself. So what do you do?

You need to know three things:

1. How to distinguish between a developer who can do a good job with your app and one who can't
2. How to work with your chosen developer to get the best result you can
3. Why 1 and 2 are important

Who This Book Is For

This book is for anyone who has an idea for an app. For the purposes of this book, I define *app* as any mobile smartphone or tablet software application that is available for download from one or more of the app stores, like Apple's App Store, Google Play, Amazon's App Store, or Microsoft's Windows Phone Store. This book talks about the skills and processes needed to make a successful app.

No matter what skills you possess (even if you're a programmer), you're unlikely to have all the skills needed yourself. So I'll talk about how to acquire those skills, either by learning them yourself or by hiring or contracting with another person.

This book is about how to turn your app idea into the best possible app, based on the resources you have.

What This Book Is Not

This book is not a "get rich quick on the App Store" book. I don't believe there is a one-size-fits-all formula for guaranteed success.

This book is not about validating or marketing your idea. I've seen apps that I thought were sure-fire hits go nowhere, and I've seen apps that I laughingly insisted no one would waste money on pull in more than $10,000 in one day.

The same old rules of marketing apply for apps: You have to find a real market, and you have to solve a real problem (or get insanely lucky, but don't count on that). If you want to know how to determine if your app is likely to make any money, start by searching online for "lean startup." Once you've decided that people will pay money for your idea, come back to this book for help building it.

This book is not about how to write code. I briefly discuss code, but this is more about process than code. This is also not a book about graphic design or user experience design.

This book is also not the One True Way™ to create an app. It's a collection of techniques and strategies that I've found helpful, but apps can be (and have been) built successfully without them. I'm not saying that you *must* do things the book's way.

Finally, this book, being a book, is not going to be the most up-to-date resource available on mobile app development. Specific how-to instructions and details placed herein would become out of date before this book went to press. Therefore, I've created a companion website and blog at http://AppAccomplished.com that contains more current information. I'll be able to keep the website updated over time, as new tools and platforms are released and old ones fall by the wayside. This way, I can keep the book's content focused on the "what and why" of mobile development; you can find out about the "how" elsewhere.

Why This Book

More than anything else, this book is about how to get your app built while making the most of your time and money. Hiring an app developer is effectively placing a bet (or making an investment). This book gives you the tools and techniques to increase your odds of success as much as I know how.

There's nothing in my professional life I dread more than looking over the code for an app on which someone has spent tens of thousands of dollars or hundreds and hundreds of hours (or both), and having to tell them that they are much, much further from a salable product than they believe.

In addition to the personal unpleasantness, it's bad for the profession, and for everyone involved. Lots of money is wasted, lots of effort is squandered, and many apps that could have made an impact never see the light of day.

There is no 100% dependable way to make sure you have a successful project. This is very important, so I'll say it again: *There is no 100% dependable way to make sure you have a successful project.* It is, however, possible to dramatically increase your chance of success. Most failed projects that I've been asked to evaluate have failed in particular ways and had warning signs and red flags all along. This book helps you make the most of your odds, avoid the common traps, and recognize the warning signs as they appear.

How This Book Is Organized

To the extent possible (excluding Chapter 1, which is about why you need this book), this book is organized chronologically as you go through the app development process. However, I structured it so that you don't have to read it in order. You should be able to start reading at whatever place is most relevant to your particular project and find references to other relevant material as you need it.

Here's a brief summary of what you'll find in each chapter:

- **Chapter 1, "What Could Possibly Go Wrong?"**—Explains some of the common misconceptions about mobile app development and gives some reasons many app projects fail.

- **Chapter 2, "The App Development Life Cycle"**—Provides an overview of the high-level steps in the app development process.

- **Chapter 3, "Prototyping and Wireframing Your App"**—Explains how to turn your app idea into something a developer can understand how to develop.

- **Chapter 4, "Determining Your App's Components"**—Provides a list of the different kinds of technologies, libraries, features, and functionalities that are commonly used in mobile apps and explains what each is and why you might want to include it in your app.

- **Chapter 5, "Finding the Right Tools"**—Provides a list of the different services and kinds of development environments and tools that are used to build apps and explains why and when you might use them.

- **Chapter 6, "Skill Gap Analysis"**—Explains how to figure out what skills you need to get your app built and how to figure out which ones you are missing and what you might do about that.

- **Chapter 7, "Finding a Developer"**—Explains the different kinds of potential development resources you might use, where each can be found, and the pros and cons of each.

- **Chapter 8, "Interviewing and Selecting a Developer"**—Discusses the process of determining whether a particular developer might be a good fit for your app project.

- **Chapter 9, "Managing to Milestones"**—Explains how app projects can be organized and managed and gives some recommendations about strategies that have worked for me.

- **Chapter 10, "Understanding What You're Getting"**—Explains how to estimate the quality of the app you are getting and the code that is being written for it.

- **Chapter 11, "Pulling the Plug Early"**—Explains how to determine how far off track your project seems and how to decide whether it's recoverable.

- **Chapter 12, "Communicating Using Bugs"**—Explains how to use a bug or issue tracking tool to communicate with your present and future development teams.

- **Chapter 13, "Testing"**—Explains how to find and work with testers of your app to get the quality you need.

- **Chapter 14, "Submission and Beyond"**—Discusses submitting your app to an app store, what to do if it gets rejected, and how to start planning your follow-up release.

The Case Studies

You'll find sidebars like this throughout this book. These are based on real projects that had real problems and provide examples of the issues being discussed. I've anonymized them by avoiding identifying specific apps, people, and companies. Sometimes, when maintaining privacy dictated it, I also changed some details that didn't directly impact the points under illustration. They all really happened, though.

Acknowledgments

I need to start by thanking my wife, Penny, and my daughter, Tamara, for the many hours I spent writing instead of spending time with them. I love you both, and I couldn't have done this without your help and support.

The guidance of my editor, Trina MacDonald, has been invaluable, especially during the initial stages, when we were trying to figure out what this book should be. I'd like to thank my technical reviewers: Wes Miller for his writer's eye and his encouragement, Bob Wesson for his app creator's perspective, and Mark Kolb for another app developer's second opinion. Thanks also to Olivia Basegio, for herding the necessary cats (yours truly included), and Sheri Cain, for making me sound like a professional author.

Thanks also to John and Nicole Wilker of 360|iDev, who encouraged me to become a conference speaker, and Mike Lee, who pushed me to step up my presentation game—without any of whom I'm unlikely to have been asked to write a book in the first place. Likewise, I am grateful to Brandon Alexander, Bill Dudney, Kevin Kim, and Kirby Turner, who shared with me some of their experiences writing their own books, along with Joe Keeley, Graham Lee, Erik Price, David Fox, and (once again) Wes Miller, for reviewing and providing valuable feedback on the early outlines of this book as it was taking shape.

About the Author

Carl Brown (@CarlBrwn) started writing software for client companies while working at EDS in 1993. He became enamored of developing for mobile connected devices in 2005, starting with the Palm VII and moving on to Windows CE. Since 2008, he's been focused primarily on the iOS app market (with some Android thrown in). He's worked on dozens of apps, starting with the Calorie Tracker for LIVESTRONG.com. He's also been brought in to rescue a number of troubled or failing app projects, with varied success. He's a frequent speaker at the annual 360|iDev iOS developer conference and a speaker and organizer with CocoaCoder.org, the largest Mac and iOS developer meet-up group in Austin, Texas, where he lives with his wife and daughter.

Editor's Note: We Want to Hear from You!

As the reader of this book, you are our most important critic and commentator. We value your opinion and want to know what we're doing right, what we could do better, what areas you'd like to see us publish in, and any other words of wisdom you're willing to pass our way.

You can e-mail or write me directly to let me know what you did or didn't like about this book—as well as what we can do to make our books stronger.

Please note that I cannot help you with technical problems related to the topic of this book, and that due to the high volume of mail I receive, I might not be able to reply to every message.

When you write, please be sure to include this book's title and author as well as your name and phone or e-mail address. I will carefully review your comments and share them with the author and editors who worked on the book.

E-mail: trina.macdonald@pearson.com

Mail: Trina MacDonald
Senior Acquisitions Editor
Addison-Wesley/Pearson Education, Inc.
75 Arlington St., Ste. 300
Boston, MA 02116

What Could Possibly Go Wrong?

In my consulting practice, I am often asked to take over, or at least examine, app development projects that are in trouble. Usually, months of effort and tens of thousands of dollars have been expended, and I often find that the quality of the existing development is so bad that it would be less work to just start over. I dread few things more than breaking that bad news to entrepreneurs, business owners, and managers. Those conversations are unpleasant and heartbreaking.

I fervently hope the information in this book can reduce the frequency of those conversations—not just for me but for all competent contract app developers.

One aspect of most of those conversations is surprise that the situation could possibly be so bad. Part of it is pure denial: People never want to find out they've wasted their effort. But I think there's more to it than that. I think that there is a common misconception that apps are easy to make and that any developer ought to be able to make them. Unfortunately, that is simply not the case.

App Projects Are Not Small and Easy

Compared to enterprise software running on a desktop or in a web browser, it's true that apps are smaller and cheaper, but that's really not saying a whole lot. A fairly typical iPhone app project in 2014 can take two or three developers three or four months and can easily run between a hundred thousand and a quarter of a million lines of code. While that's not a lot compared to some kinds of development, it's not trivial.

Through the years, many studies have reported that a significant percentage of software projects fail (although the percentage can vary wildly). App projects are definitely software projects, and they have many of the same issues and risks as any other software project. App projects can and do fail—some of them spectacularly. I haven't seen any studies specifically on the percentage of app development projects that fail, but I'd expect it to be similar.

I would say that anecdotally more than half and maybe as many as two-thirds of app projects I have knowledge of would be considered failures under the criteria outlined in the following sections. Several examples of such project failures can be found in sidebars in this chapter (and throughout the rest of this book). This is not a scientific survey, and I don't know how representative my experience might be. I have talked to many would-be app creators about what it would take to rescue their failed projects (some I could help, many I could not), and this might skew my experience. However, I know other app developers who have also spent a significant amount of time attempting to rescue failed projects and their anecdotal estimates are comparable.

Defining Project Failure

Let's talk about what I mean by the word *failure* in the context of app development. Different people and different studies use different definitions, which is likely part of the reason that different studies reach such different conclusions. When I say a project *failed*, I mean that one of these four things happened:

- The app failed to ship (that is, didn't become available to users).
- The app failed to work (that is, didn't work as intended for a noticeable percentage of intended users).
- The project cost significantly more money than planned (more than 10% or 20% over budgeted funding).
- The project took significantly more time than planned (more than 10% or 20% over budgeted time).

Let's talk through these situations.

First, the app has to ship. I think we can all agree that if the app was never seen by any user in its target audience, then the project failed. You have to ship in order to succeed. End of story. This is the least controversial of my criteria.

Second, the app has to work. This doesn't mean that the app has to be bug-free, as virtually none of them are. But the end user has to be able to use it in order for it to be called a success. This can be a subjective criterion; there can be legitimate arguments on both sides about whether an app is "useable" or "functional." For purposes of determining via this criterion whether an app has failed, though, it's usually either clear or irrelevant. (This criterion is irrelevant if the last two criteria fail, and if the app's functionality is in question, they usually do.)

Finally, the app can't have gone significantly over budget or schedule. These final two are the most controversial of my criteria, but I stand by them. I live in a world where I have customers, and those customers are depending on me to produce an app for them. Those customers care how much it's going to cost and when it's going to be done, and they need to plan on that.

Getting Clarity on Functionality

The second criterion, "the app has to work," is necessarily subjective. It depends very much on the nature of the app and the project, and it's just not possible for a book to give an unambiguously measurable way to determine functionality for any possible project. But that doesn't mean you can't.

Every app creator should (although most don't) insist on writing into the contract (or an accompanying statement of work) criteria for determining whether an app is considered fully functional. Agreeing on that up front (and amending it as you go, if needed) can save a lot of disagreement later.

Project Success Is Mostly About Estimates

Notice that the last two criteria—the project cost significantly more money or took significantly more time than planned—make a distinction between the outcome for the app itself and the project that produced it. It's possible (and not uncommon) for an app to be launched successfully but the project that produced it to have been a failure. Many contract app developers who get paid by the hour would likely count such a project as a success. If the app makes it to market and gets good reviews and the client company paid the bill, then most contractors are happy, even if it took twice as long and cost three times as much as planned.

To me, this feels dishonest. If a contracting company tells you that they will build your app for $50,000, but in the end you end up paying $75,000 or $100,000 or more, I consider that a bait-and-switch tactic. And it's unfortunate because it creates an incentive for contracting companies to generate unrealistically low estimates, knowing that they'll just charge the customer more in the end.

Project Success Is Also About Scope

An estimate, however, is only valid for a given *scope* (a given set of features). If new functionality is added to a project, then the budget and schedule have to be revised.

There is sometimes a disagreement about whether a given feature or bug or issue is within scope. Assuming that everyone is acting in good faith, such disagreements result from failure in the communication process between the client and contractor. Scope should be documented unambiguously.

Communication failures arise consistently, though, and often contractors who work on a time-and-materials basis choose not to clearly define the scope. Assuming that they can talk their clients into continuing to pay, this is to their advantage.

Another tactic contractors use is ignoring the scope as agreed and beginning work on new features as if they are in scope. This leads to unpleasant conversations after the work has been done. It should be incumbent on a contract developer to make sure any changes to the scope are mutually agreed upon and documented before work on the new functionality begins.

The Specter of Unprofitability

There is one important factor about an app project's success that these criteria do not take into account: *profitability*. I can't consider profitability in my criteria because I don't generally have access to app revenue information. All I (or any contract app developer) can do is build the best app I can within the time and budget I promised.

But profitability (or at least return on investment [ROI]) should be important to app creators. And if I had access to profitability information and could consider ROI goals as a failure criterion, then I would expect an even higher percentage of app projects to be failures. As it stands, app projects have to make it all the way through the funnel depicted in Figure 1.1 to be ultimately successful. I don't know what percentage of apps fail at each stage, but I'm confident that a large percentage of them don't make it all the way to profitability.

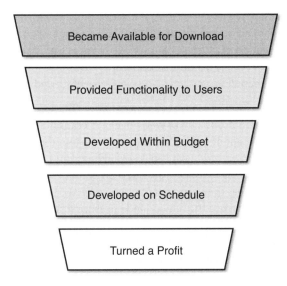

Figure 1.1
App projects must work through this funnel to be ultimately successful to their creators.

Apps Are Not Easy to Program

App development requires skill and experience. Because of the relative lack of raw computing power, one of the difficulties with mobile development is that the code in an app is fairly interdependent. It's unfortunately way too easy for this piece of code in this part of the app over here to have an effect on that piece of code in that part of the app over there. So the developer has to be extra careful.

Our Expectations Were Set by the Web…

We software developers as an industry got somewhat spoiled during the late 1990s and early 2000s because much of the exciting work being done in technology used web technologies and web servers. And the good thing about web servers at the dawn of the century is that really powerful servers could be purchased for a modest amount of money. With the rise of the 64-bit PC CPU, servers could hold more RAM than most web transactions could ever use, and it became not just feasible but expected for servers to hold entire databases in memory cache.

Add to that the fact that web protocols themselves were becoming widely adopted, and it became easier than ever to build a web application that could be reached by millions or tens of millions of users with a relatively small team of programmers working out of someone's garage. Web protocols also allowed the creation of much richer user experiences than had previously been possible for widely distributed applications because the layout rendering, font handling, and image display were offloaded to the machine running the web browser.

The good thing about this kind of web development is that each web request is mostly independent of every other web request, and the servers have enough power that each request can have all the resources it wants. Under enough traffic, that ceases to be true, but then at that point, it's relatively simple (assuming that things are engineered correctly) to put more web servers in parallel and use the networking infrastructure to share the incoming traffic load between them. Eventually if a service became popular enough, it would start running into tricky scaling problems that required a lot of performance tuning, but a lot of companies avoided this entirely.

...And Then Invalidated in the Mobile World

But mobile development has different constraints and requires different techniques. There's never as much memory in the device as the app developer wants because memory banks draw too much power, and battery life is the overriding concern of the device vendor. All the graphics have to be drawn on the device's screen as well, so you don't have the luxury of offloading it to another machine as you can with the web. And apps don't even have exclusive use of the device; there's often mail being fetched or music being played in the background, and the app could be interrupted at any instant if a phone call or text message comes in. This means that apps are constantly resource constrained. It's a delicate balancing act that doesn't happen so often in the web world.

So the situation in mobile app development today is much closer to the client/server programming of the 1980s and 1990s than the web programming of the early 2000s. The primary differences from a programming standpoint are that mobile platforms have far, far better development environments (developer tools, frameworks, libraries, and components) than existed back in the heyday of client/server, and mobile apps generally only have to implement the client half of the client/server equation. Figure 1.2 shows the major differences between web, enterprise, and mobile development.

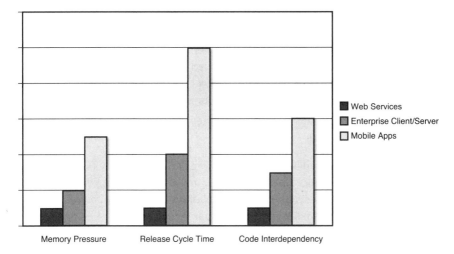

Figure 1.2
Visualization of the three largest differences between mobile app development and other common types.
(Shorter bars are better in this case.)

Mobile Apps Are Outside Your Control

The other thing that web servers made us lazy about is bugs (and I say that as a recovering ASP.Net and Ruby on Rails programmer). The nice thing about writing server code is that when something goes wrong, you can figure out what happened (hopefully) from the server logs, and you can make a change and push it to the servers and fix the bug before it affects too many of your users (again, hopefully). There were times, especially immediately after particularly poorly tested releases, that teams I've worked on have done a dozen or so different releases of web server code in a day, each one fixing one or more bugs or performance problems. And the great thing there is that as soon as the server is patched, every subsequent web request will get the fixed behavior.

In mobile app development, by contrast, you can't iterate as quickly. Once an app is installed on a user's phone, only that user can decide to upgrade to the next version of the app. Depending on the bug, the user might choose to just delete your app instead of update it (and maybe even leave a bad review). But even worse, in mobile app development, you don't ever have direct access to the machine your code is running on, so if there's a problem, you can't just look at your server logs and find it. Tracking down a bug that's happening only on a subset of smartphones and tablets and doesn't happen for the developer can be a real nightmare.

And last but not least, there's often the dreaded "Waiting for Review" lag. Although some app stores, like Google Play, will let you upload new app versions as soon as you've fixed a bug, other stores, like those from Apple and Amazon, require your update to be reviewed before it can be released, and that causes even more time to elapse between when a bug is brought to your attention and when a fix is available to your users.

Poor Skill Set Fit

Some parts of mobile development are more difficult than others, and some are relatively easy. Unfortunately, it's not immediately obvious which parts are which, and it varies from platform to platform. It's actually common for a developer who is familiar with one programming language or library to believe that familiarity is more relevant when moving to a new programming language or platform than it actually is.

Example: Threading on the iPhone

Most development platforms and operating systems these days have something called *threads*, which you can think of as containers inside an app into which commands are placed so that they can be executed. By having multiple threads, an app can do more than one thing at the same time (or nearly the same time). For example, one thread can be redrawing the app's screen as it scrolls, while another thread is downloading a video that will be displayed at a later time.

If a programmer knows how threads work, and that programmer learns that iOS (the operating system that runs on the iPhone and iPad) has threads, that programmer can easily assume that he or she knows how to make the iPhone do multiple things simultaneously. But he or she would be wrong. Although the iPhone does have threads, it also has queues, and Apple recommends that programmers should almost always use queues, and Apple's libraries then manage the threads automatically. Programmers who don't realize this often use the wrong mechanism and create their own threads, which can cause the app to malfunction under load.

The bad news is that when there isn't a whole lot going on (for example, when you're using small amounts of test data), spawning your own threads works fine. If the programmer assumes that it will work the same way with a lot of data, then he or she will likely fail to test at higher loads. Such an app may develop unexpected, undesired, and likely unacceptable behavior right at the end of the development cycle.

Your App Isn't Just Any App

The takeaway is that different apps need different skills, and just because developers did a good job with someone else's app doesn't necessarily mean they can do a good job with yours, unless the apps are really similar. Unfortunately, you can't always rely on developers to volunteer what skills your app needs that they lack (especially since it's in their best interest for you to hire them, and for you to do that, they want you to think they know what they are doing).

But don't worry. In Chapter 4, "Determining Your App's Components," you'll learn how to figure out what skills your app needs, and in Chapters 7, "Finding a Developer," and 8, "Interviewing and Selecting a Developer," you'll learn how to select the developer who is the best fit you can find.

The Case of the Videos Hung by a Thread

I was once asked to talk to app creators who were having problems with their app. It was presented to me as yet another one of the many mythical "it's 90% of the way to being done" projects (which has never actually been the case…see the section later in this chapter called "That Last 10%"). The app creators had fired the original developer and were looking for someone to finish the project before an impending deadline.

The app creators had actually done a better job at selecting a developer than I am used to seeing. The app being built was an audio/visual (A/V) app that let users create their own multimedia content. The developer who had been chosen had built several (as I remember it) disc jockey and A/V mixing apps that seem to have done well in Apple's App Store. The developer had also been recommended by an acquaintance of the app creators. So the developer seemed like a logical fit from the perspectives of both skill set and work ethic.

One critical feature was missing, though. The app required that the user would be able to upload completed A/V files to a server, and that feature was a complete disaster. First off, the app, as written, required the user to leave the phone on the *Uploading* screen until the upload was complete. There was no status indicator, so the user didn't know how long the upload would take, and the app appeared to be *hung* (also referred to as being *locked-up*, or unresponsive). In addition, if the user went to any other screen in the app, touched the Home button, launched another app, or received a phone call or text message, the upload would stop. As a result, the upload almost never worked.

The developer (I'm told) insisted to the app creators that what they wanted wasn't possible, despite the fact that there were a number of apps already in the app store that did the same thing. After some dispute to which I wasn't a party, the app creators and the developer parted ways, and then the app creators came to me.

By looking at the code, I discovered that the previous developer seemed to have no concept of threads or background tasks (discussed further in Chapter 4). It appeared that the developer had come to mobile development from Flash development, which is a technology where background tasks aren't an option. My guess is that the successful apps this developer had written previously managed to work without needing to use more than one thread, but large network data transfers absolutely require multiple things to be happening simultaneously.

Unfortunately, it wasn't feasible for the app to be completed before the deadline, so I wasn't able to solve the app creators' immediate problem.

As discussed further in Chapter 8, there are two questions that the app creators could have asked that might have prevented this problem:

- Have you ever written code that performed a large file upload? This question would have illuminated the potential risk and allowed everyone to manage it differently.

- What resources for honing mobile development skills have you recently used, and where would you turn if something unfamiliar came up during the project? Apple and many third parties have created tutorials, videos, and documents that explain how large file uploads should be done on a background thread. Asking this question would have uncovered the fact that this developer wasn't familiar with any of those.

If You Get a Good Developer, You Still Have to Worry

Although it is certainly true that inexperienced programmers have far lower success rates than established firms, despite what the established firms might want you to believe, there is plenty of failure to go around. Once cost and schedule overruns are considered, even established firms have an uncomfortably high percentage of failures.

The good news is that with well-established firms, in order for a project to fail, something has to have gone wrong. The bad news is that these days, things go wrong surprisingly often.

Inexperienced Members of an Experienced Firm

In the current app development business climate, demand is outstripping supply by a large margin. This causes a number of problems: Hiring is nearly constant, turnover is high, and responsibilities are in flux pretty much across the board. It's not unusual for most or all of a project team at a reputable development firm to have been hired in the past few months.

It's also common for existing employees to be promoted from developer to lead developer, often so there is someone to supervise newly hired junior developers placed under them. The skills needed to be a successful member of a project team are but a subset of the skills needed to lead a project team, and mistakes made when learning development supervision and project management skills can mean the difference between the success and failure of a project.

Subcontractors

Another consequence of demand outstripping supply is that firms often have more business than they can handle. Instead of turning away business, many subcontract some of their business out to other developers, taking some percentage of the revenue off the top. Since the firm that signed the deal wants to make some money, it stands to reason that the subcontractor will be working for less money than the original firm's prices (that is, the subcontractor is almost always a cheaper developer). The communication between the original firm and the subcontractor is also likely to be inferior to the communication that the original firm would have with its own employees.

Juggling Resources

When any project at any company goes wrong, the company working on it usually tries to fix it. The good news is that if your project is being developed by a reputable firm and something goes wrong, the company will likely do its best to marshal its resources and attempt to get your project back on track. The bad news is that if your project is going fine and some other project at the firm you are paying goes off the rails, the resources on your project may be pulled off (fully or partially) to try to shore up that other project. This can have a negative impact on your project and can seem to come out of nowhere, even when a project seems to be going well.

Contractor Company Overhead

Another question with large firms, reputable or otherwise, is what the firm considers *billable*. Some firms consider time spent on internal activities, meetings, emails, and conferences calls billable to you, even when those activities don't involve your project (or involve it only peripherally). This can cause your budget to get used up by activities that aren't related to your project.

Another overhead item is hours billed to project management (often at a high rate). If your firm is billing you for project management time, you need to make sure that you understand what that time is spent on and decide whether that amount of money is worth it to you.

It's Important to Know What You've Signed Up For

The solution to all these issues (and many more) is to clearly document up front exactly what you're paying for. You need to know what team is actually going to be working on your project, what their experience is, what their relationship to the firm you are paying is, and under what, if any, circumstances those staffing arrangements might change. You need to know what the firm considers billable work and what that work will be. If you're paying higher rates to get an established, experienced development firm, then you are paying to have experienced staff working on your project, and you need to make sure that happens.

The Idea Is Not More Important Than the Execution

A common fallacy is that once you get an idea for a great app, you're most of the way there. In fact, that's not the case at all. As with most other inventions, a truly exceptional idea is still only the first step in the process of making an app.

In the process of making an app out of that idea, literally thousands of additional decisions have to be made. Some of those decisions involve colors, graphics, data storage, workflow, architecture, layout, transitions, animations, and monetization, and each of these requires even more related decisions. Some of the decisions you need to make have a wide-ranging impact on the success of the app, and some have little or none. It's not always possible to tell how much of an app's success or failure is attributable to any particular decision. In general, I've found that app creators often underestimate the impact of each of the little decisions.

Each decision must be executed upon and turned into code, and that code becomes part of the final app. There are lots of opportunities for poor execution in this phase that can render an otherwise fantastic idea unworkable.

There Is No Idea So Good That It Can't Be Poorly Executed

There's a tendency I've seen among app creators to become so enamored of their idea that they don't want to worry about anything else. They often say (or think) they are looking for a developer to "implement their idea," by which they mean to make all the decisions and execute those decisions, often in return for half (or less) of the app's eventual revenue. I've never seen or heard of this strategy working out (which doesn't mean it can't, but it's definitely a low-percentage bet).

The root cause of this situation is usually that the app creator doesn't participate in the decision-making process except at a very high level. In such a case, the developers end up implementing their own vision instead of the app creator's, slavishly copying some other app, or just guessing what the app creator wants.

In the virtually certain event that the app creator is unsatisfied with the result, an adversarial relationship usually forms between the app creator and the developer. The app creators point out things that they consider to be obvious deficiencies (but generally can't articulate or communicate alternatives in sufficient detail to be implemented). The developer, frustrated, builds something else that is still unlikely to appease the app creators. And the cycle often repeats.

Programmers often refer to this as "rock fetching," and it can be hugely frustrating. Imagine the following scenario:

> Your boss: "Bring me a rock."
>
> You, after bringing back a rock: "Here is a rock for you."
>
> Your boss: "I don't like that one. Bring me a different rock."
>
> You, after getting a different one: "How about this one?"
>
> Your boss: "No, I don't want that one either."
>
> You: "What's wrong with it?"
>
> Your boss: "I just don't like it."
>
> You: "What kind of rock are you looking for?"
>
> Your boss: "A better one than that one."
>
> You: "Better how?"
>
> Your boss: "You know, better. Rockier. More rock-like."
>
> You, confused and hesitating: "Uhhhhh."
>
> Your boss: "What are you waiting for? Bring me a rock."

Most people find rock fetching irritating. It certainly doesn't facilitate a person's best work. Given enough of this, most people will eventually quit. But when app creators refuse to involve themselves with detailed questions about how an app should look or work and either don't know or can't communicate what they really want, they create a rock-fetching scenario.

A word of warning: Some developers love this kind of app creator and are happy to continue billing by the hour to write code that will be rejected until the app creator runs out of money. Personally, I find this distasteful, but some legitimate developers make the argument that they aren't responsible for their customers' whims or lack of requirements. And they have a point. Caveat emptor.

The Case of "Facebook for *Insert Demographic Here*" for Four Times the Price

I was once approached by an app creator who had been unable to get his app launched, despite having spent many months and many tens of thousands of dollars having it developed. From his initial description, I could tell that the project was in a late-stage failure mode that is always a hard state to recover from. I arranged to meet him for lunch and sat down with him to talk about what had been happening with his project.

At lunch, he spent roughly twice as much time telling me about how great his app idea was as he spent on how the project had gone. This was difficult for me because (1) I was there to figure out what was going on with his project, not how much money he thought his app would make and (2) the idea wasn't good. (Not that it matters for this story, but his idea was "I'm going to make a new social network just like Facebook, except targeted at this one particular market segment of the population." I hear that idea every few months with a different segment of the population, and none of them have gotten any traction.)

He asked his current developer to send him the latest copy of the source code they had built for him so far, and he gave it to me to look at. Based on the wireframes, the requirements, and the source control, I thought he had spent about three times as long and about four times as much money as I would have estimated in order to have built it by myself.

As I looked through the code, I realized what had been happening. The developers had built many, many different versions of the app, one after the other. They would build a version and present it to the app creator. He would tell them to do it differently, and perhaps make some vague suggestions. They would then pile his new suggestions on top of the existing code and show it to him again. Over time, they had written tons and tons of code, much of which was from several iterations ago and no longer called but had never been cleaned up. It was incredibly difficult and time-consuming just to understand what was supposed to do what and what should have been deleted. It was a horrid mess.

I wrote up my set of recommendations for getting his code cleaned up and for creating a well-defined set of features and documenting them before doing any more development. I gave him my recommendations document and never heard back (which wasn't surprising, as I didn't have time to take on more development tasks at the time, so having me do his development wasn't an option). As near as I can tell, that app never made it to any app store.

Unwillingness to Delegate: Micromanaging

If refusing to get involved in discussions about the details of their app is on one end of the app creator engagement spectrum, the opposite extreme is micromanaging, and it's no less destructive.

Some app creators insist on being far too involved in the minutia of their projects. They question the necessity of every code change and want justifications for every hour spent. They're insistent on getting exactly what they think they want and/or spending as little money as possible, but they end up forcing work to be done over (and therefore wasted) and making people wait on them. Causing developers to wait for someone to make a decision is a waste of time and money, and causing them to have to do something over is a waste of time, money, and goodwill.

It's important for app creators to have control over what happens on their projects. I'm not trying to contradict that at all. The question is one of frequency. The vast majority of the time developers spend on a project should be time spent doing development. That's what developers are being paid to do, and it's where their expertise is. That sounds obvious, but it's quite often not what happens.

There's a way for app creators to maintain control of their projects, and it's to make (and document) decisions the developer needs to have made before the developer needs them, so the developer doesn't have to wait (or guess wrong and do it over). A good developer should be able to generate a list of questions that are going to need to be answered far enough ahead of time to give the app creator time to think and decide. If you as an app creator find that your developer is having to wait on you, or that you are frequently asking your developer to redo things a different way, it's time to have a conversation about doing a better job about defining requirements.

We'll discuss this more in Chapter 2, "The App Development Life Cycle." For now, understand that it's not necessary for all the requirements for an entire app to be completely documented before any development starts, but it is important for developers to know what's required of the piece of functionality they are currently working on when they start it. Not doing so leads to wasted time and money and can put the whole project at risk.

Bikeshedding

Some projects feature endless repetitive design meetings with arguments over font sizes, RGB color values, and pixel-level control placement. The developers are paralyzed and spend a lot of (billable) time waiting for decisions to be made by the client, and progress is correspondingly slowed.

I'm not implying that control placement or color choice aren't important—they are—but they should take up a relatively small portion of the overall project budget and schedule (at least for the vast majority of apps).

C. Northcote Parkinson coined the term *bikeshedding* in 1957 for groups spending far more time arguing about things that don't matter than things that do. The canonical example is a group of townspeople tasked with commenting on plans for a nuclear reactor spending their time arguing about the color of the bike shed at the reactor. Obviously, the color of the bike shed makes no difference to the efficiency or safety of the reactor, but it's something that everyone in the group can feel qualified to have an opinion about. Everyone wants his or her opinion to be heard about *something* and to leave a mark on the project, so any trivial item can become a source of arguments. For the important things (like cooling redundancy and radiation shielding), the nuclear experts' opinions are usually left unquestioned because no townspeople in the group feel qualified to argue those points and don't want to be responsible if they turn out to have been wrong.

Most app creators don't have much (if any) experience with app programming, and so they don't feel qualified to weigh in on issues of coding style and data models. They do, however, often feel that they are qualified to give opinions about colors and fonts and graphic design. So in trying to feel in control, they cause large amounts of time to be spent on noncritical items.

Poorly Defined Requirements

With software, the old adage is true: "The devil is in the details." Software can have lots of details, and each one has to be decided upon and communicated. As discussed in the proceeding sections, sometimes the details aren't considered important, and sometimes they become the source of arguments, but sometimes the problem is one of communication. On many projects, the app creator has an understanding of what he or she wants the app to do but does a poor job of transferring that understanding to the developer who is doing the implementation.

Sometimes this is because the app creator is trying to avoid what he or she considers unnecessary paperwork. When this is the case, requirements documents, if they exist at all, often take the form of lists of bullet points—short phrases that can mean very different things to different people. Often the developers don't object to this because they don't like paperwork, either. Then the developers implement what they think is meant by a given line item, the app creator thinks that work has just started on it, and the cycle repeats for a while. It usually comes to a head when the developers check some number of items off the list, and the app creator objects because those items aren't done yet. Arguments and recriminations may follow from there, and the likelihood of a successful project is greatly diminished.

Other times, the opposite is true. On projects for very large companies, sometimes the requirements document is a large binder full of contradictory legalese that is the output of many rounds of the request for proposal (RFP) process. Verbiage from an early section implies that a feature should be implemented one way, and many pages later in the binder, an answer to an RFP question seems to say that a different implementation is required. Jargon can be a problem here, too, as large organizations often create their own vocabulary. Here, the problem is not a lack of detail but a lack of clarity.

In either case, what ends up happening is that both sides work on the project as if they understand each other—after all, there is documentation that purportedly explains what should be built. The project can go a long time like this, with both sides thinking that everything is going well. And then one day, one side says something that the other side disagrees with, and then the gloves come off. Voices are raised and accusations fly as the two sides begin to realize how far apart they are. Success is not a likely outcome.

The Case of the Required Preferences

I was once asked to look at an incomplete app project that had already passed its initial estimated completion date. It had a requirements document that was a giant list of one-liners like "The user must be able to specify preferences."

The developer interpreted this particular line to mean that the app was required to have a settings screen (which it did). On the other hand, the app creator expected an elaborate menu system that synced with the server so that if the user had an iPhone and an Android tablet and changed the preferences on one that those preferences would be reflected on the other. The app creator justified this by pointing out another line in the document that said that the iOS and Android versions should be "functionally interchangeable" (or words to that effect).

The developer had expected this requirement to take at most a day, but what the app creator wanted would take multiple developers a week or more, including adding additional capabilities to the server platform. And because this was just one of many insufficiently specified requirements, it was no surprise (at least to me) that the project had run way over on both schedule and budget.

The other problem was that the discrepancy between the developer's and app creator's expectations didn't come to light until well past the point when the project was initially estimated to have been completed, when both sides were already upset. If requirements are vague (as they sometimes need to be at the beginning of a project), the time to get clarification is early in the process, not once the relationship is already falling apart.

In the case of this app, though, neither side wanted to spend the effort to flesh out the details in the requirements document up front, so they ended up with a mess at the end.

Out-of-Date Requirements Documentation

Yet another way projects go wrong is when the requirements documentation exists but is not kept up to date as things change. This often happens in projects that involve multiple organizations and many simultaneous conversations. Decisions get made, and the two people on the phone know what was discussed, but nothing gets written down, and the rest of the folks on the project are left in the dark. Alternatively, sometimes the requirements document does get updated, but the change doesn't get announced, and other parties execute the instructions from an old copy of the document.

Requirements documents often start out as multipage documents that are basically tables of contents. Someone (usually a single person) starts the project with every intention of documenting all the requirements and begins by writing a three-page list of stuff that needs to be documented. Then as the project goes on, less and less gets written on the requirements document each day, until finally it ends up a derelict Word file on some shared drive somewhere and serves only to confuse the unwary.

Another common setup is that someone sets up a project wiki server with the expectation that people will use it to document the project, but the wiki never ends up being integrated into the project's workflow. The content on it grows stale over time, and the wiki ends up being worse than useless because no one knows whether it can be trusted.

The way to solve this problem is to force the documentation to be part of the workflow for the project—either documentation that the quality assurance (QA) team uses to do testing (so the team opens bug reports when the documentation doesn't match the reality) or in the form of a suite of automated acceptance tests that are run on a frequent (or at least periodic) basis. The automated acceptance test idea works especially well for documenting the requirements between the server development team and the mobile development team.

Without some way to bring to light discrepancies between the documented requirements and reality, documentation usually becomes out of date to some degree during a project, and this can cause headaches for everyone involved.

The Case of the API Document That Became an End in Itself

I was once a subcontractor on a mobile project that had a server component that was being written simultaneously. The project had someone with the title "architect" whose job was to oversee the technical teams. (I was the senior developer on the iOS team, and there were Android, server, and graphic design teams as well.)

One of the required deliverables to the client was a document that explained the interactions between the mobile client and the server (I presume so that if the client wanted a Windows Phone or Blackberry version of the app to be created at a later date, they would have enough information to do so). The project architect worked with a contract technical writer to build this document.

The API document was running behind schedule, and the architect was pushing to get it completed. The problem was that the focus of the document was on the document itself, and not on the service it was supposed to be documenting.

From time to time, one of the developers would run into an issue that required a change to the contract between the server and the client. For example, the iOS developer would see that the graphics designer had added an element like "date user joined" on a wireframe, but the server wasn't providing that information, or the server developer would realize that two different API calls could be combined to reduce latency since they were always called together. At that point, the developer would figure out what needed to change, and the server developer would make the change and send a note to the architect. But that information would never make it into the document. So when a different developer started working on that API call (for example, implementing it for Android this time instead of iOS), that developer would be working from a document that was now out of date.

Easily 15% (any maybe 20%) of the time spent working on the networking between the mobile devices and the server ended up being wasted because the tool that was supposed to make it easier for the developers to communicate (the document) became focused not on furthering the project but on checking a box on a checklist of deliverables.

Constantly Changing Requirements

Another thing that can cause a project to fail is indecision. Many projects start without a clear idea of what needs to be accomplished and have the design spend months changing over and over while never getting any closer to a ship date. Hundreds of thousands of dollars get spent, and there's no evidence that the design changed for the better during the process.

Sometimes the trigger for this is user testing; sometimes it's anecdotal, with someone showing the app to a friend or two and the friend(s) not immediately understanding how the app is supposed to be used. Sometimes someone says it just doesn't feel like the design is progressing in the right direction. Sometimes the desire is to find something "better" than some competitor's app, but with no clear idea of what "better" would look like. However it starts, it costs a lot of money and doesn't accomplish much (if anything).

What makes this especially hard is that there are times you can tell from user testing that an app design really isn't working. You don't want to ship a design that people can't figure out, so it's important to get a better design. The problem is the amount of money that change will cost.

When I see this happen, it's usually for apps that went from concept directly to coding and skipped the prototype phase. The point of a prototype is to get a design in front of people to figure out whether it works in the cheapest way possible. If you figure out that users aren't understanding (or liking) your app, you can try a different design (or several different designs) without needing to have a single line of code written. If there's confusion in the middle of a project, you could even hopefully move all your development effort to a part of the app that you know will stay the same (like data storage or networking or something) while you show potential users several different prototypes in an effort to get clarification. (For more information, see Chapter 3, "Prototyping and Wireframing Your App.")

But if you are well into building your app when you run into problems and you try to quickly come up with a new design that you think will be better and have your developers start coding on it before you know whether it's going to actually improve the user experience, you're starting a chain of events that can lead to months of churn with nothing useful to show.

Leaving the Worst for Last

A constant theme I hear when talking to app creators about their failed projects is that things seemed to be going very well right up until the point where they thought they were about to be done.

It's rare that a project fails a week or two after starting (and if that happens, it's usually due to an external event). This is because at the beginning of a project (or at least the beginning of the development phase of a project), there's often nothing to see, so expectations are low. It's only when the project has been going on long enough that there should be something to see that expectations are raised to the point that failure seems an option.

A common pattern is that the developer periodically meets with the app creator and says that progress is being made. Something might be shown at the meeting, but there seems to be plenty of time in the schedule to get the rest of the work done. As the time remaining in the project dwindles, the app creator might begin to be uncomfortable but is assured that everything is still on schedule, and there's nothing to worry about. It's only when the app creator looks at the list of outstanding items and sees that the schedule is almost gone that the platitudes of the developer start to ring hollow, and the app creator can no longer believe that everything is on track. This is when the failure becomes obvious.

There are two ways this can happen. First, the developer may be dishonest and just lie to the app creator, trying to get as much money out of the deal as possible. Second, the developer may be incompetent and genuinely just as surprised as the app creator when things seem to fall apart at the end. The good news is that the same remedy works for both of these cases.

To avoid failure, it's important to identify the pieces of a project that have the most risk and push them as early into the project as you can. That way, if there is going to be a problem, you can find out about it before you've spent most of your budget and you still have money to pay for a different developer.

For what it's worth, the two things that I find to be the most risky on the majority of projects are integration and performance. Not coincidentally, these are often the last two things that are done in a project before testing starts in earnest. This is not the best risk management strategy.

Figure 1.3 shows a typical project development schedule. Note how right after the project begins, many tasks are started in parallel by several different developers, and only toward the end is their work integrated (connected together) and tested for functionality and performance.

Figure 1.4 shows a different schedule for the same project. Note how much earlier the first integration and performance test occurs. This is a much safer plan because, if problems show up in the test, there is far more time to deal with them.

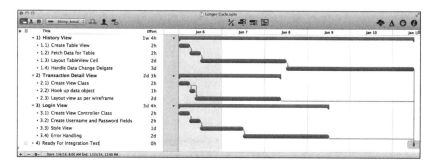

Figure 1.3
A simple Gantt chart for part of a fictitious project. Note how all three views are created and styled before the integration test starts at item #4.

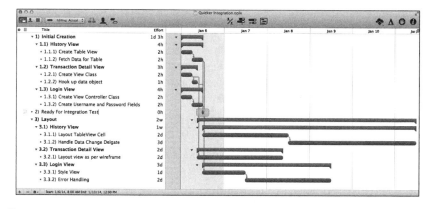

Figure 1.4
An alternate Gantt chart for the same part of the same fictitious project as in Figure 1.3. Note that the integration test has been moved much sooner in the project, to item #2.

The downside to using this technique is often calendar time. Typically you can complete an app in the smallest amount of time if the project is chopped up into many small pieces of functionality, and each piece has a different programmer, and all their work is hooked together at the end. The problem is that this is a high-risk strategy: If something goes wrong, you don't know it until the very end, and then you might not have money left to fix it. Many development shops love this model, though, because they can extract the maximum number of dollars in the minimum amount of time, and they don't have to show an app that actually works until most of the money is already paid.

But if you want to reduce your risk, time is on your side. By having your developer build a piece at a time and not moving on until it's integrated and working, you reduce the amount of your budget that you spend before you have evidence that things are proceeding the way you need them to.

The Case of Throwing Out the UI with the Bathwater

I once was brought into the middle of an iPhone project that had a fairly busy user interface. It wasn't badly designed, but it crammed a whole bunch of information into a very small portion of an already small screen.

Some time before I was brought onto the project, a decision was made that the interface would use an Apple technology called Auto Layout, which Apple had recently released to developers. Auto Layout is a cool technology that allows you to program a user interface once, and then it adjusts to different screen sizes and orientations. It's a nice time-saver for developers (once they get the hang of it) because they no longer have to write a bunch of code that figures out what the X and Y coordinates of each interface element need to be for the current screen size and what else has already been added to it.

The downside of Auto Layout is that it requires the device to solve fairly complicated equations every time the screen needs to be redrawn to figure out where everything needs to be placed. The good news is that computer processors are very good at solving these kinds of equations. The bad news is that sometimes, the processor in a mobile phone has better things to do.

Two other mistakes were made on this project that are relevant for this discussion. First, the contract didn't specify which models of iPhones the app needed to support. Second, the project schedule called for performance testing to be done at the end of the project.

Toward the end of the project, the app creator declared that the app was too slow on older iPhone models. The app had never been tested on iPhone models that old because the development team assumed that they weren't going to be supported. Effort was put into making the app faster, but it couldn't be made fast enough. The older, slower processors in the much older iPhones just didn't have enough power to solve the equations to lay out the screen while doing everything else that they needed to do.

And so, at the end of the project, long after the budget and schedule were exhausted, the Auto Layout code had to be removed from the user interface, rendering all the work than had been done on Auto Layout wasted and requiring lots of additional code to replace what Auto Layout had been doing. Earlier performance testing would have saved a lot of wasted effort.

Cost Overruns

This book spends quite a bit of time discussing risks. The cost of a project turning out to be way more than expected is probably the most likely failure mode in the contract app development space. This is sad because app development billing rates start higher than those of many (if not most) other forms of contract development right now. Costs are high under even the best of circumstances, and they become downright stratospheric if not kept under control.

Much of this book focuses on getting you your money's worth, but the following sections discuss a few of the most common ways that costs get out of control.

Unnecessary Staffing

One way that projects run way over budget is by having too many developers. The more developers a project has, the more communication effort is required. Each additional developer is not only less productive than the previous one but actually slows down the existing developers. This effect was documented in 1975 in *The Mythical Man-Month* by Fred Brooks (which I mention several more times in this book).

Especially when your development company has a number of developers on salary who are idle, the company may pressure you to have more developers on your project than you need. Make sure that the company can articulate what every developer will be doing and why each is necessary before you approve additional headcount.

Unnecessary or Wasteful Work

Not all work gets you closer to the project's goal. Some work turns out not to have been worth it. Under what circumstances should you have to pay for that?

First, understand that just because a particular piece of work doesn't make it into the final product doesn't mean it was wasteful. Sometimes there's more than one way to implement something, and it makes sense to spend time experimenting with multiple possibilities to figure out which is the best fit for your app. It's better to do that than to guess with no data and risk ending up with an unworkable solution. These experiments are often referred to as *spikes*, and we discuss them more in Chapter 2. Mockups and prototypes are also useful work that won't ever ship, and we discuss them at length in Chapter 3.

However, some kinds of work are wasted. What happens when a developer makes a mistake? What happens when fixing the bugs in a feature turns out to take twice as long as building that feature initially? What happens when the developer you got was less experienced than the developer you needed and ended up making a mess? Under many contracts, that cost is passed directly to the app creator, so there's not a lot of incentive for the developer to get it right the first time.

Unproductive Billable Time

We touched on this earlier: Developers should be developing. Try to keep meetings and administrative tasks to a minimum and make sure you aren't being billed for time when the developer is not working on your project. (For example, time spent eating lunch should not normally be billed to you.) Note that explaining and documenting the code that is being written should be considered part of development, not administrative time.

Unexpected Bugs

Sometimes projects run into bugs that take a while to fix. Sometimes those bugs are in code that the developer wrote, and sometimes they're in third-party libraries or the framework for the mobile platform itself. Bugs always happen, but most of the time they don't take a project off the rails. Sometimes they do. However, project-endangering bugs should not happen in areas of the project that are similar to what your developer has done before. Talk to your developers about what risks they see in your project before you start. (See the "Gap Analysis" section of Chapter 8 for more details.)

Unforeseen Circumstances

Sometimes bad things happen. Sometimes developers become ill or quit or have to leave a project to care for a sick family member. Developers are human, and most humans have chaotic and unpredictable periods at some points in their lives. Discuss what might happen in such a case with your developer before work starts. (See the "Contingency Plans" section of Chapter 8 for more details.)

Poor or Changing Requirements

As discussed earlier in this chapter, requirements need to be clearly decided, communicated, and understood. If they're not, they might as well be randomly generated.

Poor Initial Estimation

One of the things that can throw project costs far afield is unforeseen work being "discovered" or "found" during the development process. If this sort of thing occurs and wasn't a result of bad requirements, then it was most likely missed during the estimation process. Ask your developer before work starts about who will pay for poor estimates and how much. (I suggest that you at least should never have to pay full price for work that wasn't estimated.)

The other common result of poor estimation is everything just taking longer than expected. This could be a result of insufficient information during the estimation process (which happens a lot on projects that involve taking over a code base that someone else wrote and the code base turns out to be worse than you thought). It also happens when the developers who end up on your project are slower and less experienced than the developers that the person doing the estimation had in mind (in which case you probably shouldn't be paying the same hourly rate as the estimator had in mind either).

That Last 10%

Many people have come to me with projects that they believe are "90% complete." They never have been. It's hard to know exactly how far along a project actually is, but when someone tells you they're 80% or 90% of the way done with a project, they're almost always wrong. Why does this happen so often?

Well, first off, most people don't actually bother to go through the effort of really measuring project status but want to act as if they know what they're doing. So they tend to make up numbers, and 80% and 90% are good round, made-up numbers. Really, it's just a common and convenient lie told by developers and project managers the world over. When people tell you they're 80% or 90% done, ask them how they arrived at that percentage.

Despite the frequent fabrications, there is an underlying truth here: Most mobile app developers leave testing until the end of the project. Testing is how you find out how well a project is really going. If a developer has written code for half the features on the project, the project may be as much as half done. But if that set of features turns out to have tons of bugs, then there are tons of bug fixes that must be written before the project is half done. And before testing, there's no way to know which.

What happens is that developers write all the code to implement all the features before turning over the code to QA for testing, and they assume that testing is just a formality and won't turn up very much. They assume, for example, that the testing at the end will be 10% or so of the project time. When testing turns up a whole bunch of stuff, they stick to their guns and think (or at least say) that they're still 90% done. This is where we get the joke that "the first 90% of the project takes 90% of the time, and the last 10% of the project takes the other 90% of the time."

Avoiding this situation requires testing early, testing often, and testing the right things.

First, understand that early testing doesn't reduce risk; it just reduces uncertainty, so it's still important not to leave the riskiest parts of the project until the end. (See the "Leaving the Worst for Last" section earlier in this chapter.) Sequencing of features is still critical, even with lots of testing.

Second, each feature or component needs to be tested to make sure it's functioning correctly. Note that it needs to be tested to make sure it behaves well when expected things happen and that it doesn't behave badly when obvious but unexpected things happen. Most developers do at least an adequate job of this.

Finally, testing needs to verify that when each new feature is added, all the previous features still work. This is called *regression testing*, and lots of developers don't do a good job of it.

For more about testing, see Chapter 12, "Communicating Using Bugs," and Chapter 13, "Testing."

The Whack-a-Mole Problem

There's a specific situation that causes cost overruns and stretches out the last 10% of a project. It sometimes happens earlier in the project, but most often it shows up at the end. I call it the *whack-a-mole problem*, after the carnival game where a player with a hammer tries to hit mechanical creatures as they pop up out of holes.

The whack-a-mole problem occurs when it seems that the fix for any given bug causes a new bug to pop up. This is often an indication of a poor architecture (or poor developers). Unfortunately, if you've reached whack-a-mole, it's usually too late to change out the architecture (or the development team) without a lot of effort. There are many ways to end up in this situation, but let me take you through a common scenario.

Mobile apps are largely driven by *events*—things like the user pressing a button or new information being received from the network. Somewhere in the source code, a set of instructions gets called when a particular button gets pressed. When that set of instructions becomes too complicated, you get the whack-a-mole problem.

Imagine a banking app with a button that says Account History on the main screen. The user taps the button, and the account history screen appears. Everything works fine.

Then someone asks, "What should that button do if the user isn't logged in?" So the programmer is tasked with writing code so that if the user is logged in, that button shows the account history screen but otherwise shows the login screen. Then the login screen gets programmed to return to one place if it was shown from the login button and another place if it was called by the Account History button.

Then later in the project, someone says, "We shouldn't open the login screen if the network isn't available since the user won't be able to log in; that would be confusing." Now the programmer goes through the code and finds all the places that the login screen is called and puts a check at each one to see if the network is available, and if it isn't, it shows the screen that says the network isn't connected and asks the user to connect to Wi-Fi.

At this point, the code that is executed when the button is pressed depends on two states: whether the user is logged in and whether the network is available. The programmer isn't thinking about all the different possibilities, only the case where the user isn't logged in and the case where the network isn't available. The programmer makes the change to show the screen that asks the user to connect to Wi-Fi and checks in the change.

If the programmer wasn't careful, when the user taps the Account History button when the network isn't available, the app will ask the user to connect to Wi-Fi, even if the user was already logged in, which wasn't part of the requirement.

As time passes, more and more states can get thrown into the mix. There could be a special screen that needs to be shown on login when the users have overdrawn their accounts. There could be a special screen that's shown on the user's birthday. There could be an alert that needs to be shown when fraud has been detected on the account. Maybe an interstitial ad needs to be shown, and so on and so on. Each time a new set of behaviors is added to that button, all the previous behaviors are at risk of becoming broken, and the amount of time it takes to do a thorough test gets longer and longer because each combination of states needs to be tested. Multiply that by the number of buttons in the app, and you see how big the whack-a-mole problem can be.

Some application architectures and programming techniques do a good job of handling this complexity (assuming that the programmer is experienced with such techniques). The trick is that they have to be put in place at the right time. If they're put in place too early, they are more trouble than they are worth, but if the programmer waits too long, it becomes tedious and time-consuming to move all the existing behavior to the new architecture.

Poor Communication

Poor communication dooms any software project, but mobile projects, with their relatively smaller budgets, shorter time lines, and often remote teams are particularly susceptible. The solution, though, is not more meetings. I've been on projects that had conference calls every day, and the communication was still horrible. In fact, lots of meetings often make it worse because everyone thinks that if nothing came up on the conference call, everything must be going fine, when that's not necessarily the case at all.

It's in vogue these days for every project to have a daily stand-up meeting. I'm not going to tell you not to have one; there's nothing inherently wrong with those meetings. What I *am* going to tell you is that a daily stand-up doesn't give you information about *how well* the work is being done or whether the whole project is on track. A daily stand-up just tells you what everyone is working on that day, and what, if anything, they're waiting on to be able to complete their current tasks.

And then there are project status meetings where everyone says that his or her part of the project is going just fine. Again, these aren't particularly useful.

Making the Most of Meetings

As with requirements, good communication is all about details. And to prompt your developers to give you good details, you have to ask the right questions. The questions usually asked at meetings are either two narrow ("What are *you* doing *today*?") or too vague ("Is *your part* of the project *going okay*?").

One recommendation is that you should never have a project meeting without a written agenda, and the agenda should be circulated to everyone who will attend the meeting in advance to give people time to think about what they need to say.

The agenda should ask the questions that you as the app creator need answered, like "What's the biggest risk to this project as you see it right now?" or "What's the most likely thing that you think could go wrong on this project, and what can be done about it?" or even "What decisions need to be made in order to complete the tasks you are currently working on, and what alternatives are there for each decision?" These kinds of questions will prompt discussion of the details that you need to know.

Then, once the meeting is over, make sure that someone writes up a summary of what happened in the meeting and distributes it to the group. These meeting notes become very useful later in the project when confusion arises.

Examine the Project's Artifacts and Ask Questions Contemporaneously

Another way to facilitate communication is to look at what's happening on a project and ask questions about it. I try to review changes to the source control repository and bug trackers at least every day or two during a project to keep up to date with what's going on. (See Chapter 10, "Understanding What You're Getting," for how to do this.) If I have any questions after reading the commit messages on the code check-ins or the updates to the bugs, I send someone email and ask for clarification. If the developers know that they're going to be contacted if they don't write clear commit messages or bug updates, they eventually put more thought into what they write, and the quality of that information goes way up. (There are many discussions of source control and bug trackers throughout this book, so don't worry if these terms are unfamiliar right now.)

It's important to ask these questions soon after the developer does the work. If you wait a week or two (or maybe even a few days), the developer might not remember as well what he or she was doing, and the quality of the explanation will suffer.

Insist on Getting a Plan

Periodically (at least weekly), you need to insist on getting a plan that shows what needs to be done between now and the end of the project, with specific details about what the next few steps are. Much of the report will be the same from week to week, but as you get more and more of these reports, you should see how the things that have been done have lined up with what the plan had previously said was going to happen. As with everything else, make sure you understand what you are looking at and ask detailed questions until you do.

If at all possible, I recommend getting these plans in the form of Gantt charts (which are discussed in Chapter 5, "Finding the Right Tools," and Chapter 9, "Managing to Milestones").

Abdication of the Management Process

Many of the issues discussed in this chapter boil down to one root cause: The app creator didn't pay enough attention to managing the project or left the management of the project up to someone else (who may or may not have done it at all). Whether you are doing the programming yourself or can't write a line of code, if you want your app idea to come to fruition, you have to keep an honest and vigilant perspective on where you are in the project and make good decisions based on that knowledge.

Many app development companies provide a professional project manager to do this for you (and charge a premium for the privilege), but project managers don't have the same incentives you do, and their loyalty is not to you or your project but to their employer. Often, those project managers don't want to ask hard questions. They don't want to admit that failure is an option. They are generally incentivized primarily to manage your expectations and get you to pay your invoices.

You, as an app creator, are responsible for understanding where a project is now and where it is going, what risks are involved and what can be done about them, and whether your developer is doing a good job or needs to be replaced. If you don't feel comfortable about that responsibility, welcome to the club. This is difficult stuff to do, and anyone who says differently is selling something.

The simple fact remains that there's no one else you can trust to do it. You are the one selecting the developer, and you are the one controlling the purse strings. It's your vision and your goal. But despite the difficulty, it is possible. It can be done, and this book is here to help you do it.

Wrapping Up

This chapter discusses the different ways that app projects fail and provides some tips about what can be done about it. Here are some key points to take away:

- Despite the relatively small size of app development projects, they are still software development projects, and many of them fail.
- App projects can fail by taking too long or costing too much, even if the app produced at the end is acceptable.
- A number of factors make mobile development more difficult than web development, but inexperienced programmers don't always recognize that.

- Even experienced development companies with good reputations can have failing projects.

- Good requirements are key to getting a good estimate, a good project, and a good app. And they don't just have to be defined well but also have to be communicated well.

- To the extent possible, uncertainty and risk need to be pushed early into the project schedule to avoid catastrophic failure at the end.

- Testing should never be left until the end of a project.

- You can prevent project failure. It's difficult, but this book is here to help.

The App Development Life Cycle

Every app goes through a series of steps or phases between idea and completion. This chapter discusses a simple but iterative model that has three major phases: design, development, and testing (see Figure 2.1). Some people divide these phases further. For example, some people might make a distinction between internal testing and external testing or separate graphical design and user interface design, but for purposes of this book, those distinctions are not particularly helpful.

Some apps spend more time in a given phase than others, and some apps skimp on certain phases, but all the phases are at least touched upon.

One of the things that separates the best apps from the amateurish ones is that better apps repeat all these phases many times, and the app gets better with each iteration. So for professionally built apps, the kind I hope you aspire to build, these phases form a cycle. Each cycle encompasses a certain amount of functionality, as specified during the design phase. Some cycles are shorter and cheaper and focus on one thing, while others can be longer and cover a wider range of functionality.

There aren't any one-size-fits-all rules about how many times an app needs to repeat the cycle before it's "good enough." However, I feel confident in estimating that hundreds or thousands of apps go through too few cycles for every one that goes through too many. So when in doubt about whether to go through the cycle again, I recommend erring on the side of doing it.

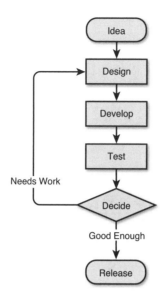

Figure 2.1
An example of an app life cycle flowchart.

Keep in mind that any given app can be in more than one phase at a time. One person can be working on testing while another is doing development, or one feature may be in development while the next feature is being designed. There isn't One True Way™ to approach app development. The model I describe here is simplistic, perhaps overly so. It is, however, a useful framework for discussion, and one that we'll come back to throughout the course of the book.

The Design Phase

When people think of the word *design*, they often think of visual design or graphic design. While having an attractive-looking app is important, that's but a small part of what designing an app entails. Steve Jobs famously said, "Design is how it works" (see www.nytimes.com/2003/11/30/magazine/30IPOD.html). For purposes of this book, I define *design* as "the process of making and communicating the decisions about exactly how an app will look, sound, function, or behave in any given situation."

Think about that for a minute. Design isn't just something that happens in Photoshop. It involves deciding and communicating. Even if you have no graphical talent at all and can't tell a Bezier curve from a cloud brush, you, as the owner of an app idea and as the person who wants that idea to come to fruition, are a designer. You are, in fact, the most vital part of the design process because without a definition or a description of how the app is supposed to work, nothing else can get started, no one else has anything to do, and the app will never make it into an app store.

Initial Design Steps

Design starts with fleshing out the original idea. It starts with describing, even to yourself, the core purpose of the app. It starts with answering the question "What will the app do?"

Just as importantly, though, design starts with answering the question "What should this app *not* do?" There's a famous saying: "Every program attempts to expand until it can read mail" (see www.catb.org/jargon/html/Z/Zawinskis-Law.html). While this tendency is annoying on a desktop computer, it's fatal on a mobile device. Deciding what shouldn't go in an app is as vital a design task as deciding what should.

The second factor in my design definition is communicating. Decisions need to be documented and communicated in order for something to count as design. I consider this to be true even when I'm designing an app that I'm going to develop all by myself; it's still important that I write down my decisions. Creating apps can take months, and life happens along the way; it's very helpful to be able to go back to your notes and design documents when you're nearing the end of the testing cycle to see if you've hit all the points that you wanted from the outset.

So your app's first design artifact is likely to be a short description of what the app is supposed to do, along with a list of potential features, as well as maybe some notes about what you don't want to include. This isn't nearly enough to get started on, but it's very important. It's the very core of the design, and you'll be using it over and over as you talk to people about what your app does. It will inform every other decision you make. It's even likely to bear a strong resemblance to the description that your app ends up with when it finally goes on sale.

Making Your App Look Like an App

The next part of the design process is usually sketches and wireframes, which then hopefully lead to interactive prototypes. This is what most people think of when they think of "designing an app." But when we're talking about design, we're talking about where design fits into your project and how it affects your outcome. This isn't a book about how to do design. If you want to learn about design (and you should if you want your app to be a good one), there are several good resources for you, including *Learning iOS Design* by William Van Hecke.

Wireframes, at a minimum, are a necessary starting point before development. You can do them yourself, or you can hire a designer to do them for you. I encourage you to at least try your hand at making a first-draft wireframe of your app, even if you are going to hire a designer. It will help you communicate to the designer what you want. A picture is worth a thousand words, after all.

But if you hire designers, you either need to understand the design they produce well enough to change it, or you need to plan on going back to them when changes are needed. It's a rare wireframe that doesn't end up needing clarification or alterations before the app is finalized. Chapter 6, "Skill Gap Analysis," talks more about professional designers.

Design Early, Design Often

Even though virtually no designs survive the development and testing processes unscathed, you still want to do as much design as you can early on. Holistically, design is the input into either the development or testing steps of the development life cycle, depending on how far along you are in your project. On some iterations, especially (but not exclusively) early ones, it makes sense to take a design directly into testing and incorporate the testing feedback directly into the next design.

In my experience, a lot of people don't do this. Some do, but usually they don't do it enough. Most wireframes I see have not been shown to potential users. The few potential users who *have* seen wireframes have generally been friends of the designer with far too much foreknowledge about what the designer is trying to accomplish. They can't give valuable feedback, and that's a problem.

In my experience, this principle holds: *The later in the process design is done, the more expensive it is.* This doesn't mean that contractors get more expensive per hour as the project goes on but that, as the project goes on, each decision and each design change represents the loss of some amount of effort. That effort, now lost, has a cost.

For example, if you decide to remove a feature, any time that you, your designer, or your developer spent thinking about that feature is now time that could have been spent thinking about something else. Alternatively, adding a feature later in the development process means that code written before that feature now needs to be reevaluated in light of the new requirement. In the worst case, some of that existing code will need to be rewritten.

All this doesn't mean that you should never change anything once you've started development; in fact, nothing could be further from the truth. It just means that, the earlier you make a decision, the cheaper it will be relative to making that decision later. Imagine that late in development, you realize that a particular feature is going to take a lot longer and be much more expensive than you thought. Cutting that feature right then will likely save you time and money and would probably be the right thing to do. Consider, though, that if you'd cut that feature out before you ever started development, you would have saved even more.

Not having a crystal ball, we can't cut features before we realize they are going to be problematic, and we can't necessarily know before testing that users will find something confusing and that it will therefore require redesign. So if you find yourself needing to make a design change late in the process, by all means do it and try not to beat yourself up about it. But if there's a question about making a decision now or later, the sooner you can make the decision, the better—at least as long as it turns out to be the right decision.

Secondary Design

Features and wireframes are obvious elements of design. And with many app projects, that's where the design process stops. That's a shame because there's a lot more to design than this.

It's fairly common—in fact, I'd say normal—for projects to start development at the point where they have wireframes of the workflows of the key features. If an app is simple enough, that could be as much as 80% complete. But on a more complex app, that could be as little as 20% designed. Why? Because there is often a gulf between your expectation of the app's use case and the way that people have to interact with the app. The following sections consider a few of the most common scenarios where just designing the key features isn't enough.

Error Handling

Error handling can require a huge amount of effort. What do you want the app to look like when something goes wrong? How do you want it to behave when an error occurs? How many different things could go wrong? How customized does the app's behavior need to be in each of those cases?

A lot of apps fail to design for error conditions at all, leaving the programmer to ask for clarification, or guess, or just hope an error won't happen. Some programmers aren't experienced enough (or don't care enough) to figure out what the error conditions could be and try to handle them. But your app needs to handle itself gracefully if the network is unavailable (or poorly available), or if the device is running out of disk space, or if memory is running low, or if the user gets unexpectedly logged out, or if the email address doesn't contain an @ character, or if one player quits in the middle of the game, or if the information it's fetching (from disk or the network) is missing or corrupted, etc. Trust me, handling errors can be a lot of work.

First-Run Conditions

What does the user see when the app is run for the first time? This is sometimes called the "soft landing problem." How do you tutor the users about how the app works without driving them crazy? How do you indicate to the users that something is selectable when there's no data there to select? How do you convince them that it's worth their time and effort to log in (or worse, to create an account)? Depending on the app, this can be the majority of the design work. Doing this well is hard, but doing it poorly gets your app abandoned before it ever gets used (and maybe also bad reviews).

Transitions and Other Animations

A lot of wireframes are lists of screens with no indication of which screen leads to which other screen. In order for this to work, not only does the order of the screens matter, but how you get from one to the other can be critical. People often think of animations as pure eye-candy, but when done well, they provide users with a context about where they are in the flow. Often when people leave a bad review saying an app is "confusing," it's because there isn't a clear flow with appropriate transitions and a clear way for the user to get back to the previous (or primary) screen.

Scrolling and Element Obstruction

Is there a condition the app can get into where the user can't see the controls? This often happens with text fields. When the user is typing, the keyboard appears. Alarmingly often, none of the wireframes show a keyboard at all. If the designer doesn't consider that the keyboard will appear, he or she might do something like put the next field to be filled out or the Submit button at the bottom of the screen, where it will be hidden by the keyboard. The user will finish entering data and be unable to figure out what to do next.

This also happens when there ends up being more data than the designer expects. I often see designs where there is a list of four or six items on the screen and then a button at the bottom. But what happens when there are several dozen or several thousand items in the list? How long is it going to take the user to scroll to the button? How is the user even going to know the button is there?

Text Length Assumptions

Many designs fail to consider what should happen when the text that needs to be displayed is too long for the space intended to contain it. Should the font shrink or be wrapped or be truncated? How does this choice affect the look of the surrounding text?

All these factors and many more need to be considered during design. Chapter 3, "Prototyping and Wireframing Your App," discusses them at length.

The Development Phase

Development, for purposes of this book, refers to programming and tasks that support programming (planning, documentation, and so on). It is almost always the most expensive part of getting an app into an app store. This means that it's important to do only as much development as you have to. If you front-load your project by designing what you really want, you can hopefully minimize the amount of money you spend on development.

Development Is *Not* About Screens

Screens are the basic building blocks of mobile design. They're the primary components in wireframes and prototypes. They even tend to monopolize conversations about mobile apps. So it's understandable that when app creators think about development, they tend to do so in terms of screens. Although it's understandable, it's counterproductive.

I can't begin to count the number of times I've heard app creators and inexperienced developers attempt to estimate development in terms of screens. I've seen people make development schedules that contained nothing but screens (Developer A is going to spend this week on screen 1 and next week on screen 3, and Developer B is going to spend the next two weeks on screen 2, since it's got more stuff on it.) This way of thinking bears very little resemblance to reality, and the more you think this way, the more confused you're likely to get.

I often explain it by way of this analogy: Estimating the effort involved in a mobile app by counting screens is like estimating the effort involved in building a house by counting bedrooms and bathrooms. While it's true that the count of bedrooms and bathrooms is important and often used as a shorthand description for the size of a house, and while it's true that, all other things being equal, building a 2-bedroom and 1-bathroom house requires less effort than building a 5-bedroom, 3 1/2-bathroom house, no one builds a house one room at a time. There's a lot of infrastructure that's the same regardless of which house you're building, and there is a lot of additional effort that goes into things that have nothing to do with those rooms—like the often-considerable effort spent on the kitchen.

As in building a house, in app development, you need a foundation with a structure and plumbing. Those things are vital, and they require time and effort and aren't measured in terms of screens.

There are much better ways to think of measuring development. One popular term I tend to use is *feature*. There are others, such as *story* in the Agile software community (though I find this this term isn't particularly useful for nontechnical folks to use for planning or estimation).

What's a Feature?

The term *feature* is hard to define without using unhelpful words like *thing* or *function*. However, I find that people can usually pick up the concept by example. For example, I would say that "store each child's name and homeroom teacher," "store the grade each child made on a given test," "send email to each child's parents with their average grade," and "provide a way for the teacher to enter the grade for each child" are all features. "Make this list have white text on a black background" is not really a feature, but "Display all the children's grades on a scrolling screen with white text on a black background" is a feature (and also a description of a screen).

It's not important to have an exact definition of *feature*. Some people might consider "post a text message to a friend's Facebook Wall" and "post a photo to a friend's Facebook Wall" to be two different features, and some people might argue that "post to a friend's Facebook Wall" should be a single feature that covers both. It doesn't matter which way you go, as long as everyone on the project understands what is involved in the feature.

The Name of a Thing Is Not the Thing

A common problem occurs with regard to feature naming: There's a tendency for people to read the name of a feature and infer from the name what that feature entails. In general, this is a bad idea, and each feature should have a sufficient written description (maybe even with pictures) for reasonable people to be able to agree on whether a given feature is complete. We talk about this more in Chapter 9, "Managing to Milestones."

Scheduling, Planning, and Budgeting

Just as a professionally built house doesn't begin with someone building a single room, a professionally built app doesn't start with someone building a single screen. An app, like a house, needs a structure, but before even that, you need to start with a budget and a plan.

The budget and the plan are irrevocably linked, but development can be constrained by either. If you know how much money you have to spend, that determines how much effort you can afford, which in turn informs the plan. By contrast, if you are sure what you want to get done, you can have the plan built first and then figure out the budget from there. Either way, the first step of the development process should be to produce a plan, a schedule, and a budget.

The schedule should list all the important features of the app and include a time estimate to develop it. The schedule should also list the infrastructure (data storage, network connectivity code, and so on) that the developer thinks will be needed. It should include testing, both as development occurs and a final round of bug-hunting right before submission. And this may seem obvious, but the schedule should add up to less than the total budget (hopefully with some padding in case the unexpected happens).

If at all possible, I recommend that you don't allow programming to start until you are satisfied with the plan.

Spikes (in a Software Sense)

There are times when a given design for a given app contains a feature that it difficult or impossible to estimate. It might be potentially technically infeasible. Or there may be more than one way it could be implemented, without a clear choice of which is preferred. Or it might be outside the experience of the development team. In such a situation, one technique is to perform an experiment to gather the information required in order to make the estimate. This experiment is colloquially known as a *spike* (or sometimes *tracer bullet*). The resulting code may or may not be able to be reused, but it doesn't have to be. The idea is to plan on spending a predetermined, fixed amount of time on a spike, which is followed up with another planning phase that incorporates the knowledge gained during the spike.

Developer as Designer

Another thing that might preempt planning is if the design is insufficient for planning to begin. Sometimes an experienced developer will find things in the wireframes that you didn't realize. Sometimes you don't have the time or desire to do the initial design yourself. If that's the case, having your developer flesh out your idea into a design is a valid strategy. If you go that route, I recommend that you get the design agreed upon first and then have the plan and budget built from there. In my experience, having design and development happening simultaneously by the same developer (or development shop) is often a recipe for cost overruns and wasted effort. Remember, the earlier a design decision is made, the cheaper it is (again, assuming that the decision is a good one).

Planning Should Not Be Optional

Among developers, especially less experienced ones, the tendency is to start writing code right away. You shouldn't allow this. My recommendation is that you insist on having a detailed plan before you allow programming to begin (or at least before you agree to pay for any of it). If the developer asks for a reasonable amount of time and money to prepare a plan, I think paying for the plan is a good business decision on your part. Look at it this way: If you're not willing to risk a relatively small amount of time and money with this developer to get a plan, are you sure you'd want to risk a much larger amount to try to get an app?

The reality is that it's not feasible for a nonprogrammer to be able to determine accurately whether a given block of code is "good." You could learn to program yourself, but then why would you outsource? You could pay an additional developer to do code reviews of the first developer, but that would reduce the amount of actual functionality you could get for your budget. And even if you were to do that, keep in mind that there are differences of opinions even among programmers, and what's perfectly good code to one programmer might not work with the biases of a second.

Instead, I recommend focusing on the characteristics of a competent developer that you *can* measure; the most useful and important of these is the ability to make a plan and stick to the plan. By paying developers to program without getting a detailed plan from them first, you are depriving yourself of your best yardstick. Any developers you're considering need to be able to give you a plan to which they are willing to be held accountable. Otherwise, you should move on.

Feature Sequencing

When you work on sequencing your app's features, first you need to choose a structure and then make some decisions about the resources and components that are going to be shared between many, if not most, of the screens. Chapter 4, "Determining Your App's Components," talks about this in depth.

Once that's done, you want to make the plan. Generally, you want to start work on the things that will take the longest, that will be the most complicated, or that will require the most testing.

Functional Before Fancy

My recommendation is to push for getting the minimum viable set of the functionality of the app complete and then go back in future iterations to add optional features and make it pretty. There's a simple reason for this. It's possible to ship a working app with an unexciting interface and then go back and make it pretty for version 2. It's not ideal, but it's a viable strategy, and many apps have done it successfully. It's not, however, feasible to ship a pretty app that doesn't provide value to the user.

I've seen many app projects run out of time or money. Sometimes, it's expected, and sometimes circumstances have changed, and less money or time is available than was originally thought. (Remember Lehman Brothers? Many software project budgets were trimmed abruptly in September 2008.)

In the event that time, money, or other resources start to run out, it's better to have something you can ship than to be left with nothing but a cautionary tale about building an app with an attractive but useless user interface.

I also recommend this order because making an app pretty has a tendency to slow things down. Beautiful custom animations can make the difference between a good app and a great one. But when those animations sit in between a developer changing a line of code and seeing whether the change was correct, those couple seconds, repeated thousands and thousands of times, add up to wasted time and money, as well as frustration and lost productivity.

Start with the Front End or the Back End?

If there is a server component involved, I generally prefer to start by writing the part of the app that talks to the server, especially if the server is being developed at the same time. Network performance often dictates changes to the API during the course of development. (*API* stands for *application programming interface*; it's the "agreement," if you will, between the app and the server about how they are going to communicate.) In my experience, those API changes can have far-reaching impacts on the layout of the user interface, so it's best to figure them out as soon as you can. I've been involved in more than one project where we had built and polished an interface that led users through a series of screens only to find out that the information we needed was available only in a different order, and we ended up having to rearrange everything.

The next thing I often choose to work on is storage. Most of the screens and most features of many apps contain some amount of data, provided either by the user or the network or both. How this data is stored and accessed influences the design of all the screens that show the data.

However, as usual, one size does not fit all: This isn't always the right order for every app. I have a tendency to work more on business and social apps than novelty or game apps. Some apps (for example, Angry Birds) feature a particularly fancy or impressive user interface and a relatively simple (or non-existent) storage model. If a particular animation or user-facing control scheme is the thing that's likely to take the longest, then likely it should happen first.

Skinning

Making an app look like the graphic artist's conception is a process called *skinning* (for putting a new skin on the existing app). In order for this to happen, the programmer needs to be provided with the graphical elements that need to be put into the app (as well as other elements, like sounds). The good news is that these elements should already exist, having been created as part of the wireframing/prototyping process. The bad news is that these elements need to be prepared in specific ways in order to look attractive across different device types and display sizes. How those elements need to be prepared varies from platform to platform. Your developer or designer should be able to help you understand how this needs to happen, as can a number of online resources. The important thing to understand at this point is that your developer's schedule likely presupposes that these assets will be made available in the correct format.

When Design Isn't Worth It

Sometimes, a particular piece of your design turns out to seem inordinately expensive. Often when this happens, it's because you specified an interface, animation, or transition that would have to be custom built when a similar item is readily available. For example, early in the iPhone's history, there wasn't a supported way to put a button in the center of the top navigation bar, where the title usually is. There were ways to get it to happen, but they were a lot of work or very fragile or both.

When these kinds of limitations come up, only you can decide if your specific implementation is worth the extra time and trouble. It's important to realize that this does happen, and you should try not to get overly attached to any particular design element. I've seen at least one project go way over budget because a detail that most users would never notice turned out to be very, very difficult to program.

So far, we've barely scratched the surface of what development entails, but we'll continue discussing it extensively throughout the book. For now, I hope that you have a feel for what development is and that you realize that planning is an important early part of it.

The Testing Phase

There are two kinds of testing: looking for bugs that need to be fixed and discovering whether new users understand the app. Both types of testing are critical, but they're different processes with different objectives, and it's important that you keep them straight. You need to understand what you are testing at any given time and not conflate the two types of testing. I've seen several apps that were only tested for bugs by people who knew what the apps were supposed to do, and the apps turned out to be too confusing for new users. I've also seen an app that "seemed okay" to casual test users, but it turned out to be riddled with bugs when it got out in the store.

Testing Should Start Before Development

I'm a big advocate of testing as much as you can before you start programming. As I said earlier, the later in the process design is done, the more expensive it is. Programming is expensive, and throwing programming effort out and doing it over because you realized your design needed to change is expensive and wasteful. It can't always be avoided. Occasionally, something unexpectedly turns out to be technically infeasible. But I would argue that the vast majority of the late-stage design changes I've seen happen were for things that could have been caught much earlier in the process.

It's a surprise to most aspiring app creators I talk to that testing *can* start before development, much less that it *should*. But I've seen more than one app fail to ship because of deeply entrenched design issues that could have been caught before a single line of code was written.

Design testing can start with a single low-fidelity sketch of an app's screen. Hand it to a few people in the app's target market with whom you haven't discussed the app. Don't explain what the app is supposed to do. Ask them what they would expect the app to do, based on the screen they're seeing. Ask them what they think is interactive and what isn't. Ask what they would expect to happen if they interacted with the screen. (Don't say *tap* or *swipe*. Let them tell you how they'd use it.) See how closely what they would do lines up with what you want them to do. Redesign and repeat as necessary until the screen makes sense to a new person.

I recommend eventually building a full interactive prototype (see Chapter 3) and giving it to users to test. Oddly (to me), few of my clients want to spend the time or effort to build such a prototype. When I ask them why, they often explain that they don't want to "waste" time or money or effort on something that won't ship. However, I've seen many of them change their minds in the middle of development when it became obvious the design had issues that could have been caught in a prototype phase. In hindsight, many of them have regretted not having done prototype testing. I've even had some clients skip prototyping, regret that, and then decline to do prototype testing on subsequent apps. Some have had multiple, serial regrets about it.

Overly Optimistic Testing Mindset

The lack of willingness to test a prototype tends to result from an overly optimistic mindset. Prospective app creators very often seem to have a confidence in their vision of their app design that makes them feel that testing it is unnecessary. They feel strongly that their app will succeed as conceived, and they don't see a need to validate it. This confidence isn't restricted to app creators; many startups and new business ventures fail for the same reason.

But an overly optimistic attitude about testing often permeates the entire creation process. Creators skimp on the time and money they allocate to testing in order to squeeze in more features, only to find the end product an unshippable mess. It's better to have fewer but reliable features than more but buggier ones.

Regression Testing

A common way of skimping on testing is testing only new features as they are developed, and not going back to test previous features again when the new features are added. Unfortunately, the tightly integrated nature of mobile apps makes it surprisingly easy to break previously completed feature A in the process of building feature B. Going back and testing features again is called *regression testing*, and it's critical to do it often, repeatedly, and consistently. The more features you add without testing the old features, the more risk you run of your old features being broken; in addition, the longer you continue to make changes after something that used to work was broken, the harder it is to figure out what broke it and get it fixed again.

The Case of the Eroding Accomplishments

I was once asked to provide advice on an app to which the former developer had added features for months without doing any kind of regression testing. When the developer had all the features developed and thought the app was ready to submit, it turned out that almost every feature had at least one thing that had been broken. The creators were shocked at my estimate for how much work it was going to take to get the app into a shippable state and chose to take it back to the original developer. As I write this, that was 10 months ago, and the app still hasn't been published. Don't let this happen to you.

Negative Testing

Another common issue with testing is a lack of negative testing. *Negative testing* is testing the software, intentionally looking for problems. Contrast that with "golden path testing," which is testing to see if the app works the way it's supposed to work. So, for example, golden path testing could consist of tapping the Login button, typing a valid username and password, tapping the Submit button, and verifying that the user is now logged in. Negative testing the same form would involve doing things like tapping Submit while the password field or username field is empty, forcing the keyboard to be dismissed and seeing if it comes back correctly, scrolling to see if you can get the Submit button stuck under the keyboard, dragging the Submit button instead of tapping it, and so on. It's testing for all the things that were mentioned earlier, in the section "Secondary Design." It's adding far more data than the programmer expected in order to see what happens. It's jumping back and forth between screens or closing and relaunching the app at inopportune times. It's intentionally using the software in incorrect or unexpected ways, trying to get it to break or misbehave.

I've also found that, as with prototyping, clients often want to skimp on negative testing. The app does what they expect it to do when they use it the way they expect it to be used, and they think that's good enough. If that were true, building apps would be much simpler and cheaper. But in the real world, your users don't always use things the expected way, and if the app misbehaves, it leads to unhappy customers, bad reviews, or even the app store review team rejecting your app (for the stores like Apple and Amazon that require reviews before the app can be made available for sale or download).

User Experience Testing

Whereas regression testing and negative testing are best done by professionals who have an understanding of the app, user experience (or usability) testing is different: It's done by people who are unfamiliar with your app but who are demographically potential users of your app. This kind of testing isn't about finding bugs (although you might find them, and if you do, you need to make sure they get captured and fixed). Instead, this kind of testing is about getting users' honest opinions about whether they can figure out how to use the app, whether they think they would use it, what they like, what they don't like, what confusion they had, and whether they would pay for the app (and how much).

Testing Development as You Go

A common mistake people make with testing is putting all the test time at the end of the schedule and not doing any testing before then. It's certainly useful to have a dedicated testing phase right before you ship to find any last-minute bugs, but please don't wait that long to start. Before development starts, there's no point looking for bugs in the yet-to-be-written code, but starting tests of the code soon after the start of development and running them continuously right up until ship (testing both new and old features) will help you produce the best app in the most predictable time frame.

Automated Testing

Automated tests are tests that are written in computer code that exercise other computer code. While this kind of testing does not eliminate the need for real people looking for bugs, it greatly reduces the need for lots of regression testing, and it helps in finding newly written bugs very soon after they're introduced, cutting down on the cost of finding them and fixing them.

Automated testing has become quite popular in the startup world and is making inroads into the enterprise software world through the adoption of a software development methodology called Agile. Automated testing is less popular in the user interface development world (for example, with web development). It seems like more mobile developers come from web backgrounds (Flash and HTML), and I probably see 10 mobile projects that contain no automated tests for every project I run across that does have any automated tests.

Automated testing isn't useful for everything, and it can be taken to a counterproductive extreme, but it's definitely something to keep in mind when thinking about testing your app. It's also a handy way to separate experienced from inexperienced programmers. Automated testing is a skill that takes some time to acquire, but there's more to it than that. Automated testing is a check on a programmer's own failings; a mythical perfect programmer wouldn't need automated tests because he or she would write perfect code the first time, every time. So, often the value that programmers attribute to automated tests is proportional to their estimate of how many mistakes they expect to make. Professional programmers realize that they are fallible, and they do their best to correct for that. Programmers who don't believe they are likely to make mistakes aren't programmers whose code I'd want to depend on.

Repeating the Cycle as Needed

Virtually every app could have one more feature added (or deleted) or go through one more round of performance testing, or have one more thing done to make it better. At some point, you have to decide whether enough is enough and you're ready to ship or whether you need to go back and design the next thing to be developed. There's only one way to be absolutely sure that you've made the correct decision, and that's with hindsight, after listening to the response from the market.

However, while there are no hard-and-fast rules, there are some things to consider. The following subsections discuss these considerations.

Considering Your Competition

Your competition is perhaps the most clear-cut consideration. It's likely to be pointless to release an app that's less functional and less attractive and less refined than an established direct competitor. Your app needs to be at least as functional, be at least as polished, and have at least one compelling feature that your competitor doesn't provide in order to have much of a chance of success.

Considering Your Budget

Budget problems happen far too often. If you're close to running out of money, you need to be shipping soon. Most clients I see don't keep money in reserve, and they plan on being done right at the time that the money runs out. They're therefore just one unexpected delay away from failing the project.

You should insist on a plan that gives you an app that, while it might have fewer features or fewer bells and whistles than you want, could at least potentially be shipped well within your budget. You can always do another cycle (or more), continuing to add features or polish with the rest of your money. But if you plan only one cycle, and it's big enough to consume almost all your budget, then you have no fallback position in the event that something goes wrong.

User Testing

A more subjective, yet still very useful, technique to determine whether you're ready to ship is to hand the potentially completed app to a number of new people and see what feedback they have. If user testing is done correctly, it is probably the most helpful way to make a decision.

Keep in mind that, in order for user testing to be a good representation of the real world, the users need to be in your target demographic, and they need to get no more explanation or assistance than your average user is going to get.

Considering Your Schedule

Releasing based on a schedule can be a useful constraint, but it's easy to wind up with a bad result when you're driving toward schedule as your primary goal. It's quite true that sticking to a reasonable schedule is a good practice to keep things from getting out of hand. Many projects have success with this metric.

But a lot of clients are concerned with how soon they can get in the store and feel that they need to cut corners to get there faster. Speed becomes all-important and trumps nearly everything else, often even common sense. This is a recipe for disaster. As a matter of fact, it's such a recipe for disaster, and so common, that many books have been written about it. The seminal work is *The Mythical Man-Month* by Fred Brooks, first published in 1975, based on his experience at IBM working on the OS/360 operating system for IBM mainframe computers. It's just as poor a strategy now as it was some 40 years ago.

Deciding What's Necessary: Apple Versus *Consumer Reports*

There are conflicting strategies for deciding what's necessary before you can ship. A decision about whether you are ready should consider where your target demographic falls in the spectrum.

On one side, you have Apple. Apple is notorious for shipping with fewer, more polished features. Remember when the iPhone first shipped? It had no multitasking, no cut-and-paste, no third-party apps, and, of course, no Adobe Flash support. All these features (save Flash, which Adobe eventually gave up trying to port to smartphones) eventually appeared over the years, presumably once Apple decided they were polished enough.

On the other side, you have *Consumer Reports*, the magazine that is known for evaluating products based on huge tables rating each product on lists and lists of individual features and totaling the scores up to recommend a winner.

Neither of these strategies is always correct or always wrong, and there's plenty of ground between them. Try to figure out which camp your target user leans toward and let that inform your decisions about whether to do another iteration, and, if so, what it should be focused on.

The Case of the Never-Ending Design Cycle

Once upon a time, I was contracted as part of a team working on an app. This app had a hard deadline. There was an industry event that was going to happen, and arrangements had already been made (and money had changed hands) for this app to debut and be heavily advertised at that event.

So a deadline was set for when the app needed to be done, and a schedule was worked backward from that. The schedule was tight, and every programmer was working nights and weekends. The "code freeze" date—the date past which the only changes allowed are bug fixes of issues deemed to be severe enough to stop the launch—was swiftly approaching. We were nearing the point when we'd switch to all-hands-on-deck QA testing, find and fix the remaining bugs, and ship. We were tired and we were stressed, but we were starting to see the light at the end of the tunnel.

And then we got *the call*. A design change had been mandated. We were to rearrange this one screen over here.

We objected. The time for design freeze had long past. We couldn't possibly incorporate the new thing. We argued. We lost.

We failed.

Now, I need to be honest here: It didn't just happen like that. It just happened like that *three times* (although, in truth, one of them was a web app, not a mobile app).

One of the three projects launched as scheduled and was a disaster (at least from a technical standpoint). We'd had no time for performance testing, and it fell over under load.

One of the projects "launched" in the sense that the advertising happened as planned. But the app, not being in a usable state, was nowhere to be found. The app arrived much later, long after most people who'd seen the marketing had likely forgotten about it.

And the last project didn't launch at all. When the scheduled app ship date arrived, there was still so much disagreement about what the design should be that no one could even produce screen mockups for the ads. The marketing campaign was canceled, any deposit forfeited. The app itself arrived in the store months later, having missed its window, was a commercial failure, and was soon pulled from availability.

Let this be a warning. In the words of Steve Jobs, "Real Artists Ship" (see http://c2.com/cgi/wiki?RealArtistsShip). Don't let the cycle go on too long, especially in the face of a deadline.

Wrapping Up

This chapter discusses the app development life cycle and defines and discusses the three phases in the process of making apps. Hopefully, this information helps you understand what you'll need to go through before your app is ready and is getting you thinking about your planning process. Here are a few final thoughts to wrap up this chapter:

- Design is not just what happens in Photoshop. Design is making and communicating the decisions about what the app will do, what it will not do, and how it will behave. It's far deeper and more important than just graphics, and design changes get more expensive as the project progresses.

- Development is not just about, or even mostly about, the screens of an app. A lot more goes into an app than just what you can see on the surface, and you need to plan for all of it.

- Testing should start as soon as you have something to test, and it should never be left until the end of the project. Don't confuse testing to find bugs with user experience testing. Automated tests are very useful for avoiding regression issues.

- Go through as many cycles as you need to. Err on the side of having too many cycles but don't forget that you have to ship to have any chance of succeeding.

Prototyping and Wireframing Your App

A good way to minimize the cost and reduce the risk of developing an app is to decide as many things as you can before you start paying developers to write code. A good way to do that is with extensive prototyping. As discussed in Chapter 2, "The App Development Life Cycle," the design phase of the life cycle is all about making decisions. To make decisions well, you need a context and a framework. The easiest and cheapest way to get that context is to build a prototype.

The word *prototype* means different things to different people, and I use it here fairly loosely, as a blanket term that covers many different activities and artifacts. I'll do my best to make it clear what kind of prototype I'm discussing as I go along. In general, however, when I talk about prototyping, I'm talking about quickly and inexpensively building some kind of artifact that moves a project in the direction of completion but that is not intended to be included as part of the final product. The words *quick* and *inexpensive* here are critical but relative. If a prototype is going to cost a significant portion of the budget for the whole project, then it isn't actually a prototype. That said, if you are building a triple-A video game title with a budget of several million dollars, a prototype could be fairly elaborate and costly. The main thing is that a prototype has to be a lot faster and cheaper than the final product.

When prototyping an app, you will hopefully go through many prototypes (or at least many iterations), keeping the parts of them that seem to work and throwing out the rest. Looking back once an app is done, it's not unusual to see that the prototyping phase took up a significant amount of your effort and the app's development schedule. Each individual prototype should still be relatively fast and cheap to build, even if they all turn out to have been a lot of effort once you've added them up after the fact.

There's a tendency to want to be done with prototyping and move on to actual development. Prototyping is often not seen as *real work* since it doesn't ship. But the information that makes the difference between your app being successful and not can usually be determined from prototyping, and it's far, far cheaper to find that information during the prototype phase than after coding has begun in earnest.

One reason that people don't see prototyping as being valuable is that they build the prototypes and then just let them sit. A prototype is largely a communication medium. If you don't show it to people and get their feedback and refine it, you are wasting your time. Once a prototype is complete and has incorporated all the user feedback that is feasible, the prototype then becomes a communication tool between you and your development team. Don't underestimate how useful that prototype will be when code starts to be written.

We'll talk later about what to do with the prototype once you build it, but first we're going to talk about getting a prototype together. While building (or iterating on) a prototype, remember two key rules: fast and cheap. Don't agonize over choices. If you can't decide, flip a coin and note what you didn't pick so you can come back to it if it turns out you don't like your first choice.

Focus on the Core Experience

When starting the prototyping process, you should start with the most useful or important action that your app provides to your user. This is sometimes called *the golden path*. Don't start by worrying about corner cases and what-if scenarios. We'll come back to those later.

The core experience is the cornerstone on which your app is going to be built. Take your time to get it right. What is the single most important thing that your app is going to provide? Where is the value? Start there and then work backward.

Many apps have multistep workflows. All those steps may be important, but you should start with the one that provides the most value—the one that solves the biggest problem or relieves the most pain.

For example, many connected apps begin by asking the user to log in to or create an account. That's fine, and when it comes time to design the flow of your app, logging in and out are critical functions that have to be considered carefully. (We discuss them at length later in this chapter.) But when you're starting to figure out the primary use case of your app, you should skip login and go straight to the most common or most valuable part of the app, from the user's perspective. We'll come back and discuss things like login later.

Write Your Commercial First

When trying to nail down app design, my favorite technique is to start by thinking about what a commercial for the app would look like. You've seen Apple iPhone and iPad commercials of users reading books, taking panoramic photographs, taking phone calls, etc. Imagine what such a commercial would be like for your app. Eventually, you'll write a script for it. That script will form the starting point of the prototyping exercise.

I think of this as being the app equivalent of what startups call the "elevator pitch." Imagine that you find yourself in an elevator with someone, and they ask you about your app. You have only as much time to describe it to them as it takes the elevator to get to the next floor. What do you say? That's your elevator pitch. Your commercial would be the multimedia-enabled equivalent of that. You have 30 seconds or less of your potential user's attention. What would you show?

Apple has made many commercials that are fantastic examples of this concept. Early on in the iPhone's existence, Apple would show commercials with someone taking a phone call or looking up something on a map. The iPhone was front-and-center on a distraction-free white background. The hands and fingers that were manipulating the iPhone were clearly visible. Think about one of those that you've seen (and go look one up on the Internet if you need to).

Now fast forward to the introduction of the iPad. Those commercials were slightly more sophisticated. You often saw a person sitting on a couch reading a book or newspaper or website on their iPad while it was perched on their lap. You never saw the user's face, but again, you could clearly see the hands and fingers touching and manipulating the device. Think about that for a minute before you go on. Again, go find one (or more) of these commercials on the Internet if you don't have a clear picture of one in your mind.

Pick Your Typical User

We start our commercial-writing exercise by imagining the most ideal user for your app. Who are they? What problem do they have that you're trying to help them solve? Are they technical? Are they too young to read? Are their eyes too old to clearly read smaller fonts?

Most people with business experience inherently start thinking about a target demographic. That's as good a place as any for us to start this discussion. But there's a factor we need to consider first: Either *your app is your business and your business is your app* or *your app is an adjunct to your real business.*

If your app is your business and your business is your app, you should use only *self-reporting capable* attributes, like *soccer mom* or *cat owner* when writing down your target demographic. There is no one who would describe themselves, unprompted, as "a person who wants an app that would help me play with my cat while my kids are at soccer." A lot of my clients have a tendency to presuppose a more specific audience than is likely to exist, which leads to confused users when the app expects them to be more focused than they actually are.

If your app is an adjunct to your existing business, be honest about who your customers really are and what they want or need from an app. Too often the marketing department wants an app to increase foot traffic, but the information technology (IT) department won't play ball and give the app access to the company's data, so the functions the customer really wants are unavailable, and marketing convinces themselves that the customer really wants something else. I've been down that road many times. You don't want to go there.

Now it's possible that your app legitimately reaches multiple demographics and has multiple use cases. That's fine (and might be useful for sales). In this case, though, you need to focus. Pick only one typical type of user for now; you can come back and do this exercise again later with a different user in mind, if you want to.

Once you have some idea about who your user is, you need to get more specific. You need to pick a typical example of that demographic on a typical day for illustration purposes. The important thing to remember here is that you are not a typical member of that demographic. The typical member is highly unlikely to want to build this app, so you don't count. If you pick an example that's too contrived, this won't work, so think about who a typical member of this demographic would really be.

Pick the Perfect Situation

Once you have your typical user in your head, it's time to put them in the situation where your app can do the most for them. It's okay to imagine a contrived setting here, although hopefully it's still a situation your typical user will encounter reasonably often.

Imagine where that person would be in the moments before starting to use your app. Are they standing or sitting? Is their device already in their hand, or will they need to get it out of their pocket or purse or backpack? Are they completely focused on accomplishing a task, or are they waiting in line, trying to stave off boredom?

Now get inside your user's head. What do they want? What are they thinking about? What are they worried about? Are they harried or bored? Are they tired or wide awake? Are they happy or sad? Try not to say "it doesn't matter." If you're not sure, just pick one, and you can refine it later. The more specific you can be, the better.

Now think about the problem. What's in your user's way? What's the pain point? What's wrong, and how does your user feel about it? Try to get yourself in that situation. Try to feel what the user would be feeling. What words describe those emotions?

You've now set the stage for the prototyping process. Write down what you've come up with so far. This is the place that you want to put yourself when it comes time to test your prototypes, and this is also the situation you'll need to describe to your initial testers before you ask them for their feedback.

Determine What the User Does Now

Now we can move on to tasks. We're not worried about screens or buttons yet—just actions. What does your user do with your app at this point? Do they answer the phone? Do they read an article? Take a picture? Share information on a social network? Record a to-do item for future reference? If it's a series of tasks, write them all down, in the order the user will perform them.

Now take a minute to think about how you want your user to feel when the tasks are complete. What words describe those feelings? These are your target words for what you want your users to describe when they've imagined themselves using your app. We'll come back to this when we talk about gathering feedback.

Flesh Out the Script

At this point, you should have notes on what your commercial would be. It should start with a particular person in a particular place or situation, experiencing a particular problem or need, in a particular emotional state. Then there should be a list of the actions the user takes with your app, followed by how you want the user to feel.

Now it's time to think about turning the actions into an app. For each action you have written down, think about how you want that to be represented in an app. Is each a button the user taps? What does the screen with the button look like, and how does the user know what that button will do when tapped? (And how does the user know to tap that button?) Maybe it's not a button but a gesture. Does the user need to scroll? Does the user stay on the same screen while performing all the tasks or transition to new ones? For now, assume that each action will involve moving to a new screen; you can combine the screens later.

Don't worry about details here; don't even think about colors and fonts. Just write down what actions you want represented and how many screens are involved. Avoid tutorials, instructions, and voiceovers (ideally forever, but definitely for this step). Right now you're just worried about the core functionality of the app, and the app needs to be able to speak for itself.

Now, hopefully, you'll have an idea of what you would show if the app were built and you wanted to showcase it. Now it's time to move to the next phase of prototyping: making wireframes.

Wireframe the App

Now that the stage has been set, it's time to build your *wireframe* (also sometimes called a *mockup*). First, let's quickly discuss about what a wireframe is and what it isn't.

A wireframe, for our purposes, is a series of static representations of app screens. They usually have callouts on them or arrows between them or text that indicates how to get from screen A to screen B.

Some people have specific requirements about the level of detail that has to exist (or not exist) in order for something to be called a wireframe. Some people insist that wireframes have to look like crayon drawings, so that the observer doesn't get too caught up in the details. Some people insist that wireframes have to be picture-perfect representations of what the finished app will eventually look like. For purposes of this book, I don't care about any of that. Use the level of detail that makes sense to you for the particular point in the process. It's not unusual to do several iterations of wireframes, each at a different level of detail. That's fine. The important thing is that the wireframe needs to be quick and cheap relative to what the next step will be. Don't worry about perfecting your colors and gradients before you decide how many buttons you need and where they should be.

As I said in this book's preface, this is not a book about app design or graphic design. I'm not going to argue the pros and cons of putting buttons at the top of the screen versus the bottom of the screen. There are plenty of books on that subject, and it's arguable whether there is one always-correct answer for any of those questions. For our purposes, it doesn't matter.

What we're going to talk about here is an iterative process. Pick something, anything, and show it to people and get feedback. Then pick something else and see if the feedback is better or worse. Keep repeating that process until you find the one that gets you the most positive feedback and then go to the next step. That's iteration, which is the core of prototyping.

Design skills and information will certainly make the iteration process faster—maybe thousands of times faster. I'm not trying to imply that you don't need to know anything about design or say that the layout doesn't matter. It absolutely matters when it comes to how much iteration you end up needing and how long it takes before you have a design that works for your user.

But for purposes of this discussion, I'm not going to talk about the principles of app design. I'm not primarily a designer, and if this book tried to include everything, it would never get finished. You can find lots of good design discussions online and in books. Go find one, or use your own taste.

Sketch Your Initial Screens

A few pages ago, I asked you to think about the tasks your user would perform in your app for the single workflow in the situation in which your app is most valuable. Now it's time to figure out how your user might do those things.

From your script, you should have a guess at how many screens you would need to show in your mythical commercial. Think about each of them in turn. What should each screen look like? Grab some paper (or a tablet and stylus) and draw a quick sketch. Don't get stuck. Don't worry about content or details, and don't worry about what else might be on that screen. Just sketch the things that the user would interact with for that part of your script.

Chances are, you're not doing what I just asked you to do. You don't have a pencil or stylus in your hand, and you're not sketching. That's okay. I expected that. So let's talk through one. For illustrative purposes, I'm going to use a purely hypothetical banking app as an example throughout the rest of this chapter. Figure 3.1 shows a first draft of the first screen. Note that, at this point, the sketch is crude, and you don't need to know where on the screen the button will be placed. That's fine: You will refine it over time.

Figure 3.1
An initial sketch of the Home screen, with a History button.

The screen in Figure 3.1 is probably uglier than what you were expecting. That's kind of the point: You have to start somewhere, and if you wait to start development until it's good enough that people want to pay you for it, you might never ship. If you can make it better now without getting stuck, then feel free, but if you need to stop and think about it, just do the minimum and come back to it later.

Now we repeat this for every action that we have written down for the use case that's going to be in your commercial. Once we have a few rectangles with stuff in them, we need to connect them.

The easiest thing to do at this point is to draw arrows between them, with text describing what triggers each transition, as shown in Figure 3.2. Drawing arrows between screens works pretty well at first. Eventually, though, you will end up with too many screens to fit on a page. That's fine; we'll worry about that in a while.

This is the basic process for making a wireframe: sketch screens and then connect them together; then you sketch more screens and connect them, too. Lather, rinse, repeat, and you're done.

There are some tricks, and some ways to make it easier, and we'll get to those. But for the moment, reflect on how amateurish that illustration looks and how little it looks like an app. Then understand that even that wireframe conveys information; I've had customers hire me with way less to go on than that.

No matter how artistically challenged you may be, you can make wireframes. And even if you want to bring in a professional designer (and you probably should, depending on the complexity of your app), the wireframes you create can be a huge help in communicating your ideas to your designer.

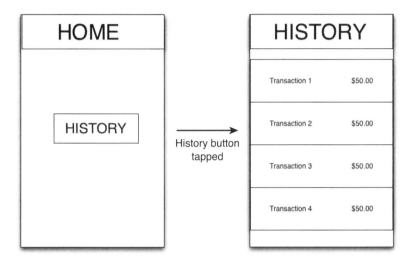

Figure 3.2
An initial quick sketch of the connection between the Home screen and the History screen.

Variations of Drawing Tools for Wireframes

Before we go further, let's briefly talk about wireframe/mockup tools. There are a ton of them, and they all have strengths and weaknesses. There's no right answer (although I'm sure some of them are horrible, so there are definitely many wrong answers).

I tend to use a Mac app called OmniGraffle for wireframing. (Or for you Windows-only people, whenever I say "OmniGraffle," just pretend I said "Visio," and you'll have an idea of the kind of tool I'm talking about.) I don't use it because it's perfect but because I've been using it for years, and I'm used to it. A lot of people make wireframes in Photoshop, but that would take me forever. There are also a number of dedicated wireframing tools on the market. (Balsamiq seems to be a popular one with some of the folks I've worked with.)

There are roughly three kinds of wireframes that can be created, and different tools produce the different types:

- Barebones wireframes, which is where the name *wireframe* comes from
- Standard interface stencil wireframes
- Photorealistic wireframes, which are typically called *mockups*

Balsamiq was created to do the barebones style, OmniGraffle can do barebones or stenciled, and Photoshop could do any of the three styles but is used primarily for the photorealistic ones (see Figure 3.3).

Figure 3.3
A screen from the iPhone Settings app, presented in different wireframing styles. On the left is a barebones style, the middle is in the stenciled style, and the one on the right is photorealistic.

The Barebones Style

Each style has advantages and disadvantages. The barebones style is the easiest and quickest to put together, but that's not why it's so popular. The barebones style conveys the functionality of the wireframe without running afoul of (or instigating new) preconceived notions about what people think the app should look like.

Back in Chapter 1, "What Could Possibly Go Wrong?" we talked about *bikeshedding*, which is the tendency of people to argue about trivial things that are easy to argue about and to miss more important things that require thought. Bikeshedding is a trap that's easy to fall into with more fleshed-out wireframes. I've seen meetings called for the purpose of grouping user interface elements into screens completely derailed by objections to the shade of color in a wireframe's gradient that was never intended to be permanent. Wireframing in the barebones style can help avoid this trap.

The downside of the barebones style is that some people have difficulty visualizing what an app might be like from just a line drawing, and that can interfere with the amount of information the design can communicate. I've had customers approve a wireframe sketch and then upon seeing the fleshed-out design exclaim, "That's not what I told you to do at all!" Once those folks saw the new design and the original wireframes side-by-side, they realized their misconception, but the design still had to be done over, and a lot of work was still wasted.

Common UI Stencils

Stenciling provides the next level of detail up from the barebones style. This style emulates the look of the default controls and interfaces of the chosen platform. You copy and paste the generic user interface elements from the stencil onto your wireframe, change the text, move some things around, and you're done. It's more work than the barebones style, but it's not too bad. This is the style I use to do most of my wireframing.

To use this style, you would have to acquire a stencil that's appropriate for your platform and your wireframing tool of choice. In general, that's not too difficult these days. Back when the iPhone first came out, there were a bunch of them available for free. Now most of them have an associated fee, but it's usually on the order of $100. Since a developer can cost $100,000 or more, I'd say it's probably worth buying a stencil if it helps you communicate your ideas more effectively and prevents duplicate work and wasted effort.

Photorealism

The final style of wireframes is the photorealistic ones, often called *mockups*. If you're going to have custom controls or graphics in your app, you pretty much have to end up doing this one at some point. Later, the photorealistic assets (buttons, backgrounds, images, and so on) from the mockup are usually extracted and given to the developers to use in the app. This is often referred to as *slicing*.

The problems with doing your initial wireframes in this style are that it takes a lot longer (at least for most people), and it can lead to bikeshedding.

Briefly Jumping Ahead

There's one other alternative to the wireframe types we've just examined. Some *interactive prototype* tools (discussed later in this chapter) can be used for wireframing, so if you're going to build an interactive prototype (and you probably should before development starts in earnest), you can choose to do all your wireframing work there. I usually don't do this (at least in the initial stages), just because I find that static graphics are easier for me to build in a static tool. Your mileage may vary, though, so do what works for you.

Make Static Wireframes of Dynamic Screens

The thing about wireframes is that they're static, and app screens aren't. This often leads to confusion, although the solution is pretty simple: Represent dynamic app screens in a static mockup as multiple static screens, one for each state (see Figure 3.4).

Figure 3.4
A single scrolling table screen, displayed at three different scroll positions. Note that there should really also be another screen here with the keyboard visible and the Search box on the left being filled in, and there should also be a screen that shows how the search results should be displayed.

Figure Out Your Options

The trick to creating a usable set of wireframes is figuring out all the different states in which you need to display each screen. Many teams neglect this step and create only one representation for a screen like the one shown in Figure 3.4. The developer must then either ask what the screen should look like as scrolling happens (especially at the bottom) or guess what the app creator or graphic designer intended and risk being wrong.

And there are often other states for a screen as well. Take the example of a scrolling table of rows like the one in Figure 3.4. What would this screen look like if it were being edited (assuming that the table isn't read-only)? How should rows be deleted? Is the table searchable, and if it is, what does that look like? Are there any kinds of data that need rows with a different layout? Are the rows selectable? What would that look like?

If the screen has images in the rows, what happens if one row's image is missing? Should a placeholder image be used, or does the text move over to fill the space where the image should be? For any buttons, what are the different states they can be in? What do they look like when tapped? Are there other actions or animations, like a Pull to Refresh action? If so, what does that look like?

For every screen that takes user input, make sure to wireframe it with the virtual keyboard present and with the virtual keyboard absent. You might find that things might need to scroll or move around to be visible when the keyboard is onscreen. It's better to decide how that should look now than after it's already been programmed.

You should go through all the different things that can be manipulated on each screen and think about how the manipulation would affect the screen. It's not strictly necessary to wireframe every single interaction, but if you have any doubt, err on the side of documenting too much. I've seen confusion about details I thought were blatantly obvious on several occasions.

Make Copies of Your Screens

Once you figure out what all your states are, make copies of the screen inside your wireframing tool and then make changes to it to show the different states. If you want to save space on your wireframe, you can copy only the part of the screen that's relevant to show that state, as in Figure 3.5. Once you get to the point of making an interactive prototype, you'll probably need to have one screen per state (unless your tool supports partial screen changes; see the section "Adapting Screens for Tablets" for more information).

If you have multiple screens that are subtly different, be sure to label the conditions that cause one screen to be displayed instead of another (for example, "Update button selected," or "scrolled to bottom," or "holding Pull to Refresh before releasing it").

You'll likely end up with more screens than can all fit easily on one page or screen of your wireframing tool. That's when it's time to start breaking them into groups and using indicators to show how they connect (see Figure 3.6) instead of leaving them all on one screen with arrows drawn between them, as shown earlier.

These indicators make it much easier, later in the process, to change screens around to incorporate new designs and user feedback. It's much easier to change or add a new indicator icon than it is to move around long arrows that connect different screens in the larger wireframe document.

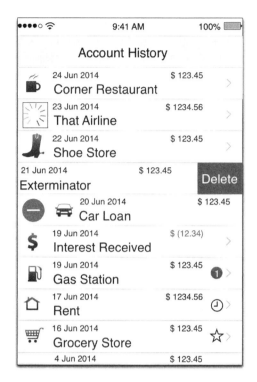

Figure 3.5
Multiple rows with buttons and images in different states.

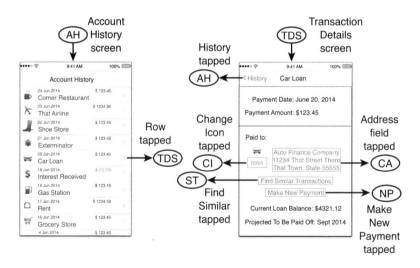

Figure 3.6
Multiple screens tied together with indicators.

Adapting Screens for Tablets

When building phone-sized apps, the tendency is to make each screen do one thing and to have lots of transitions between screens. This makes sense because when you divide up a hand-sized screen into several different areas, each area ends up fairly small—often so small that it's hard to read and its buttons are difficult to tap.

Tablet apps don't have this problem, so it's common for an action that a user takes on a tablet to cause only part of the screen to change. Unfortunately, that's not the easiest thing to represent in a wireframe. What I generally do (and recommend) is just make a copy of the full screen in the wireframe document and then superimpose the changed area on top of the relevant portion of the copy. If you were to print out the wireframe document, this would cause a large waste of paper, but I don't know anyone who prints out more than a screen or two.

This method does have the unfortunate consequence that, when refining your wireframes later, you'll have to do duplicate work when the format of the original screen changes. If you have one screen that has six or eight or more variants and that screen gets overhauled, it becomes necessary to alter the underlying graphic for each of the variants. This is tedious and annoying, but it really isn't that much work.

Determine What Other Commercials You Could Make

By this time, you should have a wireframe that shows all the features and functionality and states of all the screens needed to build your commercial for the most popular or most important workflow for your app. Now it's time to go through the other workflows that people can do with your app and add them.

You likely already have a list (on paper or in your head) of things other than the one you picked for your commercial that you want your app to be able to do. Now is the time to get that list out and make sketches of the screens that each feature would need. For each new feature, just repeat the same process that you used the first time through.

Now—and this is important—*don't get stuck here*. The tendency I see at this point is that people start agonizing over button placement and what should be on what screen. Now is not the time for that. Now is the time to get everything down on paper (and by paper, I mean some drawing program or wireframing tool). You'll be going over this again and again and refining your design—either by yourself or in conjunction with a user experience designer. Don't worry about flow or graphics or button placement or any of that yet.

Just get all your features represented by buttons and screens at this point. Refining comes later.

Also, this is the time to throw the kitchen sink at it. Even features that are a low priority or that you aren't sure are worth it have a place in early wireframes. Some features will inevitably get thrown out in the process. I often find that, once user feedback is taken into account, features I didn't think were important end up in the final design and features I thought were core to the product end up getting cut. At this point, adding a new feature is really, really cheap, so do it. If it gets cut later, you've lost the minutes of time it took you to add a new screen to a drawing document. If you have to add or cut features after development is well under way, it's much more expensive. That's why you're prototyping in the first place: to answer questions in the cheapest way possible.

Once you've added more stuff to your wireframe, you might end up with something like Figure 3.7. Note that this screen has a bunch of buttons in no particular order. This is not a good design; it's cluttered, unorganized, and visually boring, but it's an early work in progress, so that's not a problem. It successfully enumerates what the user's options are, and that's what you're going for here.

Figure 3.7
A new iterative design for the Home screen from Figure 3.2, this time more fleshed out and with more buttons that facilitate more features of the hypothetical example app.

Identify Your Error Functions

At this point, you should have a bunch of screens hooked together with arrows and indicators. These screens and the flows between them, once implemented in code, will enable a number of features that you want your users to be able to use. This is well and good, and you'll be able to improve it over time.

But what you have now constitutes only what is called the *golden path*— the workflow that happens if everything goes right and nothing bad or unexpected occurs. But you also need to account for that other stuff.

You need to go back through your wireframes and, at each step, ask yourself, "Is there anything that could go wrong here? If so, what? What should happen then?" As you're doing this, keep in mind that many things can go off the golden path, including things that eventually work but take longer than the user expects (in which case you might want to throw up an indicator of some kind), or things that happen when the users change their mind and want to go back to where they were, in the middle of your workflow. You'll likely find that at many points several things could go wrong, and you should make a screen for each one.

Now you need a way of showing how multiple things can happen from a single action. I recommend that you change your indicators that connect one screen to another to look more flowchart like, with decision icons that point to different indicators. Figure 3.8 shows an example.

Before long, you might find yourself on track to have more screens with pop-up errors than screens that the user would actually want to see. This is not unusual, and it's okay. Don't worry too much about the content that goes into these error screens, yet; you will address that in time. If you have to, instead of making a screen for each error, you can just make a list and refer to the item number in the list on the indicator.

For ease of management and to minimize confusion, I generally try to group the screens associated with the normal flow of the application together in my wireframe document and then put the error screens later in the document.

If this seems like this is a lot of work, you're right: It is. But it's work that needs to get done. All those screens need to be estimated and programmed, and your developer can't do the estimation if he or she doesn't know it should be there. Also, someone has to make decisions about what should happen if something breaks. In order to do that, the different things that can break have to be captured and written down, and this is my preferred way of doing that.

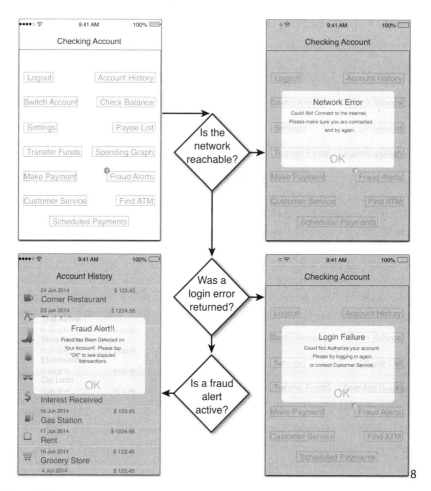

Figure 3.8
An example of how to indicate branching, which is how different things can happen in response to a user, depending on state. These conditional indicators can become quite common in your wireframes as the number of things that can go wrong expands.

Figure Out Your First-Run Workflow

Now you should have at least the majority of your features diagrammed, along with a lot of the ways that external factors could cause your app to work in ways you don't expect or want. You're almost done with the wireframing. There's really only one more workflow that needs to be wireframed, and that's what happens when the user sees the app for the very first time.

This so-called *first-run* workflow is both very important and different from the rest of your wireframing. It's important because unless the users successfully navigate this workflow, they will never become successful (or happy) users of your app, much less the enthusiastic supporters and promoters that you would ideally like them to be. It's different because the users are not yet familiar with the workings of the app, and any initial configuration the app might need has yet to be collected (for example, the users need to log in or create an account, grant the app any permissions it needs, and set any preferences they want).

So the first-run workflow has two often-contradictory goals: Teach the user how to use the app and get the information the app needs. This is unfortunate because both of these are difficult tasks, and trying to do both at the same time is even harder. Because of the difficulty, and because app creators and designers tend to focus on showcasing the core features of the app, this aspect of app design rarely gets the amount of attention and effort I think it deserves.

The most common issue I see is apps starting with nothing but a login screen. I've seen an analytics report for one app that said that more than half the users made no attempt to log in or create an account and never launched the app again. Obviously, not all apps are like that (especially ones with well-known brands behind them), but many are. When as many as 22% of apps may only ever be run once (see http://www.localytics.com/blog/2013/localytics-app-user-retention-data/), do you really want to take that chance, or would you rather give the user a good experience first and a reason to log in later?

Another common problem is apps having a set of static tutorial screens that purport to tell the user how to use the app. In most user testing I've seen, many (if not most) users move quickly through the tutorial without really paying attention to it, and then later they don't understand how to use the parts of the app that the tutorial was intended to teach them. Remember that many apps are used infrequently and are subject to interruptions, so even if the user does pay attention to the tutorial, that's no guarantee that he or she will retain that information when it's finally of use. The trick here is to understand when the user is in the right frame of mind to absorb a given piece of information about how to use your app and then present it to the user helpfully and unobtrusively.

So spend some time thinking about how you would want to be introduced to your app if you weren't already invested in using it. Then mock it up as described here, and then—and this is the most important thing—*get it in front of real users* to see what they think.

Getting Feedback on Wireframes

The best way to get feedback on the screens of an app is to give those screens to a real user at the right size on a real device and see what happens. To do that, you need to turn your wireframes into an interactive prototype, as discussed later in this chapter.

However, you can get a lot of useful information from just showing people your wireframe document, which requires less work than transferring it onto a device. I'm especially likely to show wireframes to other people who are already familiar with the app (like the app creator or other members of the development team) to both communicate what I'm proposing more effectively and illustrate alternatives (for example, to say, "Which of these two potential screens looks better to you?"). I can do this because I'm confident that the people to whom I am showing the wireframes have enough prior context to understand what the screen means without having to see it on a device.

There are also times when you don't really have enough information yet to go to the prototype stage. I use a wireframe when app creators come to me with an idea and perhaps a vague interface description but no screens well defined. I throw together a wireframe document, and then we can sit down and discuss it together. I find that having something to look at and point to, even if it's just a strawman proposal, sets the stage for more productive conversations about what the app should do and look like than I can ever get by just having a verbal conversation. The old adage about a picture being worth a thousand words seems an underestimate to me when the picture is a user interface.

The downside of doing user testing with wireframes is that you have to ask people what they *would do* instead of actually being able to *watch them try to do it*. It turns out that this makes a huge difference because what people say they would do and what they actually do are often surprisingly dissimilar.

The basic process of getting user feedback goes like this:

1. Give the users just enough context to understand what they are looking at, but no more.
2. Tell them what you want them to do but not how to do it.
3. Find out what they would do next (ideally by observing but by asking, if necessary).
4. Find out why (to the extent they can explain) they made the choice they did.

The biggest mistakes I see are giving a test user far more context, help, and information than a real user would have, making the user feel pressured to give positive feedback, and downplaying or minimizing the actual feedback. This can be caused by the app creator or developer standing right next to the test user and talking, making suggestions, gesturing, pointing, making excuses, and explaining. Another way this happens is when the same test users are consulted over and over, so that each time they collect more understanding of what the app is *supposed* to do, until they are no longer representative of the target customer. These things are all problematic. You want to start with test users who are unfamiliar with the app, give them as little direction as possible, leave them alone until they've had time to make up their minds, and collect their feedback in a nonemotional and nonconfrontational way.

Ideally, you want all interactions between the test users and the app building team to be in writing, and you don't want to ask the same user to look at the app twice. This eliminates most of the tendencies to steer users toward what the builders know they want the users to do and reduces the tendency of the users to attempt to protect the builders' feelings by saying what they think the builders want to hear. Obviously, though, that takes longer and requires more effort. You might therefore want to do these ideal tests less frequently and to do more frequent tests in person with repeat users in between the ideal tests. There's no strict formula, and it isn't a one-size-fits-all situation.

Remember the maxim discussed in Chapter 2: The later in the process a design decision is made, the more expensive that decision will be. If you have fresh eyes look at your app so infrequently that you put a lot of development effort into what turns out to be a bad idea, you'll end up wasting a lot of time and money.

Consolidate, Organize, and Refine

Once you've shown your initial wireframes to other people (or even looked at them again after a good night's sleep), you'll likely start collecting notes about screens being crowded, confusing, cluttered, too busy, too numerous, and on and on. Don't worry. It's still early, and the design will get better over time.

Now is the time to incorporate the feedback you've gathered into your wireframes. Take the complaints you are given to heart and try to address them as best you can. Make a new and (hopefully) better set of wireframes and repeat the process, and your design should get better.

Specific advice about how to address the design issues that arise from user testing, or what makes one user interface better or worse than another is beyond the scope of this book. For more information on resources to help with that process, see the "User Experience Design" and "Graphic Design" sections of Chapter 6, "Skill Gap Analysis."

Whether you use trial and error or more sophisticated techniques for making changes to your wireframes, keep in mind that, ultimately, your wireframes need to be converted to code. As you refine, improve, and add detail to your wireframes, it's important to recognize what factors will facilitate or inhibit your developer's eventual attempt to build the corresponding app.

The primary elements of any wireframe document are the screens. They certainly should not be the only elements (although unfortunately often they are), but they're the most obvious ones.

As you wireframe your screens, a good rule of thumb is that the more screens there are, the more your app is going to cost (all other things being equal). So consolidating (or eliminating) screens not only makes your document more comprehensible but is likely to reduce your development costs as well. On the other hand, packing too much stuff into too few screen isn't good either.

Group Together Like Data

For screens that contain a lot of data, like scrolling lists of items, try as best you can to have only one kind of data on each screen. For example, if the screen has a list of transactions on it, try to keep nontransaction information like "what ATM machines are near me" off that screen. Not only will it be less confusing to the user, but it will make it easier for the programmer to organize the data so that the screen can scroll quickly. This isn't strictly necessary, but if you have a bunch of different kinds of data on the screen at the same time, you run the risk of getting an app that's more expensive, slower, or both.

For tablet apps, you're far more likely to need disparate information on the same screen, so if you can, try not to make them load at the same time. Using the previous example, if you have a list of transactions but you want to provide a map showing at which ATM machine the transaction took place, you could have the map displayed only in response to the user tapping a button on the transaction. This way, when the list of transactions loads, the screen doesn't have to be updated with transaction amounts and map locations simultaneously.

Simplify Scrolling Areas

Try to avoid putting areas of the screen that can scroll inside other parts of the screen that can scroll. When that happens, the two different screen elements can easily get confused about which one of them is supposed to be handling the user's input at any given time, and it can be frustrating to the user and time-consuming for the programmer.

This is also the case with swipe-driven gestures, including switch controls. When the developer has code that is supposed to detect the user flipping a switch from left to right inside a scrolling area that lets the user move the switch around the screen, it's very difficult to interpret the user's desire correctly every time. Often the switch will end up relocating instead of changing value, and the user will be annoyed.

Understand That Buttons Are Cheaper Than Gestures

All other things being equal, programming buttons is cheaper than programming gestures. And the more gestures you have, the more time will need to be spent making sure the correct gesture is triggered. I'm not saying that you should avoid gestures entirely; they're integral to the smartphone and tablet experiences. Just keep in mind that gestures take more effort to get right than buttons used for the same purpose.

Reuse Phone-Sized Screens as Tablet Screen Elements

For apps that work on a variety of device sizes, from 4-inch phones to 10-inch tablets (what Apple calls "universal apps"), you can reduce costs if you can incorporate your phone-sized screens into a portion of your tablet-sized apps. Think of the built-in iPad Mail app as an example. The left panel is essentially the list view from the iPhone version of the app, and the right panel is the preview pane. Again, this isn't strictly necessary, but it can save you time and money. Figure 3.9 shows an example of this in action.

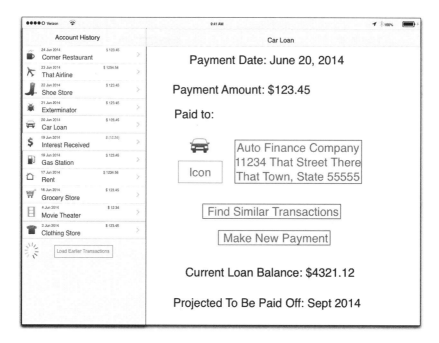

Figure 3.9
This iPad app screen reuses both screens from Figure 3.6.

Build an Interactive Prototype

In order to get a realistic impression of the kind of app your wireframes will become, but without having to spend the money to build the whole app, you can create an interactive prototype. It's not a perfect representation of what the app will be, but it's a very useful one, especially for the amount of money it costs.

There are different ways to make such a prototype, but if you've already created the wireframes discussed previously in this chapter, you already have the material you need to build the prototype (well, at least one kind of prototype). All you need is one of the many available tools that allow you to display one of your wireframe screens at a time and move between them as people tap things and otherwise interact with the device.

At the very least, it's useful to see the wireframes you've created in context at the correct size. I've seen several apps that had to be overhauled late in the development process because the buttons or other controls were too small or hard to trigger. It's much easier to see what the real size of a control is when looking at it on the real device than when looking at a wireframe on your computer screen.

Another thing that's easier to see on a device is contrast. It's far easier to understand if you can still read the screen and text by walking out into bright sunlight with your phone in your hand than it is to do the same thing with a laptop indoors. Mobile apps get used in all kinds of environments and lighting conditions, and it's much harder to accurately imagine how a wireframe will look under various conditions than it is to just try it.

The Value of Really Interacting

The most important part of having a prototype is interacting with it. You can discover a number of details about your design only when you (and potential users) start actually using it, and for a majority of those discoveries, a prototype is just as good as a running app.

When my role on a project is to develop an app from someone else's wireframes, I usually find at some point that there is either at least one button whose action isn't documented or at least one screen that is unreachable (that is, there isn't any indication of what button or gesture leads to that screen). At that point, I end up having to ask, "What does this button do?" or "How is the user supposed to get to this screen?" But I don't want to give you the impression that I consider myself perfect; I often fail to connect at least one thing during my own wireframing. This is one of the reasons I recommend using interactive prototypes: I am a firm believer in the value of processes that compensate for the fact that I am human and I make mistakes. (I discuss this belief again in Chapter 13, "Testing," when I talk about automated testing.)

Now the fact that a button or a screen doesn't end up being hooked up to something isn't the end of the world, and usually the problem is easily corrected—*but only usually*. I've also seen entire sections of functionality left out of wireframes: app designs with no provision for login at all or no indication that a list of today's transactions should pull up older data as needed when scrolling, which would require gigabytes of information to be stored on the device. These kinds of omissions make a huge difference in the complexity of the app and the time and budget required for development. This kind of wireframing mistake can, when used to make the estimate, virtually ensure that the project cannot be completed on time or within budget.

And so far, I've only been talking about obvious errors—things that clearly can't be right (like dead buttons). Once you get into the realm of judgment calls, it's even more likely that some piece of your design that seemed like a good idea in your head and as a static diagram won't turn out to be what you want in your final app. The goal here is to figure out which piece or pieces need to be changed and what they should look like, but without the expense of building those sections in code first.

The Case of the Wizard Maze

I worked once as a subcontractor on an iPhone project that had a very long signup process. It was wireframed by the designer as several screens that had to be filled out in sequence. The first screen asked for your first and last names, then you tapped Next to go to a screen that asked for your email, then you tapped Next again to go to the screen that asked for your account number, and so on. These kinds of multistep sequences are often called *wizards*, and they've been around on the desktop since the 1990s.

The problem here was that the wizard took forever to complete, and users would often give up. Instead of fixing the poor design, the designer decided that when a user left the wizard sequence, the app would remember what he or she had entered already, and when the user tapped the Sign Up button (or invoked another feature that required an account) again, it would start the user at the point in the sequence where he or she had left off.

This was a disaster because of the Back button. If users had entered their name and email address and tapped Sign Up, they would be taken to the screen asking for their account number. If they tapped the Back button at that point, where should they go—back to the screen where they tapped Sign Up or to the screen where they entered their email? If the app sent the users back to Sign Up, then how should they update their email (or even remember what email they had entered)? If it sent them to the email page, wouldn't they be confused about how to get back to the Sign Up page?

There were many meetings and arguments about what to do about this, and it took up a lot of time and money. The designer and the app creator ended up deciding to use both Back and Previous buttons, which just confused things more, but they felt that was the best they could do because they couldn't afford to throw away the code the company had already paid for. If they had just built a prototype from the wireframes, they could have realized the annoying nature of the signup process before coding it and avoided getting trapped into a bad situation between wanting to avoid both a bad design and throwing away code.

Pick a Tool

A number of tools can translate your wireframes onto a device. Many are tools dedicated to and written just for this purpose. These come in a variety of price ranges and utilities. Some are cheaper, and arguably less useful, than others.

These tools need two pieces (or at least two functions): the piece that's used to create the mockup (which usually runs on a Mac or PC, but might be able to run on a tablet) and the piece that "plays back" the mockup (which runs on the smartphone or tablet of the type the eventual app will run on). There also needs to be some way to transfer the mockup from the creating machine to the playback device.

Although developers can write quick prototypes in code (and I have, too, under limited circumstances), that's not a good general solution for the majority of app projects. While a coded prototype may be quite useful for actually collecting user interactions, it's a poor choice as a communication medium. It can be difficult for other team members to look at a coded prototype and understand what it's doing. A document-based prototype can be viewed (and even edited) by a much wider set of the project team.

The lowest common denominator is simply a PDF viewer that supports interdocument links. You just create multiple pages in the document with anchors, one for each screen. Then you create hyperlinks on top of the buttons that point to the right pages. You won't get animations, scrolling, or gestures, and the result won't be fancy, but it's serviceable and works better than trying to understand how an app will work based on a paper representation.

On the far end are expensive and dedicated apps with at least some animation and gesture support. They're nice but not strictly necessary, and I don't expect most people to have them. Balsamiq is one such tool that is mentioned earlier in this chapter, but there are dozens if not hundreds of others. I primarily use Apple's Keynote presentation software for this task, although Microsoft PowerPoint works as well. This kind of presentation software is easily acquired, and many people are familiar with it already. I find it has better organizational support than most PDF editors and can do basic animations to give your prototype an app-like feel.

The main reason I use Keynote is that it's a tool I've been familiar with for a long time. I was using it for making presentations back before the iPhone existed, and I was using it to make mockups back before the current crop of dedicated tools existed. Building prototypes with it is relatively easy (though somewhat tedious), and you can easily share those prototypes, unaltered, with anyone who has Keynote themselves, or you can export them to a variety of file formats.

Using Keynote (or PowerPoint) is also a portable skill. Time spent getting better or faster at creating slides in Keynote is useful to me both when giving presentations and creating prototypes. If I were to spend time learning a specific mockup tool, the effort I spent on it wouldn't necessarily carry over to other areas of my professional life.

All that having been said, I am not trying to influence what you use. Just because a particular tool fits my experience doesn't make it universally superior. You should use whatever makes sense to you. I do, however, use Keynote as an example throughout the rest of this chapter. I've met very few app creators who have not written or given a PowerPoint or Keynote presentation at some point in their careers, so I think it's the most useful tool I could use for illustration purposes, and techniques illustrated with it should be fairly similar to many, if not most, other tools.

Maintain a System of Record

One objection that you might have at this point is that you just went through the process of creating wireframes, and now I'm talking about creating an interactive mockup. Is it necessary, you might ask, to do both?

The answer is both yes and no. There are two goals here. The first is to document, explain, and communicate what the app will eventually do to the developers who will be writing the app. The second is to test and iterate the design in an inexpensive way. Both of these goals are important (although I've seen projects skimp on them, often to their detriment).

Wireframe documents are better for the documentation task. They not only document screens but lend themselves to including additional information, such as the ancillary functions and flowcharts and explanations of what the buttons and gestures on each screen should do. You can try to include this information in a Keynote or other prototype document, but there's often no convenient place to put such information. In addition, at some point, you are likely to want to take graphic elements (buttons, gradients, and so on) from your wireframe and use them to make assets (such as PNG files) for use in your development process. If so, having your wireframes in a drawing tool will probably be your best bet.

Conversely, wireframes are not good at being displayed at actual size on the device and being interactive.

So what we're talking about is two tools serving two different goals. You don't have to use both, although I do, and I recommend it because I find it the best way to meet the two different goals.

Having two different tools doesn't have to mean twice the work. By keeping track of what you are trying to accomplish with each tool, you can reduce (but not entirely eliminate) duplicate work.

You need to decide which tool is your system of record—the one that is considered the authoritative source for documenting what is going into your app. Personally, I use the wireframes for this. You can use either one; you just have to be consistent. At all costs, you need to avoid confusion about which tool or document contains the latest or correct version.

If changes are made to both the wireframes and the mockups, it becomes easier for changes to get lost and never make it back to the document the developers will be using as the design for the final product. This can cause frustration and wasted work all around, and it can contribute to producing an app that's not as good as what you deserve.

Always Working from Wireframes

The method I use and recommend is to always work and make changes to your app's design in your wireframe drawing tool. Then you can copy from your wireframing tool into your mockup tool for testing. I do this so that I always know where my source material is, I always know what the latest version is, and I don't run into confusion about where I am in the process.

The downside of this method is that if I'm looking at the mockup and I realize or decide that I want to make changes to it, I end up having to switch tools, make those changes in the wireframing tool, and then export the changes from the wireframing tool and import them into my mockup tool. (I'll say more about that process later in this chapter.) Some people find this to be tedious (and I can't really disagree), but it's a quick, straightforward process that I've gotten used to.

One reason this works for me is that I usually only test mockups for one part of an app at a time. The feedback from those tests is then used to decide what changes need to be made. Normally, to keep the different screens of the app consistent, those changes are made throughout the app. Not putting all the screens in the mockup reduces some amount of work.

Abandoning Wireframes for Mockups

Another option is to build a full mockup of every screen of an app when you get to that stage and then use the mockups as the authoritative source going forward. If your mockup tool supports the documentation and annotation needs of the project and everyone on your team has access to that tool, then this might be a good choice for you.

A benefit of this option is that it minimizes the iteration time between prototype tests. When you get feedback about something during your tests, you just grab your prototyping tool, make the change, and re-create the prototype. With some tools, you can even do that directly on the device on which the test is happening.

If this is the direction you're going, you might want to skip having a wireframing tool altogether and do everything in your interactive mockup tool—assuming that it meets all your documentation and communication needs.

Transitioning Back and Forth

Yet another option is to cycle through phases where you re-create everything from your wireframing tool into your mockup tool, make changes to your mockups as you test, and then copy all the changes back into your wireframing tool.

Personally, I find this to be extra work, but it has advantages—mainly that the iteration process inside the mockup tool is faster. It's a perfectly valid strategy, though. I have done this in a limited form for specific screens that I expected to need to make a lot of changes to.

Convert Your Wireframes

Once you're ready to go to user testing with the interface that you've built in your wireframes, you need to get your wireframes into a mockup tool. There are many ways to do this, and there are no purely correct or purely wrong answers. But I'm going to walk you through the process that I generally use.

I created my process within two constraints: I try to do as much of the work as possible in my wireframing tool, and my prototyping tool forces me into what is usually the wrong orientation. I've previously discussed why I prefer to do most of the work in the wireframing tool (it lends itself better to documentation and makes it easier to extract image and other graphics assets for use during actual development). Why the orientation constraint? Keynote on an iOS device can play back slides full-screen only if the slides are in landscape mode, so if I am building a portrait application (and I often am), I have to rotate the screens as I import them into Keynote (the rotation is awkward but not too bad). If your constraints are similar, this process should work well for you. If your constraints are wholly different, you might need to make your own process.

The process I use is to export each screen from the wireframing tool as a single (usually PNG format) graphic image file and then drop that file into one slide in a Keynote presentation, rotating it by 90 degrees as I import it. I then add links and annotations as needed (as discussed later in this chapter). This is a quick (though repetitive) process, and it's very easy to delegate to a junior member of the development or design teams, if such a person exists on the project.

There are also times when someone else (such as a professional graphic designer) is responsible for creating and maintaining the wireframes (usually in Adobe Photoshop), and this technique works splendidly in that situation, as well. It's easy for the design group to create one PNG file for each screen and hand off all the files to me (or someone else in the development group) to put into Keynote. I've even had designers put the files into Keynote themselves, with very little instruction from me.

This isn't a perfect solution, primarily because when each screen is its own static PNG, it becomes impossible to animate only portions of a screen. In other words, there are times when I want to be able to mock up something like a list scrolling with the rest of the interface (for example, the title/navigation bar at the top and the tab bar at the bottom) unchanged. I can't make such a scrolling effect with this technique. It also makes it impossible to move just part of the interface in the prototype tool. For example, if I decide from testing that I'd prefer a button to be 10 pixels bigger or 5 pixels lower, I can't do it right there but have to go back to the wireframing tool, make the change, and repeat the export/import/rotate process.

The advantage of this process is that it works for pretty much any wireframing tool. All these tools have the capability to export to an image file, it doesn't matter who is building the wireframes, and the wireframes don't have to be created in a specific way or need to be re-created. It's a very flexible process, and that flexibility is useful when you're working with different clients with different processes as well as in writing a book when I don't know what kind of tools the reader might have.

Figures 3.10 through 3.14 show the steps in importing a screen into Keynote from OmniGraffle. Your tools may be different, but the process should be similar.

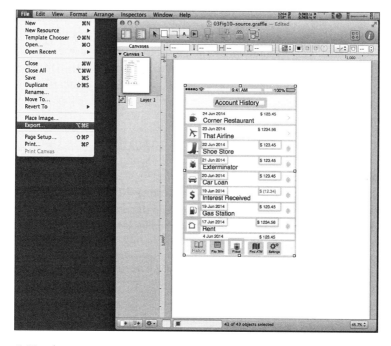

Figure 3.10
Choose the screen to export.

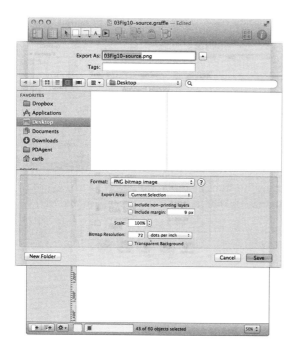

Figure 3.11
Export as a PNG with no margin.

Figure 3.12
Create a Keynote document with a custom size equal to your target device, rotated by 90 degrees (so an iPhone 4 would be 960×640, and an iPhone 5 would be 1136×640). Note that Presentation Type on the right side is set to Links Only. This prevents clicking anywhere from advancing to the next slide and gives you control of what slide is next.

Figure 3.13
Drop the exported file into the new Keynote document.

Figure 3.14
Rotate the picture 90 degrees (using the Rotate Angle setting on the right side) and set the dimensions of the image to exactly those of the screen you are targeting.

Hook Your Screens Together

Once you've imported your graphics into slides, you need to hook them up as indicated by the arrows and indicators that are (hopefully) included in the wireframe document. Figures 3.15 through 3.19 show the steps for linking one screen to another so that the tester can tap the button to see the next screen in the sequence.

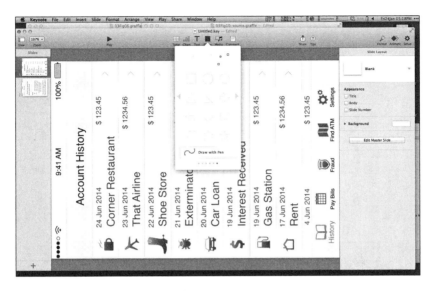

Figure 3.15
Add a rectangle with no fill to be your button.

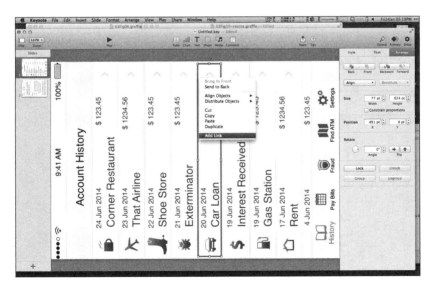

Figure 3.16
Put the rectangle over the button and add a link.

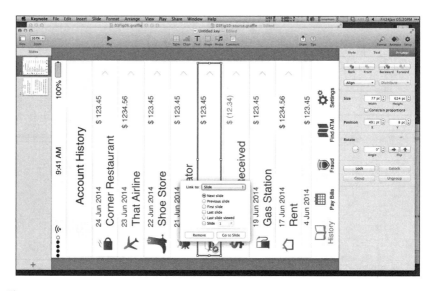

Figure 3.17
Set the link destination to be the target slide. Don't forget to remove the stroke from the rectangle afterward so the user isn't confused.

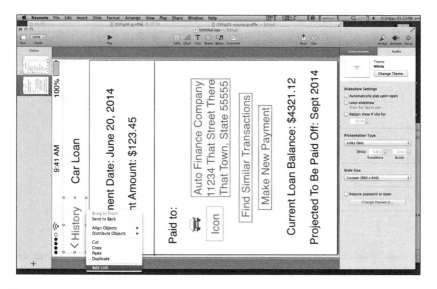

Figure 3.18
On the target slide, repeat the process with the Back button.

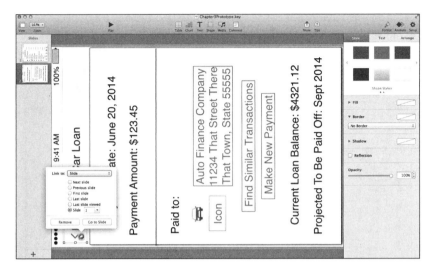

Figure 3.19
Set the destination for the Back button to be where you came from.

Duplicate Screens as Needed

As you hook things up, depending on the scenario you are trying to test, you might need duplicate wireframes in your interactive mockup. For example, if I want to show people how an app will behave when the network is having issues, I do the following:

1. Build out my golden path workflow in Keynote (that is, the way the app will look and behave if things are fine).

2. Make a copy of that Keynote file and name it "network trouble" or something.

3. Consider each network attempt that I want to simulate an issue with, such as retrieving more details for a particular transaction from the server (see Figure 3.20).

4. Add the network error slide that I want to test and make a duplicate of the first slide in the network flow.

5. Wire the first of the duplicated slides to the error message and then wire the error message to the second of the duplicated slides (see Figure 3.21).

Figure 3.20
A transition that might involve the network (assuming that the data hasn't been retrieved yet) that is a candidate for a network error screen.

You might need to do this for a number of slides, depending on what you want to test during this round. Over time, I end up accumulating a number of Keynote mockup files—one for each scenario I want to test independently.

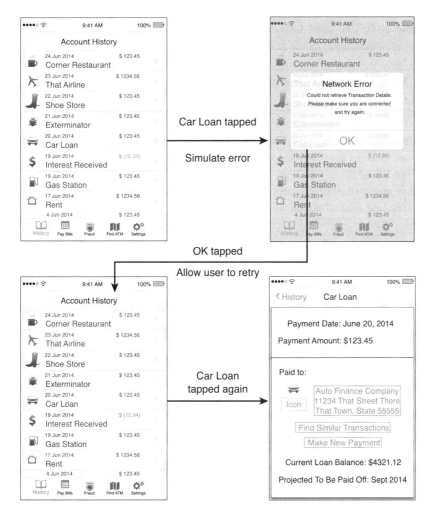

Figure 3.21
The new workflow of the screens from Figure 3.20. Note how the network error screen has been inserted into the middle of the workflow, and the first (History) screen has been duplicated.

Prototyping Tips and Tricks

Certain user-experience issues that tend to pop up require special attention. Although you can deal with them after development has started, I find it a lot cheaper to make sure they're covered during the prototype phase.

Make Sure the User Can Always Get Back

One of the problems I commonly see when trying to implement interfaces is a lack of thought to how users might get back to a previous screen (or state) if they change their mind about the current action.

It should always be possible for users to get back to a previous state with relative ease. If it isn't possible, users may become confused about where they were or where they are. You want users to feel free to safely explore the different parts of your app and to be comfortable with it. If they become concerned that they might become confused, they're less likely to become long-term users of your app and are less likely to tell other people about your app. That isn't what you want.

When exploring (or learning) your app, users will often tap the wrong thing or use the wrong gesture. When that happens, you owe it to them to have a clearly marked, consistent way for them to recover from their mistake.

As you create your interactive prototypes, don't neglect to pay attention to Back buttons and Cancel buttons and the like. Your users (and hopefully your revenue stream) will thank you for it.

Make Sure Users Know Where They Are

A couple years ago, Facebook released a version of its iPhone app that had buttons along the top of the screen where the screen's title usually goes. This was desirable for Facebook (although it's since abandoned the practice, at least on iOS) because those buttons were common across all its web and mobile user interfaces, and the commonality of the experience was more important to the site (at the time) than were the conventions of any specific platform.

Unfortunately, Facebook's design led to a rash of app designs that had buttons in the title bar. This caused confusion among those apps' users because it was hard for them to figure out where they were in the apps. It also caused confusion among the developers who were trying to interpret wireframes because we didn't have a consistent way to tell which wireframe screen we were looking at during development.

I'm not telling you that you have to have a title at the top of each screen (although I usually prefer that). I'm just asking you to make sure there's always a consistent way, when looking at a single screen of your app (either while running the app or examining the wireframes), to know which screen you're currently on.

Don't Forget the Keyboard

Make sure your prototype includes what things should look like when the keyboard is visible. I usually make the keyboard appear when the text field is tapped (by putting a transparent button covering each text field) and then show the fields get filled in when any part of the keyboard area is tapped (by putting one big transparent button covering the whole keyboard). See Figure 3.22.

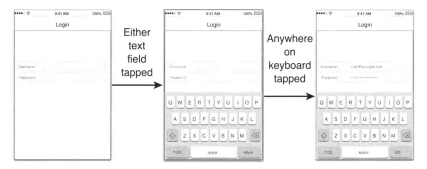

Figure 3.22
An example of how to mock up the keyboard appearing and fields being filled in.

Special Case: Logging Out

For apps that have a server component that requires users to log in, there's a special case where things get complicated.

As discussed earlier, there needs to be a first-run workflow that collects the users' credentials and gets them logged in. This is normally a unique set of screens that the users must navigate before the parts of the app that require the users to be logged into the server get unlocked.

The trick comes when the user logs out (either deliberately or as a result of the server indicating that the user or session is no longer authorized). At that point, the user needs to log in again, and the user might want to log into a different account, in which case any old data belonging to the old account needs to become inaccessible to the new account.

The seemingly simple answer at this point is to pop up an alert box over the existing screen and ask the user for login and password again. The problem with this is that the application still has state and data, and there are screens queued up in memory that were instantiated when the user was logged in. These screens, and the data associated with them, need to be purged from memory. It's hard to do that when they are visible under the username/ password dialog box.

Another possibility is to throw the user back into the first-run workflow by transitioning from the logout screen to the initial login screen. This can cause complications in the view hierarchy, and it can have unintended side effects (like retriggering the tutorial parts of the first-run sequence and annoying the user).

I therefore encourage you to make a dedicated "logged out" workflow that gets the user reauthenticated in such a way that the developer has an opportunity to move any old data off the screen (so it can be deleted safely) and that doesn't risk odd behaviors by reusing existing screens. You don't have to do this, but if you do, it will make your developer's life easier.

Get Feedback from Yourself and Others

As discussed earlier in this chapter, you want to try not to influence a test by giving a user too much context or too many instructions.

With interactive prototypes, you can interpret users' intent not by asking them but rather by watching what their fingers do. Often users will react to a situation on a prototype with their fingers and without conscious thought. It's good for you when this happens, because that's what users do in the real world (and it's not the kind of thing that users do when looking at static wireframes).

And developers and designers and app creators often find themselves doing the same thing. I've found myself reflexively hitting something on a prototype because habits or muscle memory have kicked in, without active thought. These gestures are very instructive.

Another way to get better feedback is to give yourself a series of tasks to accomplish on your prototype in a short period of time. Use a countdown timer that you can see with a loud buzzer at the end (there are many apps for that). I find that when part of my mind is occupied by anticipating and glancing over at the timer, I react more naturally to the app in front of me, without overthinking.

Wrapping Up

This chapter discusses how to turn your app idea into a prototype and use that to communicate with users and developers. Here are some key points to take away:

- Focus on the core experience of your app first and don't worry about anything else until this is done.
- Thinking of your app as if in an Apple iPhone or iPad commercial is a good way of focusing on that experience.
- Once you've written out your core experience and script, go back and flesh out the other features.
- Start your wireframes simply and add more detail over time.
- Simpler screens are better at first, and you can consolidate them later.
- Once you have your screens and the lines and actions between them, move to an interactive mockup.
- Interactive prototypes and mockups allow you to try out designs and workflows for very little money.
- Don't get confused about which tool or document holds the authoritative source of your app's design and try to reduce redundant work.
- Try to make your user tests real by not giving too much context or instruction.

Determining Your App's Components

Chapter 3, "Prototyping and Wireframing Your App," discusses the process of deciding and communicating what you want your app to look like. That's very important, and many app creators don't do a good job of that. But it's not sufficient. There is far more to an app than screens, transitions, and animations. Your app needs to function, and it needs to function well.

In order to find a developer who is an appropriate fit for the needs of your app, you need to figure out what your app needs. This chapter goes through many of the common needs of different kinds of apps and helps you decide where your app should fall in the spectrum of possibilities. It looks at the various *components*, or specific pieces of technical functionality that define what your app can do for your users.

Chapter 8, "Interviewing and Selecting a Developer," talks about using the components you decided on to determine whether a particular developer is a good fit for your specific project.

Dealing with Devices

Deciding which mobile devices your app should support involves a trade-off between market reach and development costs. In theory, it would be ideal to have your app, the way you want it, available on all devices from all vendors running all operating systems on day 1. But that's just not feasible.

Each operating system has specific unique development costs. There are different strategies to mitigate those costs somewhat, and we discuss them later in this chapter. But fundamentally, you can't be all things to all people, and some compromises have to be made. The trick is to figure out how to make the best use of the resources you have at your disposal.

Choosing Your Mobile Platforms

Generally, the first choice that needs to be made when planning your app is what mobile app platform(s) you want your app to be available on. *Platform* means the operating system you want your app to run on and, to a lesser extent, the development environment and app store you're going to use to get it there. Your platform could be iOS, Android, Windows Phone, or Blackberry, or maybe even something else. You could try to distribute your app via Apple's App Store, Amazon's App Store (if the app runs on Android), or Google Play.

I'm not going to tell you what platform(s) your app should be on. I have no idea what the needs of your app or users might be, and I do not believe there is a one-size-fits-all answer for every app market. In addition, the positions of the various platforms change as new devices and operating systems and apps and frameworks are released, and the pros and cons of each platform may well have changed by the time you read this book.

You can find a lot of opinions on the Internet about which mobile platforms have what advantages and disadvantages. There are constant arguments about what platform is "winning" or which one is easiest or cheapest to develop apps on. Such articles are easily found with a quick search. And if you want to find and read those articles, then they are available to you.

But I think that's missing the point. I think the important question to ask is "Who is your app *for?*"

In my mind, there are two potential groups of people that your app should be written for. The most obvious is the target market for your app. The other is your company's investors (or potential investors). Let's talk about the least obvious first.

Exit Strategy Platform Selection

I interact from time to time with venture capital–backed startups. What they are most concerned about is their *exit strategy*, which is who might buy the company. If your company hopes to leverage the app you are building into a high valuation or acquisition, then consider first the desires of your potential acquirers. Look at the companies that might buy your app and see what startups they've been buying and what platforms their apps were built on. You might find yourself choosing to build on Android if you want to get bought by Google, Windows Phone if you want to get bought by Microsoft, or iOS if you think you might get bought by Apple.

There are also market perceptions to consider. There are times when the startup community (or the venture capital community) becomes convinced that one particular platform is the hot one. It's the platform that's getting all the buzz, and the startups that are building apps for it are the ones raising the big investment rounds at the big valuations. If that's your game, pick that platform and try to get traction. Good luck.

Platform Selection for the Rest of Us

If your goal is not to either sell your company or go bankrupt trying, you've got a different group of people to please. Consider this question: Who do you want to be using your app, and what kind of device they have? Finding an answer won't necessarily be easy. But this is a far more useful question to consider than most of the questions that actually get asked when trying to decide what platform or platforms to target when apps get built.

One thing that gets lost in many (if not most) conversations about picking an app platform is that apps are products. And as with any other product, there are groups of people who might find a given app appealing, and there are groups of people who won't. It's basic marketing.

A number of groups of people tend to use each app platform, and certain attributes and advantages appeal to certain demographics or personality types; these change from time to time as new devices and features are released for each platform. By finding the demographic characteristics that are most favorable for your app, you can better determine what platform is likely to be attractive to your model user.

Finding a Starting Point

Some companies build apps simultaneously on multiple platforms. They don't bother to try to discover which platform would be the best fit for them because they know they'll be building for all of them (or at least the most popular of them). While this seems reasonable, it isn't always.

Building for multiple platforms can be a valid strategy, but only if you're sure about what you want to build. It's fairly common for an app to be redesigned soon after launch, once it gets traction and the creators understand the way the app is used in the real world. It's often prudent to build an app on one platform first, iterate with it until you understand what it really needs to do, and then expand to other platforms.

The problem is that when you're iterating on an app and trying to get traction, keeping multiple versions running on multiple platforms in sync slows down the iteration process and increases the cost. If you choose not to keep the versions in sync, you run the risk of alienating users on your secondary platforms.

So unless you are sure you know exactly what your users want from your app, your money and resources seem inexhaustible, or you are in a must-win race for market share, I recommend that you spend the time and effort to decide what platform is the best fit for your users and start there. Only when you've achieved traction is it usually worth expanding.

Form Factor

Once you decide what platform or platforms you are going to target, your work isn't over. Each platform comes in a number of form factors, and deciding which one or ones to support can make a huge difference in both how well your app might be received by its intended audience and how much it might cost to develop.

On some platforms, like Apple, there are currently two form factors: phone and tablet. On other platforms, like Google Android, it gets more complicated, with a whole range of sizes and screen resolutions and aspect ratios. In the future, the number of form factors will likely grow on each platform. Luckily, you can usually just design your app to look good on a few representative sizes and ignore most of the rest, and it will look good enough for most people.

On Apple's App Store, you can choose to build two versions of your app, one for the iPhone and a different one for the iPad, or you can make a single version that works on both. On Google Play, you have even more options, including multiple binaries for a single app listing.

Rotation

Even when you've decided what form factors you want to support, you have to remember that devices can rotate. So you need to decide if you're going to support rotation and, if so, how your app will need to change for the two different aspect ratios.

Rotation is far more important in the tablet form factor than on the phone. Many apps that run on phones choose not to support rotation. It can be a minor annoyance, but users generally seem okay with it. Tablet apps, however, are used in many different orientations, and there are a plethora of different tablet cases that prop up tablets at all different orientations and angles. Your app will be expected to run at the natural orientation of the user's tablet case, so not supporting rotation on a tablet app can lead to frustrated users and will likely result in poor reviews.

Supporting Older or Future Devices

Developing for every possible hardware and software combination that can run a particular platform's apps is usually not worthwhile. Procuring one of each of the possible permutations of device and operating systems for testing would be prohibitively expensive, if it were even possible.

Supporting Older Hardware

Graphics and animations and other features that look good on the newest devices often are so slow as to be unusable on older devices. Old devices have much less memory and slower processors, often with fewer processor cores or limited graphics processor capabilities. It's just not possible for them to scroll currently popular user interfaces as quickly or smoothly as the newer devices. On the other hand, if you make an app that will perform smoothly on old devices, it could likely be perceived as boring by people who own shiny new ones.

But unless you're writing an expensive app with high-end features and wide appeal, supporting only the most recent device released might limit your market too much for you to make back your development costs. So it's important to carefully consider the trade-offs between the effort required for supporting a particular generation of devices and the number of potential users in your demographic that are using them. That said, you should be careful in deciding what devices your app does not support, as that can result in poor reviews if users do not understand until after buying the app that their device will perform poorly or is not supported at all.

Supporting Older Software Versions

Supporting older versions of the operating systems that run on older devices is also problematic. Each vendor puts new features into each new version of its core software in order to encourage new users to switch to their platform and to attempt to retain existing users. Using these features enables users with the latest software to have the experience they want, but the app won't run or won't run reliably for users with older software versions. Avoiding these features means everyone gets the same experience, but users of newer devices might prefer a competitor's app that has more bells and whistles.

It is possible to selectively enable features on new software and hide them from users on older software, but that requires more effort and is more expensive. You have to write extra logic for showing or hiding each feature, and you have to test each feature on old and new software, and you have to make sure the user experience is still acceptable with the new features disabled.

Supporting Newer Software Versions

There's a period of time each year, at least in Apple's ecosystem, when there's a new, unreleased version of the operating system that's available for developers to begin developing and testing on. This period usually starts each June at their developer conference, and runs until September or October, when Apple releases its new devices. During that period of time, each app creator has an opportunity to take advantage of the new features provided in the new operating system and to release a compatible app when or soon after the new devices and OS launch.

When those new devices are released, millions of them are generally sold in a short time, and millions more existing devices upgrade to the new software version. At the point when a user first runs a new operating system, the tendency is to go to the App Store and look for apps that showcase the new features that are now available. If you have an app available that showcases the new features, there's a very lucrative opportunity to get your app downloaded by a lot of users—and potentially even featured by Apple.

That opportunity is also a double-edged sword. Each and every app can take advantage of it, including your competitors' apps. If you choose not to take advantage of that opportunity and your competitor does, you might find yourself losing a number of existing users.

The disadvantage of building an app with the new features is that it can be a lot of work. As the summer progresses, generally different developer-only software versions are released. Each of these releases has some changes from the previous version, and the version that will eventually be released is likely to be different as well. This means extra work when development that you've already had done needs to be reworked to match the new version.

There are also usually bugs in the new operating system (especially in the early developer preview versions) and in the new development tools. This means you'll need to pay extra for your developers to work around those bugs.

If your app manages to become a hit when the new devices are released, then all those costs are obviously worthwhile. But if not, then you paid extra when you could have held back on development until the new devices were out and then started development with the production versions of the operating system and development tools (although even in Apple's ecosystem, "production" releases are usually followed up with minor updates to the OS and development tools again several times in short order).

Device Sensors and Capabilities

Many apps take advantage of specific capabilities of the devices they will run on. Some examples are cameras, microphones, accelerometers, gyroscopes, and GPS receivers. Some devices have special and unusual capabilities, like built-in stylus support, near field communication capabilities, or fingerprint readers. Typically, a few new sensors or features are added to a new device each year. They're generally promoted readily on the marketing literature and discussed in the reviews for each new device, so getting a list of the currently popular ones shouldn't be difficult.

Each of these features can be seen as an opportunity to provide more functionality to your users, as well as a potential time sink that can run your project over schedule and over budget.

Some of these features might be required functionality for your app to run at all. Others you might want to support if they're present but not insist on. Each of these choices can alienate some users and delight others, so take some time to make an appropriate decision, ideally in collaboration with some typical potential users.

Some of these capabilities, like basic camera use, are very straightforward. However, even the simple features can lend themselves to very complex implementations, such as when the output of the camera isn't quite what you wanted, so you want to crop or edit or filter the picture.

It's easy to fool yourself into thinking that getting a GPS location shouldn't be a big deal, but then you might find out too late that your quick-and-easy GPS implementation is draining the device's battery unacceptably quickly.

So take the time to think about what you want to do with each of these capabilities, and talk to your potential developers about their experiences, your options, and their recommendations.

Native, Web, and Hybrid Apps

While I spend the majority of my programming time developing native iOS apps, that isn't the right solution for every problem. In addition, many customers have asked me about HTML5 and hybrid app frameworks. Many native developers think HTML5 apps are garbage, and many HTML5 developers think that native apps are byzantine and ridiculously expensive to develop. The truth is both—and neither. While there do exist both garbage HTML5 apps and ridiculously overengineered native apps, there are good examples of both. Each development practice is a tool, and some tools are better for some problems than others, and each tool has advantages and disadvantages.

Before we dive into pros and cons, let's spend some time defining some vocabulary. Each of the terms we're going to talk about is somewhat fuzzy, and there is often disagreement in different communities about when and how they overlap. Someone somewhere is bound to disagree, so I'll just try to use the terms as consistently as I can.

HTML5 Apps

HTML5 is, for purposes of this book, a set of web technologies that incorporate the recent standard specifications for HTML, CSS, and JavaScript, as well as modern libraries and extensions to them, such as JQuery. Generally speaking, these are the same set of user interface technologies that would be used to write the presentation layer of a web application.

Mobile Web Apps

A *mobile web app*, for our purposes, is an HTML5 app that is installed on a web server and accessed on a mobile device solely via the device's browser. The first year the iPhone existed, this was the only officially supported way to write an app for one. These apps can, after they've been run once and installed themselves, run without a network connection. These apps can also have an icon on the device's home screen or store local data and even be functional enough that some less sophisticated users might not realize that they aren't native apps.

Native Apps

Native apps, for our purposes, are apps written directly against the SDK provided by the device's hardware or software vendor. In the case of the iPhone or iPad, this would be apps written in Objective-C, using Apple's Cocoa framework, using Apple's Xcode development environment. In the case of

Android, this would be apps written in Java using Google's Android SDK in the Eclipse editor, using Google's Android Studio, or with ANT on the command line. For Windows Phone, this would be an app written against Microsoft's libraries, likely in Microsoft's C# language using Microsoft Visual Studio.

Now there's a gray area here, and I'm significantly oversimplifying things. There are apps that many mobile developers would describe as native apps that would not meet this definition of *native*. We'll pick up this topic again later in this chapter, in the section "Dealing with Third-Party Frameworks." But for the purpose of simplifying the imminent discussion of the pros and cons of native, web, and hybrid apps, it's easiest to ignore the gray areas, so that's what I'm going to do.

Hybrid Apps

A *hybrid app*, for the purposes of this discussion, is an app that was written as an HTML5 app but is not installed via a server but rather downloaded from an app store. This is usually accomplished by means of a third-party framework that encapsulates the HTML5 code and allows the app to be packaged as if it were native. Adobe PhoneGap and Appcelerator Titanium are two examples of such frameworks, and there are probably dozens more.

Some companies choose to, in effect, build their own hybrid frameworks. They create a native app that displays only (or mostly) HTML5 content by means of the web page user interface controls built into the various platform SDKs (Apple's UIWebView class, Android's WebView/WebClient class, or Windows Phone's WebBrowser class). The primary differences between this strategy and a third-party hybrid framework is that building your own framework is more work, but you eliminate the risk of the third party abandoning support for your framework and have a simpler code base, since you implement only enough of the hybrid functionality to suit your needs.

For purposes of the following discussion, though, these two approaches—getting a hybrid framework from a third party or writing one yourself—are effectively equivalent.

"Write Once, Wrong Everywhere"

Back in the mid-1990s, before mobile apps, in the heyday of client/server software, there was a movement toward writing *cross-platform applications*, which were defined at the time as applications that could run unmodified on any client operating system. One of the strong proponents of this movement was Sun Microsystems, which used the marketing slogan "Write Once, Run Anywhere" for its Java programming language. The detractors of this strategy started using the phrase "Write Once, Wrong Everywhere" to point out the disadvantages of Sun's cross-platform approach.

Most of the advantages, disadvantages, and discussions that happened back then in the client/server world are happening again now in the mobile world, and the HTML5 and hybrid apps are the catalyst for that argument resurfacing in the 21st century.

The advocates of the HTML5/hybrid approach say that it's possible, and often even preferred, to write apps once using HTML5 technologies and have those apps run on iPhones, Android phones, Windows phones, Blackberry phones, and even yet-to-be released phones running operating systems that will run presently unknown but standards-compliant operating systems.

The advocates of the native approach point out that these HTML5 apps look and behave differently than native apps, in some subtle and some not-so-subtle ways. Their argument is that over time, users get used to the way that the native apps that ship with their devices work. They go on to argue that when those users try to use apps that don't have the same behaviors, they become frustrated and have to retrain themselves to adjust to the new way of working. Some go even further and claim that the existence (or at least the prevalence) of these hybrid apps introduces a cognitive load that makes the users of the platform more inefficient (since they're constantly having to remember what apps use which behaviors) and wastes countless hours of human productivity when aggregated across all mobile users.

Hyperbole aside, HTML5 and hybrid apps are generally slower than native apps. And most of them do behave somewhat differently, especially when scrolling (they often lag more than native apps and act differently when the end of the scroll area is reached), responding to less common gestures (like pinch to zoom, copy/paste, or jump scrolling), or performing animations or transitions. But that doesn't make them unusable, and the claims of massive productivity losses are nonsense. On average, each app (be it native or hybrid) has its own differences and quirks, and most of those differences are much more dramatic than the ones that result from whether the app is native or not. Figure 4.1 illustrates the relative speed and effort of different app approaches.

There are some other issues with the hybrid approach that bear discussion.

First, when device vendors unveil new features, those features are made available through the native app interfaces alone. Only after someone has taken the time to write (and hopefully debug) a native library that makes the new feature available to the JavaScript interface can those features be used by an HTML5 or hybrid app. This means that, in the race to take advantage of the newest and most talked-about features of the latest devices, hybrid apps are always going to be running behind. If you want your app to appeal to users looking for apps that show off their new device's new features, a hybrid app might not be the best choice for you.

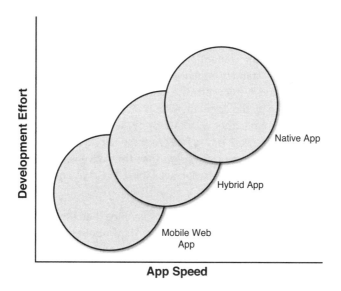

Figure 4.1
In general, native apps are faster and more responsive than HTML5 apps, but developing them takes more effort (especially developing for multiple platforms).

Second, there's channel marketing and promotion to consider. One of the most lucrative things that can happen to an app is to be featured in an app store. By publishing a hybrid app, you are greatly reducing, if not eliminating, your chances of being featured in the relevant app store. The vendors that decide which apps they are going to feature generally seem to prefer apps that showcase the best and latest aspects of their device platform because that makes users more likely to want to get a new device (or to tell their friends to get new devices). In addition, these app store vendors seem to prefer to showcase apps that are exclusive to their store or platform (because, again, that increases demand for new device purchases). If you build a hybrid app, then by definition your app was not built exclusively for their platform, and so the odds they will showcase your app will likely be reduced.

These are the primary reasons the customers I work with generally don't want non-native mobile development. The vast majority of the customers I speak with usually want the fastest apps they can get that can take advantage of the latest features and have the best chance of getting featured in their app store of choice.

There are still more downsides to hybrid development.

Hybrid frameworks always have bugs in them. I can say this universally and without qualification because it's true. That's not to say that the people who write the hybrid frameworks are incompetent—far from it. But think about it: All the native mobile platforms have bugs in them. Virtually every native software update from every smartphone and tablet vendor has release notes that contain some variant of the phrases "bug fixes," "performance improvements," or "stability enhancements." If there are constant bugs in the native operating system software written by the team of professional programmers paid by the company who is in business to get you to pay for said operating system (either with cash or by viewing ads), what are the odds that the hybrid framework is bug free? And the hybrid frameworks typically have worse developer support systems than the native vendors. So their bugs typically have less information available to help you get your work done despite their bugs.

And hybrid apps are also likely to have more bugs than the native equivalent because they are more complicated. Again, think about it: Each hybrid framework has to have enough code in it to support every feature and action that any hybrid app using the framework could possibly need. In general, that's far more features than your app will use, but you still have the potential to be affected by bugs that were introduced when those features were implemented.

And those bugs are generally harder to find and fix than they would be in their native equivalent. This is because native code has a plethora of development and debugging tools that are provided by the vendor of that operating system and associated libraries (and often many third-party tools as well). Those tools were designed and built to develop and debug native apps. Hybrid apps don't have the same kind of development support. Generally you end up using one set of tools (the native set) to debug the app part and another set (often part of the browser development toolkit) to debug the HTML5 part. It's much more complicated, and so it's harder and takes longer.

One final point here is that hybrid frameworks, like all third-party frameworks, have an increased long-term support risk. What if they cease to be maintained by their creator? We'll discuss this issue again and in more detail in the "Dealing with Third-Party Frameworks" section later in this chapter.

Situations Where Hybrid App Frameworks Make Sense

I just painted a dismal picture of hybrid apps, but keep in mind that my interactions are primarily with one segment of the app creator market. There are many valid situations when hybrid apps make a lot of sense.

Rapid Development for Market Validation

The best reason I can think of for building hybrid HTML5 apps is to develop and iterate an app quickly to see whether there's money to be made in a particular market niche. For a fraction of the time and cost of native development, it's possible to create a minimum viable product (MVP) that is available to the vast majority of the smartphone and/or tablet users in the United States on each of the major platforms.

If your app finds traction with your potential audience, then you can use that traction to try to raise money to follow up with native development. If it doesn't, then you can try to make relatively inexpensive changes across all of those platforms at the same time; or you can give up and pat yourself on the back for determining that your idea wasn't viable without spending hundreds of thousands or millions of dollars.

I once told an entrepreneur to take the angel investment he had raised and get a PhoneGap developer to build his app idea instead of giving the money he had raised to me for building him a native app. It just made more sense for his business situation, and the app he wanted built didn't require new features, fancy gestures, or fast UI response.

Leveraging Existing Development Talent

Some companies have a large, existing investment in HTML5 development talent. They have a large staff of web programmers with JavaScript skills and want to make the best use of those skills.

Now let me caution you here: Many companies have gone with this strategy and regretted it. Mark Zuckerberg, the CEO of Facebook, famously said in September 2012 at TechCrunch that "the biggest mistake we made as a company was betting too much on HTML5 as opposed to native."

But that having been said, if your company's choice is between a hybrid app and no app at all, a hybrid app is probably a better choice.

Reusing Existing Web Resources

Another reason that people choose to go the hybrid route is when they have already built a mobile website that does most or all of what they want their app to do. In that case, using a hybrid framework is the minimum-effort way to leverage code they've already spent time and money building.

If the work is already done, then you could just leave it as a website, as discussed in the next section. But if you want your app to be in an app store, using a hybrid framework can be the easy way to get it there.

Now before you think that this is easy, take a deep breath and think for a minute. The assumption that started this section—that you have already built a mobile website that does most or all of what you want your app to do—is a big assumption. It's a huge assumption, and most people I talk to who think that their websites are ready to be apps are very, very wrong.

In Chapter 3, we discussed at length what an app does and is and how to build a prototype of what you want your app to be. If you can read that entire chapter and at every point think "yes, my website already does that" and you can read through Apple's Human Interface Guidelines or an iOS or Android Interface Design book and think that your website already does all of that, then you might be ready to turn your website into a hybrid app.

If not, a hybrid app may or may not be the closest path to getting into an app store. It depends on how close your website is to that standard.

Could Your Idea Be Done in a Website?

From time to time, I talk to customers whose idea for an app could be done entirely within a website. They primarily want to display content, and they don't have many interactive features or controls. Some of them decide to go the website-only route, but some of them end up wanting to make apps anyway. A number of factors inform this decision.

Discoverability

Some companies want their customers to be able to find them in the app store for a given platform. A website, however good and app-like it might be, doesn't meet their customers' requirements.

Imagine that you are trying to sell a large enterprise software system to the government (or maybe some other large enterprise). A common process for the government to take is to send out a request for proposals (RFP), stating what they want; your company and others send in proposals, and then the government narrows the field down to a short list of vendors, does some investigation, often has the vendors come and provide demos, and eventually selects a winner. During the phase when the field is being narrowed, a matrix or spreadsheet is usually created, showing which vendors have which features, and then the shortlist is made by eliminating vendors whose feature list is inadequate. More and more frequently now, "has a mobile app" is one of the features that appears on those spreadsheets, and vendors that don't have an app get eliminated before their mobile website is ever examined. I've been told that some RFPs now even state that products without an accompanying mobile app will not even be considered.

That is only one example, but it's a useful one. And it happens frequently on a smaller scale as well. When faced with an overwhelming number of service choices (for anything from banks or car insurance to retail outlets to streaming media), more and more people are making the number of choices more manageable by choosing from among those they can find in their platform's app store.

Monetization

Somehow, some way, you need to get some return on the investment you are making in supporting the mobile platforms. It might not be easy (or even possible) to measure, but you need to be confident that what you're getting is worth the money you've spent on your mobile website, or app, or both.

Some apps make money intrinsically because people either pay for the app itself or pay for features through in-app purchases. If this is the way you want to recoup your mobile investment, then an app is your only way to go.

Other companies make money via a service. For example, my bank has an app. That app is free because the bank doesn't make money from the app; but it makes money by charging me fees and lending out my money to other people and collecting more interest than it pays me. The app is worth the investment to the bank (I would guess) because if it didn't have a good app, many of its customers would go bank somewhere else that did (I know I certainly would). If your primary product is a service, you may or may not actually need an app, depending on what your service does and what your customers expect, but monetization won't be a factor in your decision.

Still more companies make money by selling advertisements. If this is you, then you may or may not make more money from an app, depending on how many more users you get from having an app than you would have with just your website and the spread between what mobile ad impressions are paying and what website impressions are paying. This second factor is the wildcard. Ad revenue can vary wildly, it varies by device platform, and it is hard to predict in advance. (And frankly, it can be hard to understand why you got paid the amount you got paid even in retrospect.)

Dealing with Third-Party Frameworks

Hybrid app frameworks like PhoneGap have a number of advantages and disadvantages that aren't specific just to the question of whether the content in your app is going to be presented via HTML5 or native code. Inherent trade-offs are involved when any piece of third-party software becomes incorporated into your app for any reason.

Better, Faster, Easier, Cheaper

There is an obvious advantage to using third-party software components or libraries: You don't have to take the time or spend the effort (or money) to have them written yourself. Often, the component you are considering was written with more care, time, and effort than your budget or schedule permits for the equivalent functionality. In addition, the component has likely been tested in the real world far more that your testing schedule and budget would permit, and it's quite likely that bugs have been found and fixed that you or your team might have missed.

But, as we used to say at one of the startups I worked with, "Just because it's *better* doesn't mean it's *good*."

Bugs

A third-party component almost certainly has bugs. If it were simple enough to be written perfectly, it would probably be simple enough that you wouldn't need a third party to write it. The bad thing about the bugs in third-party libraries is that it's almost always harder for a programmer to find bugs in unfamiliar code than in code he or she understands. Fixing bugs in other people's code can be one of the most time-consuming, frustrating tasks that programmers undertake.

But the good news about bugs in third-party components (at least good ones) is that a lot of the bugs in them get found and fixed without your having to be involved. It's often the case that, upon revisiting a GitHub project after some time away, issues will have been found and fixed that you were unaware of (although sometimes these fixes introduce new bugs, so caveat emptor).

Correlating Quality with Popularity

It's difficult to determine the quality of the code of a component without having a lot of programming skill (and, honestly, even experienced programmers get fooled from time to time into thinking a library is better than it is). There are, however, some things even a nonprogrammer can look at to try to increase the odds of not incorporating bad code that they will regret later.

In my opinion, the largest contributor to the rise in the popularity of third-party software components and open source in general in the past five or so years has been from a source control hosting service called GitHub (and the competitors it spawned), and by extension from git, the source control system that GitHub is built on that we discuss further in Chapter 5, "Finding the Right Tools." GitHub, through its pricing structure, has encouraged more free and open source software (FOSS) to be released. Once the code is public, GitHub makes it easy to search for and find the code and tell other people about it.

But the thing that GitHub has done that is relevant here is to provide metrics about the history, quality, and popularity of third-party projects. GitHub provides a forum for people to report bugs in the code to the developers, and that allows people interested in using the software to look at what bugs have been reported and how the developers have responded to those issues. GitHub also shows the number of people who are interested in a project and the number of people who have made their own contributions to it.

In general, the vast majority of components that can be found are of poor quality, and many of them are unfinished or abandoned. If you grab a project at random from GitHub, chances are the project will be garbage. But you don't have to grab a project at random. By comparing the popularity, issues, and history of software components that seem like they might meet your needs, it's much easier to determine whether the code seems to work well for the people who use it and whether the developers seem responsive to issues.

Getting Locked In

The biggest problem with building a third-party component into an app is not being able to get it out again if it turns out that it sucks. It's almost inevitable that you (or your programmers) will need to tailor the way your app works in order to match up with the way the component expects to be used. This might be trivial, or it might be a considerable amount of effort, depending on the complexity of the functionality of the component and how dependent your app is on the component. In the event that the component doesn't work out for you (either now or in the future), that tailoring work is now not only useless, but it's an obstacle between you and a better solution.

In general, the smaller the third-party component is (as measured by number of lines of code) and the fewer places your code calls the component's code (as measured by the number of errors generated when someone tries to build your code without the third-party component in place), the easier it will be to replace, and the safer that component is to incorporate.

Finding Developers Experienced with the Component

Assume for a moment that you hired a developer to build an app for you, and that app got built around a third-party component that is very tightly integrated with your app. The good news is you probably paid a lot less for that app than you would have if you'd paid to have the whole app written from scratch. But the bad news is that you might not be done paying because at some point, if your app is successful, you're probably going to want to release another version of it. Some vendor will release a new device or a new operating system that will require you to put out an update. And at the point that you try to find a developer to build the next version, you'll realize that you need a developer who is familiar with (or can be paid to take the time to become familiar with) your integrated third-party component. This could potentially narrow the field of developers that you can choose from, and that might drive up your costs dramatically.

Even if you choose to replace that component, whoever is replacing or rewriting that functionality will need at least a working understanding of what the component was doing and how it was doing it in order to move forward.

The Case of the Unholy Grail(s)

I once was asked by a friend and former client to review the code of a startup that a group of investors was considering purchasing. The potential investors were happy with the valuation, the demo they had received, and the potential market. They just needed someone to validate that the technology was capable of doing what they needed it to do.

What I found was not good news. The programmer who had formerly worked for the startup had built the server infrastructure (without which the app was useless) on a web platform called *Grails*, which is based on a programming language called *Groovy*. Groovy, simplistically speaking, was a language created to emulate some of the success of the Ruby language but with better performance characteristics. Grails was written as the web framework for Groovy in much the same way that Rails had been written as the framework for Ruby. Groovy and Grails aren't *bad* languages, but they've never become all that popular. The startup was locked in to a relatively obscure development platform.

So I informed the investors that in order to make the changes that they wanted to make to the service (and hence the app), they would either have to find a programmer versed in an unpopular third-party framework or budget for the code to be rewritten for a more popular platform.

The projected financials couldn't support the development costs of a server rewrite, so the investors would have to find a Grails programmer—as would anyone they might want to sell it to in the future. In the end, the deal fell through.

One can never say with certainty what would have happened under different circumstances, but I feel that if the startup had only been built on a more popular framework in the first place, the investors would probably have gotten another app for their portfolio, and the startup founder would probably have gotten his exit.

Abandoned, Fractured, or Rewritten Component Fates

Over time, the development landscape changes. Platform vendors create new development tools and add new features. Bugs in a component are found (and hopefully fixed), and mistakes in components' designs become apparent. Nothing stands still for long.

Also in constant flux is the importance of your component to the people who developed it and are maintaining it. If the trouble of updating the component becomes more onerous in the maintainers' minds than the value they derive from the component, they might abandon it. If that happens to a component that's an integral part of your app, then it's bad news for you. And it does happen. It's happened to some of the most popular FOSS iPhone libraries ever, including Three20 (which was written and released by Facebook) and ASIHTTPRequest.

If a component you rely on is abandoned, you can choose to replace it, rewrite the functionality, or hope that someone else will begin to support it. And if it passes to someone else, you can hope that it just passes to *one* someone else. Because some FOSS projects become fractured, ending up with several people—sometimes dozens of people—who all start with the original component and make their own series of usually incompatible changes (usually called *forks*, as in "a fork in the road"). If that happens, it's really hard to tell which fork is going to turn out to be the best one in the long term because they all start out the same, and it takes time for them to differentiate themselves. And forks seem to get abandoned at a much higher rate than original projects, likely because it takes much less effort to fork a project than to start one, so the people who fork projects are less invested in their success.

Some components get wholly or partially rewritten, which might be the worst fate of all. Some maintainers decide (with justification or without) that their library just can't be maintained in its current state and needs to be "fixed." Often at that point, the developer/maintainer decides that it's too much trouble to maintain backward compatibility with the old way of doing things. After all, users of a FOSS component aren't paying customers, and supporting them can be a lot of work. It's a lot simpler to say "we're starting over from scratch" either for the entire component or for some part of it.

For example, a popular FOSS library for iOS called RestKit recently fixed some design issues by changing the networking stack in a way that was incompatible with existing installations, causing problems for the people who had adopted the previous versions. If you need to update your app, this is effectively abandonment. You're not going to be able to get any of the library's bug fixes for your app without rewriting your app to incorporate the library's new design.

Poor Documentation

In addition to developers feeling it can be too much trouble to maintain backward compatibility with old versions of their software, they often feel that documentation isn't worth the effort. This is one of the real drawbacks of FOSS software. Unlike with the platform vendors that (presumably) employ professional technical writers, FOSS developers generally try to avoid writing documentation (and to the extent that they do write it, they usually write it poorly). This can be especially problematic in the case where the developers choose to rewrite part of the library but don't update the documentation to reflect it.

Adapting to New Features

New features, such as new processors, are unveiled all the time. That clock is ticking for your app, too. If a new phone model comes out, and a library you depend on doesn't yet support it (usually because there's a new processor that has a new instruction set), you might have a problem.

When this happens, it usually (but not always) happens with libraries that are available only as binary distributions. (In other words, their customers aren't given access to their library's source code.) Analytics libraries are particularly notorious for this.

I've seen several companies get stuck. They wanted to put out a new version of their app to catch the wave of downloads that occurs whenever a new iPhone is released, but their app incorporated a library that did not support the new device's processor. That left them with the choice of cutting the library (and its associated functionality) out of the app temporarily, replacing it with another library under a time constraint that likely wouldn't allow thorough testing, or waiting for the vendor to finally update their binary library distribution.

Licensing

One quick final word about third-party components: Each component comes with some sort of license (explicit or implied). There have been companies that have gotten in trouble for failing to live up to the terms of the licenses of the software they've incorporated into their apps. Make sure that you (or someone in your organization) understand the licensing requirements of every third-party component that you or your developers or representatives place in your app.

Mitigations

We've discussed many risks you take when incorporating any piece of third-party software, and there's no way to completely avoid them. (Even Apple and Google deprecate pieces of their APIs over time.) What you can do (at least with third-party components) is limit your exposure by picking only components that are relatively small and simple (ideally doing just one thing) and that don't require changes across large parts of your app for integration. As discussed earlier, your dependence on a library can be measured (or at least approximated) by the number of errors generated when someone tries to build your code without the third-party component in place. Minimize that number, and you'll be in a better place to survive issues with the components you (or your developer) have chosen.

Game Engine Apps

I'm not primarily a game programmer, and I don't do a lot of work on dedicated game apps, but no discussion of app types would be complete without some discussion of game engines.

OpenGL

Games are portable between devices (or at least can be) in a way that's different than with non-game apps. This is because many games (at least the ones that use dedicated game engines) bypass the layers of programming libraries and SDKs provided by the various mobile platform vendors and talk more directly to the hardware.

Most modern graphics hardware supports much of the same set of programming calls. This is because the graphics processor in an Xbox or a PlayStation is not too different (relatively speaking) from the graphics processor in an iPhone or a Samsung Galaxy. Many dedicated game engines talk to these processors via a specification like OpenGL, bypassing Apple, Google, and Microsoft user interface libraries and common controls. Once a game is written in OpenGL for and running on the iPhone, it's a much, much simpler matter to get that game running in OpenGL on the Samsung Galaxy than it would be if the iPhone version had been written in Objective-C for Apple's Cocoa and the Android version were to be written in Java using the Android SDK.

I would definitely consider OpenGL games to be native for performance purposes. They are not, however, native in the sense that they conform to the user interface conventions of the platform. Angry Birds on the iPhone is much closer in user interface behavior to Angry Birds on a Samsung Galaxy than either is to your average iPhone or Android app.

Unity

The most popular third-party cross-platform game engine at the time of this writing seems to be Unity. It has its own suite of development tools and can produce impressive 3D games that run on a variety of hardware platforms—from smartphones to tablets to game consoles—from vendors from Apple to Samsung to Sony to Microsoft.

If you want to build a cross-platform mobile game, Unity certainly seems to be the way to go these days.

SpriteKit and Cocos2D

Cocos2D (which is a FOSS framework) has been the most popular iPhone 2D gaming platform for some time now, although from what I can tell, it's starting to be eclipsed by Apple's own SpriteKit for 2D games that have started development recently. These frameworks aren't cross-platform, though; they are a layer on top of the Objective-C language used by Apple.

Still Third-Party Frameworks, but Better

In theory, the frameworks just discussed have the same kinds of issues as any other third-party frameworks, including lock-in and needing to find developers familiar with the framework. The support burden should be lower for Unity and SpriteKit, though, since they have popular vendors behind them. Cocos2D might be a risk now, as there's some doubt as to how well it will survive in a world with SpriteKit.

Corner Cases and None of the Above

There are a couple other corner cases that are arguably native and arguably not; they convert code written in one language by the developer into the native language for the platform being built.

For example, there's a project called RubyMotion for the iPhone that attempts to allow programs written in the Ruby programming language to run as native Cocoa apps. There's another called Xamarin that allows you to write code in C# using the associated tools and then build for iOS and Android (as well as Mac and Windows). I'm sure there are others, and there will be countless more. As long as there's a programmer with a favorite language, there will be some attempt to get that language to run on the currently most popular platform.

The corner cases have the same kinds of risks previously discussed for third-party frameworks. You'll likely get locked into a framework and require developers familiar with that framework to do any future development for you, and you're at the mercy of the third party for support if something goes wrong. However, if you're willing to live with those restrictions, these frameworks (and others like them) might be viable for you.

Dealing with Analytics

Analytics is a hugely valuable tool for developers and app creators who want to understand how their apps are being used and how they could be improved. It's unfortunate how often, when I am having conversations with app creators about how to prioritize improvements to their existing apps, I discover that an app creator has no idea which features in the app are important to their users and which ones are never used. Trust me: When you have a conversation about what features your next version should include, it helps to know how many of your users are using the latest generations of smartphones and tablets and how many are using the oldest one you support.

The time to start gathering this information is long before you need it. It takes time to gather and analyze this information because you can only get data when a user is running your app and analytics is installed. The longer the analytics information is being gathered, the clearer a picture you will have.

Services

Many services are available—some free and some paid—to give you analytics on what goes on in your app. You can find the most popular ones by searching the web for "app analytics" or something like that. Typically, there's a call at app launch that takes your identifying key string (provided by the vendor). This call sets things up for you, connects to the server, and records that the app was started. Then there's a call (usually a single line of code) you can make whenever you want to record that something interesting has happened.

Many of these services are notorious for creating problems for developers. (I'm not going to name names, but a quick web search should turn up any complaints about any service you're thinking about using.) Many have collected more information from the users than they've said they would do, some have caused the apps they are embedded in to be rejected by Apple, and there are often delays between when a new phone is released and when the analytics libraries are ready to support it.

These services are generally easy to use, and they usually provide comprehensive and attractive reports, but they usually only report on the things that you tell them to report on, and that's most of the work.

What to Collect

Deciding *what* to collect is the really tricky part of analytics. Most people either collect nothing at all or way too much. The problem with collecting way too much is that it can drastically affect the performance of your app and even result in negative reviews from users whose devices are consuming too much data. So you want to collect only what is most important.

My recommendation is that, as you work on designing your app, and through the process of refining and developing it, you write down all the decisions you're concerned about making and the things that you wish you knew that would help you make those decisions. Through the process of making that list and thinking about it as you develop your app, you will hopefully get a feel for what you really need to know.

We've already talked about needing to know what kind of devices your users are running. You also want to know what features of your app your users care about and how much they care. This might be as simple as recording when a user switches to a new screen. I wouldn't recommend connecting to the server every time the user switches screens, though. Talk to your developer about recording such events to a file or something and uploading aggregates at reasonable intervals.

Dealing with Video and Audio

Pretty much every modern smartphone and tablet system has hardware support for low-power audio and video playback. But to get access to the acceleration, you have to go through the vendor SDKs. It's not the most difficult thing, and it's fairly well documented, although it's complicated and easy to get wrong, and there are always little performance issues and tricks that it takes a while to learn.

The important thing when it comes to media is to write down everything that you need your app to do and discuss it with your developer. But if you're doing your own development, you should budget some extra time to do some extra reading to figure out the tricks.

Dealing with Peripherals

Some apps take advantage of specialized hardware and peripherals. Programming apps that do this is a fairly specialized skill, although it's becoming more common as time goes on.

Originally (at least in Apple's ecosystem), the only peripherals that worked with apps were part of Apple's "Made for iPhone" program that had a lot of specialized rules or performed hacks to connect devices through the headphone jack. In the past couple of years, though, that has changed.

There are two primary means by which most (but not all) peripherals connect with smartphones these days: Bluetooth (especially the newer Bluetooth LE) and Wi-Fi (802.11). Even if you don't have a dedicated peripheral to go with your app, it might be worth it to spend some time thinking about what (if any) peripherals exist that your app might take advantage of.

Bluetooth

Bluetooth is a short-range wireless protocol most commonly associated with small, wireless headsets and people talking loudly in public to no one in particular. More recently, the new Bluetooth LE protocol has allowed for a new generation of far more varied Bluetooth devices that also consume far less power.

You're likely familiar with the exercise of having to go into the system's settings or configuration and "pair" your headset or keyboard to your phone or computer. Now, however, an app can be written to talk to Bluetooth LE devices without those devices having to be configured specifically for that phone (or tablet).

One such example is a Bluetooth heart rate monitor (the kind people strap around their chests while jogging or doing other exercise). Any app running on a Bluetooth LE–enabled smartphone and programmed to use the Bluetooth profile for heart rate monitors (HRMs) can get a list of the HRMs that are within range and choose one to get a feed from. At no time do you have to configure that HRM in the Settings app.

Bluetooth LE has enabled a range of other smart peripherals, ranging from smart watches to dice to thermometers. If your app's functionality could be enhanced by connecting to such a peripheral (assuming that the user has one), then by supporting that peripheral, you have made your app more valuable to your user. In addition, people who have just purchased a peripheral are likely to search the app store to see what apps support their new purchase. That is a marketing opportunity that you shouldn't pass up, as there will be fewer results for that app store search, and your probability of getting a download should be correspondingly higher.

Keyboards

One Bluetooth peripheral that most apps could support but most don't think about is the Bluetooth keyboard. If your app has text input (and especially if it has a lot), I recommend taking the time to find yourself a Bluetooth keyboard and see what your app's experience is like when using it.

Wi-Fi (802.11)

The other exciting advancement in the market for peripherals is the development and subsequent price drop of single chips that can implement an entire Wi-Fi network stack, some even with a built-in web server. It's now possible to inexpensively add an ad hoc Wi-Fi network to any piece of electronic hardware without adding much in the way of complexity or power requirements. This has permitted many app-enabled Wi-Fi–connected products from thermostats to remote-controlled flying quad copters.

Dealing with Accessibility

The iPhone has had a dramatic impact on the lives of people all over the world, but perhaps none so much as people with hearing or visual impairments. The accessibility features built into the iPhone's operating system have made possible apps that have revolutionized life for many, from apps that can tell a person with limited vision what color their clothes are or what denomination of paper money they are holding, to FaceTime video calling that allows hearing-impaired people to sign to each other.

But many apps are not accessible because the developer didn't care to enable or test accessibility. This is a shame because it's easy to do, and the built-in support is really powerful.

I encourage you to think about budgeting some time and money as part of your app development process to ensure that your app is accessible (if that's appropriate). It's not difficult and can make a world of difference to some portion of your app's users.

Dealing with Custom or Complex Animations

Most apps have some amount of animation in them, often just provided by the use of built-in controls. But there are usually opportunities to use animation to inform your users about the way your app works. A good designer (or a good design book) can help you understand what some of those choices might be (and we touched on that in Chapter 3).

Although basic animations are relatively easy to program on modern mobile platforms, there are things you need to think of that might not be obvious, like what should happen if an event (such as an error) occurs in the middle of an animation or what provision you want to make for the user changing his or her mind between the animation's beginning and ending.

With custom, complicated, or multistage animations, these decisions (and their associated implementations) get even more complicated.

For planning purposes, it's important to think about how many animations your app might need and how complex you expect (or want) them to be. This will help you, either via conversation with your developer or through research on your own, get a more realistic idea of what is involved in these animations so you can decide what they are likely to cost in time, effort, and budget and whether they are really worth it to you.

If you want to plan for custom or complex animations, I recommend that, as with all other noncritical features, you plan for them to be developed later in the project so that if unexpected complications arise elsewhere, you can decide to cancel them or defer them to a later version. If you develop the animations first, and then later run into time and money constraints, you'll find yourself with an attractive animation on an unshippable app, which would be a waste.

Dealing with Conditional Formatting

Most apps use relatively static text formatting. There are labels on the screen, sometimes more than one, but each label has text in exactly one font at exactly one size. Usually each label has a small number of words and indicates a screen title or button or something.

However, some apps have more complicated text formatting. If you want your app to have a block of text that contains different fonts, sizes, or colors, then thoroughly document that need. Write down how you expect that text to look (or potentially look), ideally with a wireframe or a prototype. Make sure any potential developers you might use are aware of that need and ask what experience they've had with complicated text.

Another thing that can be far more complicated in mobile development than you might expect is text containing links, typically blue underlined text that does something when you tap it. We've become so accustomed to seeing that in web pages that we don't think about the fact that someone had to write code to make a web browser do that. If you want your mobile app to do that, too, it's usually more complicated than it seems. Not only does someone have to write code to make the text show up looking like a link, but someone has to write code to detect that it was tapped and then present whatever content needs to be shown and provide navigation options to the user so that he or she can get back to the original spot.

Conditionally formatted text is not likely to be the most difficult thing in your app (unless your app is a text editor), but I've found that it often takes quite a bit longer than app creators expect, so don't forget to plan for it.

Dealing with Localization

Although most of the customers I deal with are focused on the U.S. market, according to one source (http://blog.appannie.com/localization-entry/), the United States accounts for only 34% of Apple's App Store revenue and 28% of its downloads. I haven't seen a similar statistic for Google Play or other app stores, but it seems almost certain that most of them have significant foreign activity as well.

If you want your app to be fully functional in foreign markets, you should consider localizing it. *Localization*, sometimes referred to as *internationalization*, or *I18n* (where 18 stands for the number of letters between the first i and last n in internationalization), is the process of displaying the content in your app in different ways at runtime, depending on the local preferences of the user running the app. It's usually thought of as translating all the text in your app into languages other than English, but it also extends to things like displaying date values correctly. (For example, 1/5/2014 could mean January 5, 2014, or May 1, 2014, depending on the local conventions where you live.)

Localization isn't extremely difficult to implement, but it's something that needs to be considered early on in a project. I've seen app projects waste a lot of time on localization because it wasn't considered early enough in the project. The issue, primarily, is one of design and space. Different languages have different characteristics, and if the graphical design for your app fails to take them into account, you can wind up needing to go back to the drawing board. The most frequent instance of this I have seen is when people try to translate English apps into German. German words are often much longer than their English counterparts, and often the graphic designs created by English-speaking designers using English example text don't leave nearly enough space to fit the equivalent German translations. From the code-writing side, localization is more straightforward, although it can be time-consuming, tedious, and error-prone (it's easy to translate most of the app and not realize you missed one spot).

If you want your app to be localized (or think you might), then speak with your potential developers about their experience localizing apps.

Dealing with User Preferences

Most apps of any size and complexity have some sort of user configuration or preferences in them. If yours has only a few, then it's not really anything to worry about. All the major mobile platforms have a simple mechanism for managing short lists of preferences, and they do a fine job for most apps.

However, if you need dozens of preferences, or multiple nested screens of them, or if you want to store something more complicated than a short string or number or the value of a switch, then you might need to make sure extra planning is done for managing your app's preferences. In any case, you should ensure that your app honors the default approach for managing setting preferences rather than implement a custom solution.

Dealing with Data Storage

Most apps, at some point, need to store data to make dynamic information available to the user without pulling it live off the network. This can be implemented in a myriad of ways; which mechanism for storing and retrieving data is right for your app depends on the answers to a number of questions and scenarios.

What Data Do You Need to Keep?

The first thing you need to figure out is what kinds of information your app needs to store and retrieve. It could be emails or map locations or book titles or financial transactions or any one of hundreds of other things. Usually, the primary kind of information that an app will manage is easy for an app creator to determine. But sometimes there's more to it than that.

Not only do you need to figure out the information that will be shown to the user, and where that information is going to come from, but you need to specify any ancillary information or metadata that needs to be stored as well. You might need to store login credentials to get information from a web service on the user's behalf. You might need to keep information for searching or sorting that doesn't always show up onscreen. You might need to keep metadata, like information about the last time a piece of data was refreshed or viewed, for purposes of deciding when it needs to be updated. You might also need to keep information that is normally hidden, such as to-do items that have already been completed (along with the date they were marked as done).

You should be able to determine the majority, if not all, of the kinds of information you need to store by looking at your screens and answering questions like "Where did that information come from?" and "How is it being sorted or filtered?" Any additional kinds of information you might need will hopefully become obvious early in the development process.

How Big Will It Get?

Once you have an idea of what information you're storing, the next question is "How much of it will there be?" The more information you need to store, in general, the more space the app will take up on disk and the longer it will take to retrieve it. So you don't want to keep much information you don't need or keep much of anything for any longer than you have to.

In the event that the app doesn't have a server component (as discussed later in this chapter), anything you might need to show the user has to stay on disk in the app. But even when it's possible to get data from the server, it's important to remember that if the user is likely to want to look at it, it's much better to have it locally than to have to go and get it from somewhere else. The trick is figuring out what the user truly is or isn't likely to want to look at in the near future.

So think about how much information a single installation is likely to need. Then think about what the worst case is likely to be, and then think about whether there's really a worse case than that. In many instances, users have complained about an app's performance, and the developer, upon learning how much information the user was storing, was shocked to discover that the user had 100 or 1,000 times more data than the developer ever considered, and the developer was shocked that the app worked at all under those conditions.

Now there's an argument to be made that it's not worth trying to support users who put far more information in an app than you've planned for— because there aren't likely to be many of them, and developing an app that can deal with that much data might be noticeably more expensive than developing an app that can't. The flip side of this argument is that those power users who have far more data than other people are more likely to tell other people about their experiences with your app, either positive or negative. So decide how much data storage you think you want to support and what you're willing for users to experience when they exceed that threshold by a significant amount.

Once you understand how much data you need to keep around, that determines what technologies are feasible to be used to store it. Very small amounts of data might be able to be stored the same way as user preferences, while very large amounts might require the creation of a custom storage component.

How Does It Need to Be Accessed?

The next question after how much data will be stored is "How much of it is going to be displayed at any one time, and how will the determination be made about what data is displayed when?"

Structured, or Relational, Data

Many apps store much more data than they show, and they filter what's going to be shown according to a number of criteria, such as the date and status. Think about an app that tracks to-do list items or calendar appointments. These items are stored and retrieved according to date and filtered according to category or status (such as whether they've already been completed and whether they're assigned to the Home or Work calendar).

This is often referred to as *structured data* (also called *relational data*) and can be thought of as the kind of data that is stored in a Structured Query Language (SQL) database. SQLite is currently the most common implementation of a SQL database on mobile platforms. (But the specific details of a particular SQL implementation aren't likely to matter much for most apps.)

Performance of SQL databases, in general, degrades as you put more data into them, so keep in mind that you can't keep adding new data forever and expect the app to still function. You need to think about when data can be deleted. There are also a number of performance optimizations that can be made (such as adding indexes to the data or denormalizing for query speed). Discuss the pros and cons of each option with your potential developers.

If your app tracks items of some sort that have various attributes (such as names and dates and categories and status fields) that need to be sorted and filtered when the data is displayed on the screen, you probably have structured data.

Direct Queries or Mapped Objects

If an app is going to have a SQL database in it, someone needs to decide how that data is to be accessed. One way is to use raw SQLite queries to extract relational data directly from the SQLite database. Another way is to use an *object relational mapper* (*ORM*), which turns the relational data into objects to be programmatically managed by Objective-C (iOS), Java (Android), or C# (Windows Phone).

The most common ORM in the mobile space is probably Apple's Core Data framework. It's complicated, especially when background tasks are going on, but it's far more robust, stable, and fast than any solution a development team is likely to be able to build from scratch during your project. It's designed to handle a number of common issues such as updating the user interface with new information as new data is added to the application as a result of a network fetch. It also has the advantage of being well documented (both by Apple and in a number of third-party books) and well known, so if your app is built on Core Data and later you're looking for a developer to work on the next version, it shouldn't be difficult to find one who knows the framework.

In the Android and Windows Phone spaces, there are multiple ORMs, and quite a few projects use raw SQL queries, so there's no clear ORM favorite.

One word of warning though: Don't mix and match an ORM and raw queries (and don't let your developer do it, either). The people who develop ORMs assume that they have exclusive access to the database, and if your developer violates that assumption, bad things can happen. Worse, things might work fine now and then start crashing when any minor bug fix to the ORM framework is released at any point in the future.

Whole-Screen Data Files

Sometimes apps have data that is displayed to the user in groups, and an entire group is displayed at once. While it would be possible to build such an app with structured data, it's probably overkill.

For example, imagine an app that shows a weather forecast. It might have a screen that shows the temperature and rain chance for each of the next 7 days and another screen that shows the same information for the next 12 hours. It also might have several cities for which forecasts could be displayed.

In this case, one easy solution would be to write two files to local storage for each city, one for the next 7 days and one for the next 12 hours. When the user went to that screen, the whole file would be read from local storage into the device's memory and displayed on the screen. There wouldn't be any need to run queries to filter data.

The data could be stored in a native format (like Apple's property-list format) or XML or JSON, and one easy way would be to store it in the format returned by the server. That way, when the forecast is updated, you can just copy the server's response directly to local storage. There's no point in keeping old information because people generally only want to see the most up-to-date forecast. This would be a fast and clean solution for small amounts of data that are displayed all at once.

Document Format Apps

Some apps use large amounts of data that are displayed one screen at a time and can be scrolled around. Some of these apps are word processor or spreadsheet-type apps (like a mobile equivalent of Microsoft Word or Excel), and others are readers, maybe whole-book reader apps like Amazon's Kindle app or Apple's iBooks app or PDF file viewers.

Although they are managed and displayed differently, large binary files like photos, audio tracks (mp3 files), and videos also fall into this category. If your app needs to include these, make sure to plan for it.

Each platform has a number of different ways to read and write large files, and there are various trade-offs for performance and disk space. Talk to your developer or find a book or documentation about how best to plan for this case.

Full Text Search

Sometimes you need to search through large amounts of text as the user is typing and find things that match (much like trying to find a particular email from a couple of weeks ago on your smartphone). You can implement this kind of searching with structured data and SQL queries, but for large amounts of text (as in an email app), that might take longer than the user wants to wait (and might take more memory than the device has).

The solution is to precompute indexes that are much easier to search. An open source library called Lucene from the Apache project can do this, and full-text search is built into some versions of SQLite as well.

All of the Above

Keep in mind that you aren't limited to just one of the previously discussed data storage retrieval types. Imagine writing something like Amazon's Kindle app or Apple's iBooks. You might use a whole-screen data file to display the user settings (fonts, text size, background color of the page), have a SQL database to track each book in the library (when it was last read, what page the user is currently reading, what bookmarks or comments the user has added), and use a document format file (probably ePub or PDF) to store and display each book's text with a Lucene full-text index file for each book to let the user search for quotes and text.

Figure 4.2 shows the different data storage retrieval types, along with the relative data sizes for which they are appropriate and the corresponding development effort.

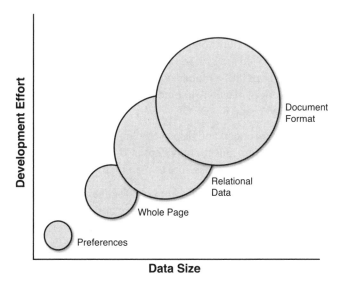

Figure 4.2
Preferences are easy to use but work for only very small data sets. As the app needs to keep more and more data, more effort must be spent on managing it.

How Secure Does It Need to Be?

Each platform has a mechanism to encrypt small amounts of data (on the iPhone, it's called the Keychain SDK), and there are a number of encryption libraries that can be used for larger files, either built into your platform of choice or as free and open source alternatives. Numerous books and tutorials explain how to use these libraries.

The important thing is to be aware of what information your app is collecting, storing, or transmitting that would be inconvenient (or worse) for the user if it were to be made publicly available. Things like passwords and credit card numbers are obvious ones, but think about everything your app stores or sends to a server, and think about how upset the user might be if that information were made public. Then treat the information as if it were just as important to you as to the customer and encrypt it properly.

How Quickly Does It Need to Be Displayed?

We already talked about some performance optimizations in the "How Does It Need to Be Accessed?" section. In general, if you need to be able to get information to the screen faster, you can use more local storage space (additional files, tables, or indexes) to store it in a format that can be found or displayed more quickly. Talk to your developer or find a book on enhancing the performance of your application.

The important thing from a planning standpoint is to make sure you understand how fast the data retrieval needs to be and what the implications might be in disk space and development effort to get it that way. Also, if display speed is important to your user experience, be sure it's tested early and often. If you wait until the very end of the project and then realize that everything is too slow, fixing the situation is going to be very expensive.

How Often Does It Change?

A final factor influencing how your data should be stored is how often your data changes and how often it needs to be updated. In general, the more often it changes, the more work will be required.

One option to reduce the effort if you have data that changes frequently is to have two different data stores: one that holds the data that changes frequently and one that holds the data that doesn't change very often. Then you can do the work of frequently changing data on a relatively small data set.

For example, imagine an app used by people looking to buy an expensive item like a house or a car. You might have one data store that has the large, searchable list of all the houses or cars that are for sale in the users' geographic area and then a different, smaller store in which the users could indicate which cars or houses they looked at, which ones they were still interested in, and so forth. That way, when users are looking at the list of the items they care about, it's a much smaller (and therefore faster) list than if the app were having to search through every item in the area for each screen.

Dealing with Servers

Many apps these days have to deal with one or more servers. Pretty much any feature in an app that lets a user share information with other users or get updated information that wasn't available when the app was submitted to the app store requires interaction with a server.

In the mobile app space, when someone uses the term *server*, and certainly when I say it here, it usually means *web API server* and generally means that there is a machine out on the open Internet running a *web service* that is listening for web requests (as if from a web browser) to a particularly defined set of URLs and is responding with well-defined structured data in a format like XML or JSON. The term *REST* (which stands for representational state transfer) is often used for this kind of API. (I'm oversimplifying here. There are specific definitions for many of these terms that are beyond the scope of this book.)

Some servers are specific to a particular app, while others (like Facebook's or Twitter's web services) provide common functionality to many, many different apps. It's not unusual for an app these days to use a combination of servers.

Servers are a huge topic, and there are a number of options and variations, and it's far too much to cover here, and most app creators I talk to generally have some experience (or at least a passing familiarity) with services they've already used. The good news is that web services have been around a lot longer than smartphone apps, so you should hopefully be able to find resources about how to write and manage the service of your choice (or your development team's choice).

The important thing about using a server with your app is to make sure all the interactions between the server and the app are well defined as soon as possible, are hooked up as early as possible, and are tested as often as possible. There are many opportunities for things to go wrong between the server and the app, and the earlier you catch those things, the better.

Writing Your Own Server

You can use a number of different server technologies to build your own server from scratch, including Ruby on Rails and Django, as well as many, many others. And then once a technology is picked, there is still the question of where to host it—either on your own dedicated web server hardware, on a shared server at some hosting provider, or on a virtual cloud like Amazon's EC2, Rackspace, or Microsoft's Windows Azure.

If you are going to have your own server built (or have a mobile API built on top of a website you already have), you are going to need a team of server developers to do that, and it will probably not be the same group of developers who are building your mobile app. These days, mobile development and server development have diverged enough that there aren't many teams that do both. Even when you have one company building both your server and your app, it's usually two completely different groups inside that company that are doing the two pieces. This means lots of opportunities for misunderstandings, blame, and finger-pointing, so be wary of that.

The other problem with writing your own server is having to maintain it. Computers have hardware failures, whether they are servers or smartphones, but when your user's smartphone dies, it's not your problem. When your server dies, all your users are affected, and you (or someone at or representing your company) are going to have to deal with it.

Platform-as-a-Service (PaaS)

Instead of building your own server from scratch, you can find a server platform (called PaaS) that you can build your service on top of. These range from services where your team writes and uploads your own server code—like Google App Engine, Engine Yard, or Heroku—to platforms where you define your service via a web interface, and all (or almost all) of the programming is done on the mobile side—like Parse (recently purchased by Facebook) or Microsoft's Windows Azure Mobile Services. There are literally hundreds of such platforms, and new ones are popping up all the time. Just search for "mobile platform as a service," and you'll be able to find lists of them, as well as comparisons between them.

I recommend that you pay close attention to the viability of the service over the long term. If the platform you choose goes defunct (and many have), it can be fatal to your app, just as we saw with components earlier in this chapter.

Social Media and Other Third-Party Services

A number of other services are used peripherally in apps. Facebook and Twitter sharing are two of the most common, but there are also remote file storage services like Dropbox and Amazon's S3.

Often, these services aren't accessed by your app's code directly but through the use of software development kits (SDKs) provided by the service itself. Sometimes, you even have a choice of which SDK to use (for example, for Facebook sharing on iOS, you can either include Facebook's Objective-C SDK or use Apple's Social framework that's built into iOS 6 and later).

You should document which services you want to integrate with and make sure you and your developer plan time to get that integration working and tested.

Dealing with Syncing

Syncing, or synchronization, is having multiple devices (like an iPhone and an iPad or an Android tablet and a website) show the same information at the same time and having a change made on one device propagate to the other device so the two devices maintain a consistent view of the data.

Syncing is difficult, especially when changes are being made on more than one device at the same time, and especially when those changes are being made while those two devices can't talk to each other. This creates what we call *conflicts* in the data, and there's no one-size-fits-all way to deal with these conflicts.

If you can avoid syncing, avoid it. Getting it right is expensive. If you can't avoid syncing, see if you can push it to version 2 of your product. Failing that, expect syncing to be harder than you (or likely your developer) thinks and plan accordingly.

Dealing with Push Notifications

Push notifications are a mechanism that Apple debuted in 2009 with iOS 3.0. It was an attempt to get some of the functionality of background tasks onto the iPhone without having to have the device's battery running down constantly while polling the network to see if there's new information for it. Since then, most of the major vendors have come to support a similar mechanism.

If you want push notifications in your app, you can build your own server to do it, with all that entails, or you can investigate one of many third-party services that will do push notifications for you. Either way, testing it is complicated and can be time-consuming, so plan accordingly.

Dealing with Background Tasks

One of the things that developers have the most trouble with on mobile apps is multitasking—having more than one thing happening on the device at the same time. Whether it's data being downloaded from a server in the background while the user is looking at something else or the user watching one part of a video while the next section is being readied for display or thumbnails being generated for images to be placed in a list that the user is actively scrolling, multitasking is one of the things developers most commonly get wrong.

You should carefully document everywhere your app might be doing more than one thing at a time. As you discuss your app idea with different developers, ask them what things would need to be done in the background and how they would accomplish that feat. Keep careful notes and ask the potential developers what experience they have with previous apps that do the same kinds of background tasks.

Remember that this is a high-risk activity, so you need to see it demonstrated as early in the development process as possible.

Wrapping Up

This chapter discusses the myriad components that can make up an app. Here are some key points to take away:

- Make a list of the different features and components that you expect your app to use. This is your shopping list when you talk to potential developers.
- Choose which platform(s) to support based on the device(s) that your target market is most likely to have.
- Make your decision about whether you want a native, hybrid, or web app early in the process; changing your mind later usually means starting over.
- Be careful about your dependencies on third-party frameworks because if your app is successful, you'll likely be tied to that third party for a long time.
- Data storage has a large impact on the functionality and performance of your app, so think about it carefully and store only what you have to.
- Your app is probably going to have to talk to one or more servers. There are a lot of ways this can go wrong, so, as with all high-risk activities, plan for it to happen early in the schedule.
- Syncing is hard, and handling all the different types of conflicts can be expensive, so plan accordingly.
- Developers have a lot of trouble with multitasking on a mobile device. Understand what multitasking you need as soon as possible and track those tasks as high-risk ones.

Finding the Right Tools

Your best chance for a successful project is to stay on top of the progress that is being made and communicate clearly, as soon as possible, what you like and what you don't like about the direction. In order to do that, you need to be actively following along with your developers, and that means being able to get access to, and make use of, the code and other assets that are being created on your behalf.

Now, before you become a micro-management monster, I need you to understand that you won't (and shouldn't) always get your way. You need to establish trust with your developers, and they with you. Trying to tell them exactly how to do their jobs isn't likely to work out well.

But you are the one paying the bills, and you deserve to get the best app you can for your investment. So you need to strike a balance between giving them feedback and getting in their way. It can be tricky, but it's doable. And a good developer will help you to do it.

You see, you and your developer want the same thing (assuming that your developer is competent and ethical): You both want to build an app that you're both happy with, and you both want it built on time and on budget. If it turns out you hate the app you end up with, then you're not going to recommend your developer to other people who need apps or be a good reference for them. In addition, most good developers truly want to do a good job.

Remember that, fundamentally, the enemy of good project management is surprise. If you and your developer work together and communicate well, you reduce the surprise and risk on both sides.

So, having established that there's a good reason that a competent developer will welcome your feedback and participation in the project, let's talk about the other reason you need to follow along: If your developers aren't competent or ethical (or if something unforeseeable happens that prevents them from living up to their potential), you need to be able to salvage what you can, cut your losses, and switch developers. When it's obvious that things are not going to end well, it's already far too late to try to get the failing developer to help package up the project's assets for transfer. That needs to be done all along, as the project takes shape.

Selecting Tools for Your Project Size

Not all projects require the same number of tools. Some apps are intended to generate large amounts of revenue, supporting many full-time employees' salaries and the corresponding overhead. Other apps are side projects self-funded by independent app creators. Not every tool is appropriate for each app project. If your app is being built on a shoestring budget, it might make sense to forgo some of these tools. Your risk will be higher, but because the amount of money at risk is much lower, it might be worth the gamble to you. It certainly is to some independent app creators I know.

The same is true if your app project isn't a full app. If you are only bringing on a single developer for two weeks to add one feature to an existing app, then a bug tracker (for example) might be overkill.

Source Control

Source control (also sometimes called *revision control* or *version control*) is a suite of software that records the current state of a development project, along with the time, the date, the name of the developer responsible for the last change, and a comment. That comment should be about what the developer thought he or she was trying to do and why he or she made the change. Source control allows someone to review the history of the development project after the fact and watch how it evolved and matured over time. For someone who is unfamiliar with a project and trying to understand it, source control is invaluable. Figure 5.1 shows an example of source control history. Chapter 10, "Understanding What You're Getting," discusses these charts and how to use them.

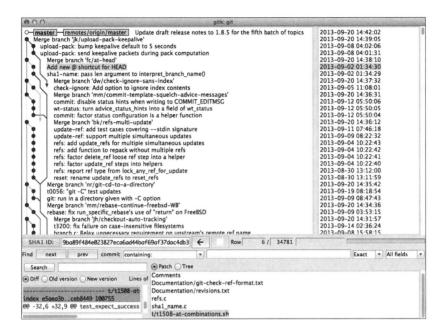

Figure 5.1
An example of source control history.

Somewhat confusingly (as is all too common with technology vocabulary), the term *source control* can refer not only to the suite of software being run that is recording the project history but also to the history itself. The collected history for a single project is called the source control "repository" (often shortened to "repo") for that project.

Again using our building analogy, having a source control repository is like having photographs, bills of materials, and foreman's notes for every day that the house (or bridge or airplane or whatever) was under construction. This might not seem all that useful under normal circumstances. But imagine if you were tasked with deciding whether it's safe to add a new wing to the structure or investigating the cause of a bridge collapse or figuring out why the plane's wing fell off in flight. How important would the project history be to you then?

Source control is also the most useful way to determine how much work has been done on a given project to date, and the best (but still imperfect) tool for deciding whether you're being billed appropriately while a project is under way. It's not a panacea, though, so don't jump to conclusions too hastily. We'll discuss this quite a bit more later in this chapter and in Chapter 8, "Interviewing and Selecting a Developer," and Chapter 10, "Understanding What You're Getting."

When I am a developer taking over a failed or failing project, source control is the single best resource that I can use to evaluate the current state of the project, figure out how it got there, and understand what's worth salvaging and what needs to be rewritten. It helps me understand what pieces of the app the former developer threw together in five minutes and didn't get around to revisiting and what pieces the developer slaved over but coded so poorly that they'll never work.

In short, if you want any real chance of transitioning from your first developer to another developer in the event that something goes wrong, you need a source control history of your project.

How Can Source Control Help Projects?

Although source control is useful for helping an outsider understand the state of an existing repository, that's not what it was designed to do. Its primary purpose is to facilitate coordination among the many people (developers, designers, testers, and others) involved in the creation of a large piece of software. It allows one group of developers to be working on new features while a group of testers are hunting bugs in a version of the project that doesn't contain the unfinished features and another group of developers are working on fixing the bugs that the testers are turning up.

In addition, once a software project reaches a certain size, developers are generally divided into groups or teams, each group working on a different part of the software. Source control allows the output of each of these groups to be rolled up and integrated with each other. This process would be impractical, if not impossible, without source control.

Source control provides a few other benefits. In the event that a bug appears in a feature that used to work (often called a regression, since the code regressed to a nonworking state), going back and figuring out when the bug reappeared is often the most efficient way to find the source of the bug. Source control also has the convenient side effect of providing a backup of the source code on the developers' workstations to a central location. No one wants to lose all their work because their hard drives died.

What Source Control Choices Are There?

There are two main types or families of modern source control: centralized source control (which, up until a few years ago, was just called "source control" because it was the only game in town) and distributed source control (which is the new, shiny thing).

There are a number of commercial source control systems, but they're rarely used outside large enterprises. If you already have one of these, you know it already. If not, you probably want to use one of these three: SVN, git, or hg.

The most common centralized source control system currently in use is called Subversion, and it's now maintained by the Apache project. It's often referred to as SVN (pronounced "S. V. N.") because that's the name of the command you type when you are using it. It uses a central server that all the developers and testers talk to. They check out code from it (getting other developers' changes copied to their workstations) and commit code to it (putting their changes on the server so other people can see them). It has the advantage of being pretty simple to use. It has the disadvantage of being slow and requiring the developer to be connected to the server any time he or she wants to do anything with SVN.

There are two popular distributed source control systems: git (pronounced like "gift" but without the *f*) and Mercurial (often written as hg, since that's what you type to use it, but even when written as hg, it's still commonly spoken as "Mercurial"). They effectively do the same thing. They have the advantage that developers can do most of their work without having to be connected to the server (which is handy in today's distributed and often mobile world). They have the disadvantage of being far more complicated than reliable old SVN. I'm much more a fan of git, but that's mostly due to familiarity. I've used Mercurial, and it's perfectly capable and useful.

There's one more thing that git and hg do well that SVN doesn't, and that's branching.

What Is Branching?

Branching, in source control parlance, is maintaining two (or more) different versions of a project that are being simultaneously developed. One "branch" could be where new features are being developed and another where old features are being tested. Or there could be four or more different features all being worked on, each in its own branch.

The problem with having four different branches being actively developed is that all those features are going to need to be brought together in order for you to ship your app with all four features in it. The act of combining branches is called *merging*, and that's where git and hg really shine. Because git and hg allow developers to work on their own, away from the server for extended periods of time, merging is something that the distributed source control systems had to get right in order to be usable at all. And so they're designed to be much better at merging.

Which Source Control Software Is Right for Your Project?

Personally, I'm a fan of git (and GitHub, discussed in a bit), but like I said earlier, that's primarily a matter of familiarity. If you don't have a strong preference between git, SVN, and hg, wait until you find a developer you like and then ask him or her what he or she prefers (as long as it's reasonable). The truth is that the developer's going to be using it much more than you are.

What GUI Should You Use?

Whichever source control software you pick, there is a good graphical user interface (GUI) to go along with it. It will greatly help simplify the complexity of distributed source control for you. Also, you're unlikely to be doing serious branching or merging, so a simplified tool should be a good fit for your needs.

A number of good GUI tools for SVN, git, and/or hg are free or reasonably priced. Most if not all of the paid ones have free trials. Also, many source control services (especially GitHub and Bitbucket, discussed in the next section) provide their own GUIs for you to use.

In addition, many integrated development environments (IDEs), like Apple's Xcode or Google's Android Studio, have source control support built in. (You'll learn more about IDEs in an upcoming section of this chapter.)

Which tool you prefer is a matter of personal taste. I recommend that you grab a few and try them out. If in doubt, use the one your developer is most familiar with, so that if you get really stuck, you can ask for help.

What Should You Use as a Server (or Service)?

I recommend that you get a service that hosts your source code repositories for you. There are many of them, and the costs are nominal. GitHub, Bitbucket, Beanstalk, and Kiln are but a few of them. Pick the source control software you want to use and then pick a service that supports it, possibly in conjunction with your developer.

It is important, however, that whatever source control service you use, you manage the access to it, instead of your developer. The account with the service needs to be owned and controlled by you. This is true of all such services and accounts, and we'll talk more about it later, but it's important for you to own the code so that the developer can't hold you hostage.

How Should App Creators Use Source Control?

When you're paying a group of developers to build an app for you, source control is your best way of keeping track of what they are doing, measuring the quality of their progress against their schedule, and having an insurance policy in case you end up needing to switch developers (either because they aren't doing a good job or because something prevents them from finishing, like being hit by the proverbial bus).

Now there's a potential conflict here because once you have the source code, you can build the project yourself. More than one developer has given a client access to the source control repository and then had the client use the code without paying for it. That has happened to me a couple times. But it's resolvable. We'll talk more about how to get your developer to agree to it in the "Get the Code, Even if There's Nothing to See in the UI" section of Chapter 10.

So you should use source control to keep up to date on what your developers are doing, but it's also a way to share files with them. If you need to provide your developer with updated wireframes or graphical assets from your designer, source control is a handy way to do that.

Must App Creators Use Source Control Themselves?

In a word: No. Many app creators have successfully interacted with developers without ever touching the source control systems themselves. Some app creators specifically hire developers because they want someone to manage all that for them.

However, without looking at source control yourself (or hiring another programmer to watch your first programmer), you will have to trust the developer's word about what's going on with your project. I've seen developers take advantage of this. See the sidebar "The Case of the Missing Source Code," later in this chapter, for just one such example.

The issue is really how much risk you are willing to take. If your app is relatively small, it might not be worth it to you. If your app is very large, it might be worth it to hire someone technical specifically to verify your developer's work.

What Else Is Source Control Used For?

Source control is also a useful mechanism for including third-party libraries in your projects. A number of open source components are available that can be freely incorporated into your app, and that can save your developers time and you money. Source control facilitates the inclusion and management of such additional components with a minimum of fuss.

What Should Be Checked In to Source Control?

It's important that enough code, graphics files, other media, and project information (called *dependencies*) be checked in for anyone who checks out the project to be able to build the same app as everyone else. If not, the developer could be looking at a different app version than the tester is testing—and that's a recipe for confusion, if not disaster.

Some development environments make validating dependencies easier than others.

Bug Tracking

No software is ever perfect while under development. I would even go so far as to say that if the software is perfect after development, you almost certainly waited too long and spent too much money before you shipped it. But many of the imperfections in software (also referred to as *bugs*, *issues*, and *defects*) do need to get fixed before you ship, and in order to make sure that happens, you want to make sure the bugs are logged and tracked. Figure 5.2 shows an example of how bugs move through different states.

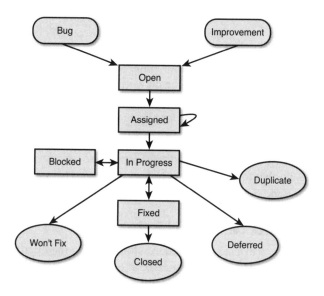

Figure 5.2
A common set of states for a hypothetical bug tool, with arrows showing potential state transitions. We'll discuss these states and what they mean in Chapter 12, "Communicating Using Bugs."

Decades ago, software developers created software products to keep track of these imperfections. (You might notice the running theme that pretty much whatever problem software developers encounter results in them creating more software; it's an occupational hazard.) These software products are called *bug trackers* (or *issue trackers* or *defect trackers* or something like that). Most professional software developers are used to working with them, and they are very useful for making sure that bugs, once identified, are communicated, understood, fixed, and documented. If you've ever had to dig or search through your old emails, trying to find the one that you sent that mentioned that thing that you thought you'd asked someone to do for you to see if they'd replied, you know exactly what bug trackers were intended to avoid. In addition, the bug database (the list of bug and their descriptions, comments, and solutions) helps you remember and understand why something happened long after the fact and can be a valuable asset when you're planning or developing the next version.

Do You *Really* Need a Bug Tracker?

As an experienced software developer, any time a potential client asks me this question, my answer is always going to be "yes." To me, working without a bug tracker or source control would be as professionally irresponsible as billing a client for hours I spent while drunk.

But not every app creator agrees with me. Some are perfectly happy to track bugs on a spreadsheet, and some have success doing so. If the app is small and the number of developers is small (meaning one or maybe two), it might make sense. Certainly if the project is a quick two-week single task to change one thing in an existing app, it might not be worth it at all.

But if your app is at all complicated or if you have more than two other people involved, then I would argue that you really need to use a real bug tracker.

In addition, not wanting to use a bug tracker (or source control) is a red flag for a developer. It indicates a lack of experience and maturity that should make you think twice about whether that developer can be trusted with your app.

Selecting a Bug Tracker

The biggest factor in picking a bug tracker for a small project with a small team is cost, followed closely by simplicity. Bug trackers can have all kinds of complicated workflows and integrations with source control systems and *continuous integration systems* (more on these later). In all likelihood, those features are going to be overkill for your project.

First, look to see what bug trackers you might already have access to. Many source control services have bug trackers built into them. (GitHub, for example, has a feature called *GitHub Issues* that is free with your GitHub account.) That might be a perfectly reasonable tool for your needs. If not, or if you just want more options, you can find a number of reasonably priced hosted bug trackers. Search online, try out a few, and, if all else fails, talk to your developer about what he or she has used in the past or likes using.

But as with your source control service, you want to make sure that you are the owner of the account associated with the bug data.

Using a Bug Tracker

However you use your bug tracker, it will almost certainly be better than not using one at all. But how well you use your bug tracker can make a huge difference in the productivity of your developers. It's not very difficult, but there are a few simple things to keep in mind.

Describe Only One Problem per Bug

Trying to work on a bug that has several different problems listed in it is difficult for a developer. If I have fixed number 2 and number 3 out of 5 items, how do I indicate that? I can't close the bug because pieces are still broken, but anyone who's trying to figure out the state of that bug isn't going to be able to tell easily without reading through all the comments, which means people will be wasting time and effort. It's not too much trouble to put every problem you find into its own bug, and it will make it a lot easier for the people trying to fix the problems.

Be as Specific as Possible

The easier it is to understand what you found and what went wrong, the easier it is to fix. Try to add screenshots and explanatory text if it's relevant. (A picture is worth a thousand words, after all, and a bug hunter especially appreciates this.) Phrases like "broken" or "doesn't work" are rarely, if ever, helpful in bug reports. Try to be specific and descriptive in your explanation.

Try to Explain How to Reproduce the Bug in Steps

As important as describing the problem is describing the steps you took to get there. Make it clear that, in order to see the bug, you need to launch the app, then log in, then tap this tab, then click this row, etc. Don't assume that whoever is trying to fix the bug will know where in the app the bug lives. The code of an app often bears little resemblance to the usage of it, and we as developers spend a lot more time looking at the code than at the interface.

Try to Explain What You Expected or Wanted to Happen

In addition to saying what went wrong, it's often useful to explain what would have been the correct thing for the software to do at that point. Don't assume that it should be obvious. If the developers are sure what it's supposed to do, it's much easier not to have to fix it more than once.

Use the Bug ID in Any Correspondence Related to It

If you're going to ask someone about a bug (maybe because it hasn't been updated or commented on, and you want to know when it's going to be fixed), include the bug number or ID and/or the URL that points to the bug to make it easier for your developer to figure out which bug you're talking about. (Many bugs have similar descriptions, and duplicate bugs can happen, so it can be easy to get confused.)

Copy Any Correspondence or New Information into the Bug

If you get an answer from your developer about a bug (or have a verbal conversation about it), put the information from the conversation in a comment on the bug. It's very useful to have all information associated with a problem in a single place.

Bug Versus New Feature

There is a distinction between a bug (something that was specified to do X, but did Y instead) and a new feature (even though the wireframe looked like X, I think that Y really makes more sense). Whether this distinction is important depends on the agreement between you and your developers. If it's a bug, and they're working on a fixed-cost or a fixed-time frame contract, then they're expected to fix it. If it's a new feature, though, they might need more money and/or time in order to do so. Also, some developers get upset when you call something a bug when it's a new feature. They feel that the word *bug* means that you're telling them that they made a mistake, and some people get offended when they're accused of making a mistake they believe they didn't make.

That said, I'd argue that, whether something is a true bug or a new feature, it should be tracked. Even if you decide not to address the feature or bug now, it could make the list of things that should go into the next version. A bug tracker, if you have one, is a natural place to capture such things for future reference, even the ones that aren't bugs. Just be aware of what you call it, and, if in doubt, have a conversation with your developer before you start logging new features in the bug tracker so that you can minimize the chance of upsetting anyone.

Tracking Things That Aren't Bugs

Bug-tracking tools are generally designed and intended for tracking small, specific defects and tasks. Although you can put full-blown features into them (and many do), these tools don't really do a good job of tracking larger tasks that have several subtasks. But most importantly, they just generally don't have a way of tracking times and schedules. Schedule tracking is probably the single most important thing you need to have in place in order to figure out whether your project is on track.

Project and Schedule Tracking

When I discuss failed projects with app creators who are asking me for a project rescue, one of the things I'm most shocked to find is that many, if not most, of the failures aren't recognized until the point when the project is supposed to have been complete. It seems normal to many of them to hand off an app idea to a developer, occasionally get a short, boilerplate status email like "Everything's on track," and not see any results or take delivery of any code until right before the end of the project. While it's possible for that type of process to work, it's a low-probability event.

Let me take you through what life is like on the contract mobile developer side of the fence so you can understand why such a process is a bad idea. There are many different kinds of developers you could choose, so I'm going to pick a couple of examples and talk about each.

First, let's assume that you are using a small development group, perhaps even a solo developer, and that your project is the only project they're really working on. From the point of view of getting the most focus, this should be a big advantage for you. But imagine that you're the developer, and you don't have anything "due" for a few of months. What's the likelihood that you're going to procrastinate? Well, maybe *you* wouldn't, but most people would. Many studies (see http://people.duke.edu/~dandan/Papers/PI/deadlines.pdf) have shown that people do better work when they are given more frequent, externally defined deadlines than when nothing is due until the last minute. When I work with my own customers, I try to make sure I have frequent deadlines to avoid this tendency in myself.

But maybe you're not working with a small developer. Maybe you're working with a large firm that has its own development staff and its own designers and project managers. Surely such a setup wouldn't have a procrastination problem, right? Well, yes and no.

Here's the thing about large development shops in a popular field like mobile development: They're frequently approached by people and companies who have projects that need to get done, often with short deadlines and often for lots of money. The desire to take these projects even when their programmers are fully engaged is very high; sometimes it is financially irresistible. So here's the question: If the firm working on your project gets overly committed because it took on one too many projects, what's the strategy that provides the best outcome for you? The answer, again, is more frequent milestones and deadlines (ideally attached to payments) because if the group has to take resources off one project to do a new high-priority short-term project, it's going to take the resources off the project with the least oversight and the furthest-away deliverables.

Traditional Project Planning (Gantt Charts)

So now that I've (hopefully) convinced you that you need to have frequent milestones and that you need to track them, how do you do it? The standard tool for this task is called a Gantt chart (see http://en.wikipedia.org/wiki/Gantt_chart). This type of chart, invented in 1910, helps you visualize time frames and schedules. If you've ever seen a chart with tasks and durations, it was probably one of these. Numerous software tools let you track tasks like this, including Microsoft Project (by far the most popular) and (my preference as a Mac user) OmniPlan from the Omni Group. Figure 5.3 shows an example of a Gantt chart. Chapter 9, "Managing to Milestones," discusses these charts and how to use them.

Kanban Boards

You can use a tool called a kanban board to track tasks in progress (see http://en.wikipedia.org/wiki/Kanban_board). It's closer to 10 years old than 100, and it has become more mainstream with the rise in popularity of the Agile software movement. These boards were originally created with sticky notes on a board, but it wasn't long before software people made a program for it (as they are wont to do).

A kanban board shows a number of cards, each one representing a task on a project. Each card is labeled with the name of the task and is put in one of a number of sections (or areas or lists) on the board, which represent the status of the task (in progress, done, blocked, programmed and ready to be tested, tested, etc.). Generally there's a list that contains things that need to be done for the next milestone, another list of things that need to be done before this version ships, and another list of things that would be nice to have but aren't expected to be done for this version. (Usually these lists have shorter names, but they vary from team to team.)

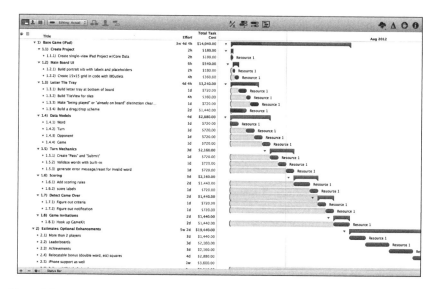

Figure 5.3
An example of a Gantt chart from a recent app proposal.

In more advanced variations of kanban, each task/card also has a *point value* that is supposed to be a representation of how difficult, complicated, or time-consuming the task is estimated to be. These point values are arbitrary but are supposed to be relatively consistent (for example, a three-point task should take roughly three times as long as a one-point task). As the project progresses, the software calculates a *velocity*, which is the number of points' worth of tasks the team completes in a given time (on average). From that, the software can estimate how long it will likely take to complete the rest of the tasks that are pending on the project and approximate a project completion date.

Kanban software, unlike Gantt chart software, tends to be online and collaborative, which is handy. A number of web services provide kanban software. Often, you can get the developers to move their own cards when a task is completed, which gives more accurate timing and is less work for you.

External Services

In addition to the tools and services that help you interact with your developers and track the status of your project, there are a number of services that continue to be used not only throughout the development process but also as part of your app throughout its lifetime.

This section talks about many of those tools, but the most important thing to remember for any service that's required for your app to function is that *you* need to be the owner and contact for that service. Not your developer. No exceptions.

However unlikely, it's always possible that your developers may fail to fulfill their duties under your contract, maybe through no fault of their own. If that happens, and you need to part ways, it's *immensely* more complicated if they own any vendor or service relationships.

App Store Accounts

You're going to have an account with the vendor of each of the app stores that you're planning on selling your app through. Do not wait until the last minute to set up these accounts. It can take time for an account to get created, and it can involve sending legal paperwork and proving you are who you say you are. In addition, having the account is a prerequisite for some development tasks, as well as for reserving the name that you want for your app.

These accounts aren't difficult to set up, and instructions are readily available, but the setup work can be time-consuming, and I've seen more than one project stalled because the account setup was left until the last minute.

Facebook/Twitter

You might want your app to post things onto Facebook or Twitter, or you might want to give it a mechanism for your users to share information with or to invite their friends. The easiest way to enable such things is to use the sharing mechanisms built into your mobile platform or platforms of choice (Share Sheet on iOS, Intents on Android, etc.). If, however, it's important to you for your app to have its own identity inside Twitter or Facebook (that is, for your user's post or tweet to appear as having come from your app), you'll need to sign up your app with Twitter and/or Facebook. Be warned, though: Twitter and Facebook like to change the way that apps talk to their systems, and if you have your app talk directly to their servers, you will likely have to update (or pay a developer to update) your app from time to time to keep up with their service changes. You may also have to remove features from your app if Twitter or Facebook decides to disallow certain functionality from external apps.

Push Notifications

If you want your app to be notified about external events, you're going to want to set up *push notifications*. This way, from your server or service, you can let your users know, through your app, that something has changed. For example, if you're making an app where users communicate with each other (for example, a text message app or a multiplayer game where a user gets notified that it's his or her turn), you'll need to have something set up that relays these messages.

You can build your own server to do this (or have someone build one for you), or you can get a service to do it, likely for less than what it would cost you to run your own server. A number of services do this, both for Apple iOS and Android. Urban Airship is the one that's been delivering this service the longest.

However, many other services (see the next section) also provide push notifications as part of their offerings, so depending on what other things you're doing in your app, you might find a vendor that includes it as part of what you were already going to pay for.

Storage Services

If you plan for your app to store files or sync data between different devices, then the app might need a storage service. Some, like Apple's iCloud or Google Drive, are built into their respective mobile platforms (assuming that you're targeting a new enough version of the mobile device software) and don't need extra accounts, per se, although they require jumping through extra hoops for configuration. Other options for off-device storage include services like Dropbox, which require users to have, or sign up for, free or paid accounts.

Platform/Software/Application as a Service

Back in the old days (2005 or so), if you wanted to provide a web service, you had to run your own server that connected to the Internet. The beginning of the end of that requirement was Amazon's Elastic Compute Cloud (EC2), which let you create virtual Linux computers "in the cloud" on demand for not much money. Over the years, the offerings have evolved, and in the past few years, they've exploded.

Many companies now provide a way for you (or your developer) to build a web service that allows your app to have functionality "in the cloud" without requiring you to think about what server it runs on. These services go by many names, including *Software as a Service* (SaaS), *Application as a Service*, and *Platform as a Service* (PaaS), and I'm sure there are others. These allow all kinds of arbitrary functionality to occur between copies of your app, from chat/ photo sharing to file transfers to collaborative puzzle solving to map location sharing, etc. Many also include push notifications and storage in some of their plans.

The options here are wide open, and the vendors are many and varied, from Google's App Engine, to Heroku, to Parse (now part of Facebook), to Microsoft's Windows Azure Mobile Services. Wikipedia's PaaS page currently lists 22 vendors, and its SaaS page lists 29. More services seem to be launching weekly, if not daily. Many of these services have gone away, leaving their customers stranded (most recently StackMob, which PayPal bought and shut down). Do your homework here and discuss with your developer before picking a reliable vendor.

Analytics Services

Analytics is a way of gathering information about how users are interacting with your app. You can do analytics while you are testing an app prior to shipping it, but it really proves its worth when your app is out in the wild, and you're trying to decide what to work on for the next version.

Assuming that you get a decent service (and there are many that technically qualify), using an analytics service is very straightforward. You just create your account, pay whatever you need to pay (depending on your plan), and then follow the directions for connecting your app to the analytics service when it starts up. Then, any time the user does something that you want to track, a line of code is executed in the app that tells the analytics service to track it, and you wait for a while and run the reports the service provides to see what your users are doing.

And there's the rub: You have to decide what you want to track. There are three competing factors at work here. First, you need information about what your users are doing, in order to make better decisions that can help to make better apps and provide a better service for those same users. Second, every time you track something, it takes a little time, and a little storage space, and a little network bandwidth (which may well be metered). If you track too much using analytics services, your users will get annoyed. Third, and probably most importantly, you need to respect the privacy of your users. I've seen many cases of app names being splattered all over the tech press because they were accused of violating their users' privacy, and if you believe that all press is good press, there are some now-defunct apps a Google search away whose creators might disagree.

You need to decide, in collaboration with your developer, what you really need to know about how users are interacting with your app. Assuming it's not sensitive information, you need to know what features are being used and how often in order to make better decisions about where to put your resources while developing future versions. You need to know when bad things (errors and crashes) happen to try to prioritize fixing them, and you need to collect enough information to figure out why an error happened but not so much that the user might get upset. You may need to know if users are pirating your app. (Or, since there's not much you can really do about it, you might not want to know.) You probably need to know other things that are specific to your app. Discuss it with your developer and figure out what makes sense.

In-App Purchasing Services

If you want to upsell your users, either because you're making a freemium app or because you have extra functionality you want to try to monetize, you'll likely need a server for that. You might be able to get away without one if you have very simple needs. (Talk to your developer about it.) But if you need an in-app purchase server, and most apps that provide in-app purchases do, you can either build and maintain your own (likely virtual) server or contract with a service to do it.

Advertising Services

If you want to try to make money via ads in your apps, you'll need a service to do that, too, maybe even more than one. There are a few major ad services— many of them provided by the mobile platform vendors themselves—and dozens of smaller ones. You can also use an add-on ad service that's called an *ad proxy* or an *ad broker* service. These services hook up to many different ad back ends (each of which you'll need to sign up for) and figure out, for a given time and user, which ad service is most likely to pay you the most (and, of course, the service takes a cut of that).

Other Services

There may be other services you need as well. Although I've touched on the major ones, there isn't room to mention all the possibilities. If you need another one, that's fine, but as I said before, make sure you—not your developer—own it.

The Development Environment

In order to develop apps, a programmer has to use special software, often referred to as *development tools* or *developer tools*. These tools include things like compilers, debuggers, linkers, and editors, as well as a host of other things. Collectively, we refer to the set of these tools that is being used as the *development environment*.

If you are going to be able to build the app your developers are working on for yourself, you're going to need a development environment materially similar to the one your developers are using. In many cases, that's fairly straightforward, as the development environment is dictated by the constraints of the mobile device vendor. For example, in order to build for Apple's iPhones and iPads, you need to use Apple's development tools, running on an Apple Mac. In the event that there is a choice of developer tools for your platform, you'll want to match what your developer is using.

Integrated Development Environments (IDEs)

The most common kind of developer tool on a modern project (which includes pretty much all mobile platforms) is an integrated development environment (IDE). An IDE is the Swiss Army knife of the development tool landscape, incorporating a code editor, a compiler, a debugger, and other development tools. In all likelihood, an IDE is the only programming tool that you're really going to need.

Your IDE is likely to be chosen for you, based on the developer you are working with and the platform(s) you are targeting. An iPhone/iPad project will almost certainly use Apple's Xcode. A Windows Phone project will almost certainly use Microsoft's Visual Studio. An Android project will probably use Google's Android Studio, although Eclipse was once the most common choice there, and some people still use it. There are other options (for example, JetBrains is a company that makes and sells IDEs for many types of development), but unless your developer is unusual, it will probably be the one provided by the platform vendor.

Simulators and Emulators

Developing apps for mobile devices is complicated by the fact that the computer on which you are doing the development is not a mobile device. Writing the software and compiling the app are not generally an issue, but what happens when you want to test it?

Even when a programmer is working strictly in the development phase of a project, there's still a lot of testing that's happening (although the scope is limited to the feature the developer is currently working on). It's a fairly constant cycle: Think about what you want to do next, write some code that you think will accomplish that, run the code and make sure it did what you wanted it to do, think about what you want to do next, etc.

When it comes time to run the code, you can't run it directly on the computer you're developing on. The device on which you're expecting to run the code likely has a small, multitouch display, and the computer you're programing on likely does not. And what's more, although you probably don't care, the CPU chip in the development computer is likely wholly different than the one in the device. This leaves you three choices:

A   You could build a different version of the app that would run on your development computer and respond to mouse events instead of screen touches.

B   You could run a program on your computer that pretends to be the hardware of the mobile device and then run the same app unaltered on it.

C   You could keep a device connected to your development computer and copy the app to it every time you wanted to run and test.

Now of these choices, A is called a *simulator* and is the fastest and least awkward, but it's also the least accurate test environment. B is called an *emulator* and is very slow: It's a lot of work to pretend to be a different kind of CPU chip. C is slow—it takes a while to copy the app to the device, especially if the app is large—and it's kind of awkward because you have to switch your focus back and forth between the computer and the device. However, it does give you the most accurate test environment. C also has the problem that you have to actually possess the device in question, which, depending on how many devices you are developing for, could get expensive.

Whatever IDE you choose will come with either a simulator or an emulator. It will also come with software that gives you the ability to copy an app to a device. I'll warn you, though: There are almost always lots of annoying hoops you have to jump through to be able to get any app running on a device during the development process. This is the case because of security concerns. For a mobile device user, this is good, but for a developer, it's a royal pain. The steps vary a lot from vendor to vendor, but your IDE should have pretty clear instructions about how to jump through the hoops. If it doesn't, the steps should be a quick web search away.

Why Bother with a Development Environment?

So, you may be asking, "Do I really have to build the project myself?" The answer is: *It depends on how lucky you feel*.

It's true that your developer will be able to give you builds that you can run on your device, and you could go through your entire project without having to build the code yourself. In fact, a lot of clients have never built their apps for themselves. And some of them have been fine with that.

But the risk is that, if you don't build the project yourself, you don't know whether the code that your developer has given you is capable of building your app. As the project is progressing, you also have to trust the developer about the state or condition of the app.

The Case of the Missing Source Code

Once upon a time, I was asked to give an estimate of what it would take to add a couple new features to an app that was already in an app store. The app creator gave me access to the source code—by forwarding me an email containing a zip file. (The developers hadn't used source control at all.) I got it, unzipped it, and it wouldn't build—not at all. Big chunks of code were completely missing.

It turned out that the previous developers had used some code from a previous project in building this client's app, but when the developers gave the client the source code, they hadn't included the relevant code from the previous project. But now the app was built, it had been in the app store for months, and people were using it. The contract with the former developers was now done (they had had a falling out), all the money had been paid, and the app's owner had no leverage in order to obtain the rest of the code. The former developers claimed that all the code had been delivered as specified in the contract, but they offered to take a look at it for a (fairly steep) price.

If that app creator had attempted to build the project before the final check had been written, he or she would have known that something was missing and could probably have done something about it. But by the time it was noticed, it was too late. Don't let this happen to you.

Continuous Integration

Continuous integration (CI) is a technique that large teams use to ensure basic quality control. It was popularized by the Agile software movement. A CI implementation consists of a server or servers that run a suite of software, including a development environment, a source control client, web and email services for displaying and reporting history and status, and often an automated test software package.

It works like this: The CI server is configured to know the source control repository that contains the project (or projects) in question. Periodically thereafter, the CI server checks whether anything new has been added to source control since the last build and, if so, the CI server checks out the latest source code from the repository, builds it and, if it's configured, runs all the automated tests (sometimes called *build verification tests*) that are configured. The server then generates a web page for the build, containing the output of any build and test processes, a summary showing the overall build/test status, and often the amount of time the build/test process took. In the event of a build or test failure, the CI server often sends email out to some or all of the team members with the error or failure message. In mobile projects, the CI server is often configured to create installable app packages that can be installed on test devices or potentially submitted to an app store.

CI servers can seem like a lot of effort until you understand the value proposition. I've seen them save teams tons of work. You see, what can happen is that a developer may be working on a particular bug or feature in a particular part of the project. That developer often concentrates on that piece of the app and pretty much ignores the rest of it. This is a useful thing for the developer to do because the better he or she focuses, the faster it will be to complete the bug fix or feature. Unfortunately, this technique has the side effect of sheltering the developer from the consequences his or her changes are making on the rest of the project. In mobile development, it's surprisingly easy to break a previously working feature that you aren't looking at when you're trying to build a new one. This is why we have to do what's called *regression testing*, which we talked about in Chapter 2, "The App Development Life Cycle."

CI servers can also be lifesavers in the event that two developers are working on two different features in different branches but doing so in an incompatible way. You can configure a CI server to do test merges of active branches and warn the relevant developers that they are on a collision course; this gives the developers an opportunity to work out the issue before much work is wasted.

But often, the most useful function that a CI server provides is simply giving non-developers easy access to current builds for testing.

CI Server Options

Unlike bug trackers and source control services, there are not a plethora of available hosted CI services supporting mobile development, at least not at the time of this writing. (There are several that don't support mobile development, so pay attention.) I've heard of a couple that support iOS or Android development, but they're still very new, they're platform specific (that is, they do one or the other platform but not both), and there's no telling if they'll still exist by the time this book is published.

So if you want a CI server, you'll either have to host one yourself or rely on one that your developer hosts. In either case, talk to your developer about getting one set up for you.

Do You Need One?

This option is far less cut-and-dried than many of the other options. I recommend your project should definitely have source control, bug tracking, and a working development environment. You definitely need to do project tracking, although you might not *need* a dedicated tool or service to do it. But as far as CI goes, if your project is simple, and you're only planning to do one, a CI server might not be worth the effort. If, however, you want to be in the business of creating apps, create complicated apps, or run multiple app projects at the same time, setting up a CI server is probably worth the effort.

Beta Testing Distribution

It's often hard to install software on mobile devices—on purpose. Most mobile devices are programmed only to accept software that's been installed via an app store. That's important for security because it makes it harder for malicious software to infect your phone. Unfortunately, as an app creator or developer, it also makes it a little bit harder to write and test your software. And while it's not rocket science to work around it for your own devices by plugging in USB cables directly to computers that have correctly installed development environments, that's not good enough. Because if you want your app to perform well and to be useful to the people that you want to buy it, the app needs to be tested before release, and it needs to be tested well. The security that protects the devices makes that very difficult.

Testing Early Builds

Years ago, recognizing this problem, a company called TestFlight was started to make it easier to install apps that were still in development on testers' phones. At first TestFlight was iPhone-only and the only game in town. Neither is true any longer.

You don't *have* to have a service for testing early builds, although you *should* because it makes things much, much easier. And if you have a service, it doesn't have to be TestFlight, although it was so dominant in the space at one time that some people still refer to distributing early builds to testers as *TestFlighting*. (This is becoming much less common, though, since the company TestFlight was acquired.)

Whatever service you choose, it will help you recruit and keep track of users and distribute new builds of your app to them. Most importantly, it will remove much of the support burden from you so that you don't have to figure out how to get the software installed on your testers' devices.

Each service has its own set of rules for interacting with testers, and they change frequently, so I'm not going to try to describe them here. The important thing to take away is that this type of service will help you get your app tested by more people on more devices, and that's critical to the overall success of your app.

Crash Reporting

Apps crash, especially in development and when they're newly released to a broad spectrum of devices. When an app crashes reliably, in front of the developer, it should be relatively easy to find and fix the problem. But often apps crash only on certain devices or only under certain circumstances; those types of crashes can be difficult to diagnose.

To combat this problem, a number of strategies have been developed. The vast majority revolve around catching the crash and writing out diagnostic information that the app can see when it's next run. Then the app can upload the diagnostics to a server, where the developer can access that information. Then, knowing where in the code the crash occurred and having some information about the circumstances and device, the developer has a much better chance of finding and fixing the bug. Figure 5.4 shows an example of a crash report.

Although code exists to help you run your own server for this, there are a number of companies that can do it for you for much cheaper than the developer effort likely to be needed to do it yourself. The important thing is that you need to be able to detect crashes both during development and after the app ships. Few things are more frustrating for an app creator than getting bad reviews and angry emails from customers about a crash that you can't reproduce to fix. Although Apple and other vendors may provide some crash dumps to you, I can assure you that many more crashes happen than the ones the platform vendors provide to you.

One important caveat: On many platforms, including Apple's iOS, in order to be able to make sense of a crash report, you have to collect and keep debug information created at build time. If you build your app and then distribute it without keeping the debug information, it's likely that crash dumps will do you no good at all. Your developer should be knowledgeable about this and about the platform vendors' requirements for crash report analysis.

As with any other service, even though this is primarily a developer tool, it's important that you be the owner of the relationship with the service.

Figure 5.4
An example of a crash report for an iOS app. This report indicates that the investigation into this crash should begin at line 302 of the file MasterViewController.m of the SeismicJSON project (see line 3, after "Thread 0 Crashed").

Also, you should understand that some of the information that you might want to collect during testing is information you shouldn't (or can't) collect from your eventual users. This means you should make sure that the crash reporting configuration that you are using when you submit your build to the app store collects only the information allowed for a shipping app on your platform—and no more.

End-User Feedback

In addition to crashes, apps always have other issues; if nothing else, the app won't do everything that your users might want or expect. So you need to determine how to get that type of feedback. If you do not provide another mechanism, that feedback will likely show up in reviews of your app; you really don't want negative feedback in the form of bad reviews.

To avoid this situation, many successful app creators provide an in-app mechanism that lets users contact them. You can use email, but if your app is popular, that can lead to unmanageable inboxes. A number of services allow you to get feedback from users in a way that's better organized, either in a web-based bug-tracking tool or in a user forum. If you choose a service that goes the forum route, users can even help each other. But forums can unfortunately become spam magnets, so there's a management overhead.

It's helpful to use such a service during beta testing. This way, by the time your app ships, you will be familiar with the service, and you will have a chance to switch to a different one, if needed, before your real users are impacted.

Wrapping Up

This chapter discusses the tools and services that can help you make a better app with less risk and hopefully less effort. Here are some key points to take away:

- Source control should not be optional. If your developer does not want to use source control or doesn't want to give you access to it (at least once you've paid him or her), find another developer.

- Bug tracking is often the easiest way to interact with your developer concerning bugs and issues that arise during the development process. Most developers are used to using it anyway.

- Project tracking is all about schedule. The sooner you know that things are running late, the easier it is to correct.

- You need to own whatever service or services are needed for your app. Don't put yourself in the position of having to negotiate with a former developer for rights to an app store account or source code that you paid for after the relationship has gone sour.

- It's important for you to follow along in the development process by building the app yourself (or having a trusted technical resource do it for you). Don't assume that the source code the developer has given you actually built the app that you shipped unless you have some verification. You don't want to find out about this after the developer is gone and it's time to start the next version of your app.

- Beta distribution, crash reporting, and end-user feedback services help manage interaction with your users and testers. If you're going to use one or more, use it during the testing process and make sure you like it before you ship your app.

6

Skill Gap Analysis

Tools are very useful, and the right tools can make a huge difference in how long it takes to build an app and how good the app ends up being. But fundamentally, apps are built by people, and those people need the right combination of skills in order for the app to be built successfully, on time, and within budget.

This chapter talks about determining whether you have access to the skills needed to build your app, and if not, how to go about acquiring those skills.

The most straightforward way to acquire missing skills, at least when software is concerned, is to contract out to people who have them. However, that requires capital, and if you have more time than money, it might be better for you to try to learn those skills yourself. Either way, it will help to understand what skills you have and what skills you still need.

Programming

In order for an app, or any other piece of software, to be created, someone has to program it. By *program* here, I mean write computer code. When it comes to who writes the code and when, there are several options. Figure 6.1 shows an example of computer code that is executed when someone taps a button in an app. Figures 6.2 and 6.3 show different perspectives on this same button.

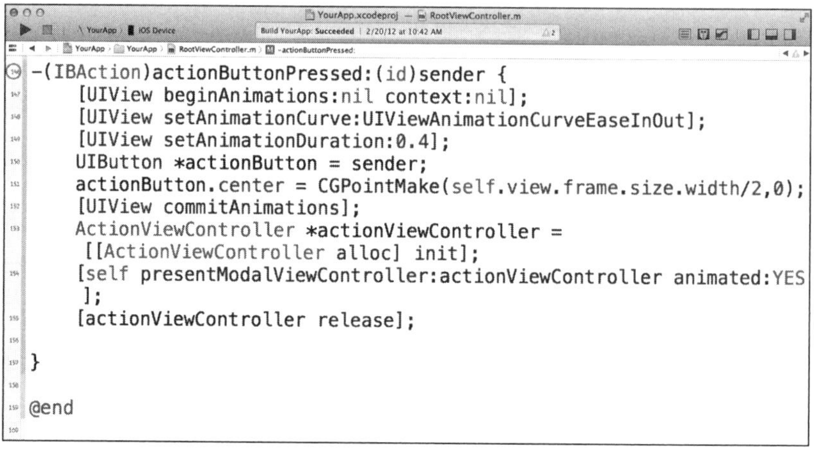
YourApp.xcodeproj — RootViewController.m
Build YourApp: Succeeded | 2/20/12 at 10:42 AM
-(IBAction)actionButtonPressed:(id)sender {
[UIView beginAnimations:nil context:nil];
[UIView setAnimationCurve:UIViewAnimationCurveEaseInOut];
[UIView setAnimationDuration:0.4];
UIButton *actionButton = sender;
actionButton.center = CGPointMake(self.view.frame.size.width/2,0);
[UIView commitAnimations];
ActionViewController *actionViewController =
[[ActionViewController alloc] init];
[self presentModalViewController:actionViewController animated:YES
];
[actionViewController release];
}
@end

Figure 6.1
An example of code (in this case, Objective-C) to do an animation in a sample iPhone app. This is the kind of code that programmers create. Figures 6.2 and 6.3, later in this chapter, show what this code does.

Preprogrammed Components

At least some of the code for your app doesn't need to be written by you or someone you hired or contracted directly. It is possible for your app to make use of existing frameworks or libraries that someone else has written and that you can license or purchase. This may save time and money, but it will do so at the expense of flexibility.

In fact, if you are willing for your app to turn into a cookie cutter, you can buy a sample app or template from various sites. It's possible to build an app with little additional coding needed, but few people are satisfied with that kind of end result.

Complexity and Experience

As discussed in Chapter 4, "Determining Your App's Components," different apps have different requirements and components. The more complicated you want your app to be, the more proficient a programmer you will need to build your app successfully. If your app is simple, you may be able to learn enough programming to be able to build it yourself, especially if you can lean heavily on existing frameworks and sample code. Alternatively, if your app is more complicated but you want to do it yourself anyway, it may behoove you to build a simpler app first to gain experience. You can get a basic idea of how complicated your app idea is by thinking about how many items you determined from Chapter 4 that you want in your app.

Ideally, you want to work with someone (or a group of people) who has built an app with each of the components that your app is likely to use. The other trick is that the more components there are, the more difficult it is to integrate them into a seamless whole. So the more feature rich your app will be, the greater your need for an experienced programmer (whether that's you or someone else).

I'm not going to spend a lot of time discussing finding a programmer because that's the topic of Chapter 7, "Finding a Developer." But I am going to spend some time on what it takes to learn to write apps on your own.

I want to make something clear to you right now: There are two overlapping but distinct skills at play here. One of them is programming mobile apps. The second is programming in general. Although it's true that an experienced programmer who has never worked on a mobile app can acquire a journeyman's proficiency in a matter of months, learning how to write computer code in a timely and proficient manner in the first place takes most people years. If you haven't done serious development on another computing platform, you are unlikely to be able to write a complicated mobile app without several years of work. If you want an app faster than that, your best bet is probably to hire an experienced programmer.

If you aren't already an experienced programmer, feel free to skim the rest of this section. Don't forget about it entirely, though. You might want to refer to it later, when you are interviewing potential developers. Any developer worth hiring should be able to describe to you in detail how he or she learned mobile development, and this section might help you determine how credible your interviewees are. We'll talk about this again in the "Gap Analysis" section of Chapter 8, "Interviewing and Selecting a Developer."

Bootstrapping Your Own Skills

The explosion of the popularity of apps has created high demand for the skills needed to build them. This in turn has created a market for educational products and services that teach these skills. There's never been a better time to try to learn to program mobile apps. Be warned, however: Programming apps is not a skill that can be learned quickly, and as time passes, the users raise their expectations and want apps to be more polished and better designed all the time.

A word of caution: When learning to program mobile apps, pick one and only one platform, such as iOS or Android, or go with a device-independent platform, like Unity 3D. Attempting to learn multiple platforms simultaneously is likely to result in more confusion and less progress than if you try to learn them individually.

Classes

Many businesses and educational institutions are currently teaching mobile app development. Only you can decide whether starting with a class is the best fit for your situation and learning style. Classes can be expensive and generally require time away from other commitments, like work and family, but can get you up and running a lot faster than some of the other methods.

My recommendation for determining the quality of a mobile app development class is to search the web for information about the instructor. Most instructors have a web presence that will list the books, articles, blogs, classes, and apps the instructor has worked on. Many classes also publish course outlines or synopses on the web. Look at some of these materials yourself and see if the information is clear and understandable to you. Also, compare and contrast this information with the most popular existing courses, like the ones from Stanford or MIT, that are available for free on the web. Another longstanding, proven, popular set of courses and books comes from the Big Nerd Ranch. Those folks have been teaching and writing on iOS and Android programming for years now.

Videos

The major mobile platform vendors make videos from their developer conferences available to their developer communities. I watch all the videos from the Apple Worldwide Developers Conference (WWDC). I usually watch them while I'm exercising, and it takes me months to get through all of them. But they're invaluable in my line of work. I also keep a folder on my laptop that contains all the PDF files of the presentation slides from all the WWDC sessions. Then, when I'm having a particular problem, I can search through that folder for keywords related to my problem to find out which videos I should go back and watch again.

You can also find videos from university classes online, often for free. At the time of this writing, the best such course I've seen is from Stanford Online.

Books

As previously mentioned, the Big Nerd Ranch has made a name for itself over the years by providing training for Mac and iOS programming. It recently branched into teaching other mobile platforms, like Android, with its usual mix of clarity and breadth.

There is also a *Learning* series of books from Addison-Wesley (see www.informit.com/imprint/series_detail.aspx?ser=2725799). Many of these books cover aspects of mobile development and are written specifically for people wanting to bootstrap their programming skills.

Conferences

All the mobile app platform vendors have developer conferences: Apple has WWDC, Google hosts IO, Microsoft has Build, and Unity hosts Unite. These are usually annual, although some vendors have smaller traveling conferences as well. The primary advantage of these conferences is getting to interact with the people who are building the platform. If you need to have specific questions answered, attending one of these conferences can be invaluable.

In addition to the vendor-sponsored conferences, there are smaller conferences as well. Some, like 360iDev, CocoaConf, and AnDevCon target one platform and draw speakers from the active developer community. Others, like M3Conference and App Developers Conference, have tracks for all aspects of mobile development. Regardless of focus, conferences are one of the best ways to advance from being a competent mobile developer to a masterful one.

Local Meet-Up Groups

Many cities have meet-up user groups that get together regularly to discuss mobile programming. Meetup.com is a good site to find groups in your area. Most of these groups encourage newcomers to their platform and are happy to help and answer questions.

Keeping a Sense of Perspective

No matter what resources you consume, programming is an act of creation. To get better and stay better, you must write code. There's no substitute for practice, and your next app is almost always better written than your previous one.

Getting started is hard work, and getting good enough to write a complicated app takes time—often years. If you're in it for the long haul, more power to you. If not, hiring or contracting an experienced programmer is likely your best bet.

The Case of the NDA Days

Back in 2008, when the Apple App Store first launched, Apple kept all the iPhone development resources under nondisclosure agreement (NDA) for several months. I wrote my first app with one other developer and a part-time QA resource in five months, with only Apple's documentation and books intended to teach programming on the Mac.

I had been programming computers for a living for more than 15 years at that point, and that first app was truly poorly written. Once the NDA finally was lifted and books started coming out and the community got to share resources with each other, I learned what I should have been doing, and I was mortified.

Despite my lack of information, the app was quite a success. But it was a much simpler app than would be acceptable these days, and the bar for the App Store was still pretty low. Several versions later, the app was finally something I could be proud of. Thinking back on that first version, though, still makes me cringe.

There are two takeaways here. First, even with a decade and a half of professional coding experience, it still took me months to become a beginning iPhone developer; the two types of development are really different. Second, you should take advantage of the resources available to you. They're much better than developers and app creators used to have, but then, so is the average app. Consumers are far more jaded now, and you have to step up your game if you want to compete.

Testing and Quality Assurance

The quality assurance (QA) function is the last chance in your process that you have to avoid shipping an app your users will hate. While it seems like it ought to be easy to tell for yourself the level of quality in your app, experience has shown me that that isn't necessarily the case. In addition, there are very few, if any, good resources of which I am aware to teach someone how to thoroughly test an app for quality.

So you're almost certain to need to enlist the help of other people when testing your app. These may be professional testers, they might be potential users, or you might want a mix of both. Either way, see Chapter 13, "Testing," for more information on testing and interacting with your testers.

Server Support and Troubleshooting

Any app that has a server component becomes vulnerable to a number of network and server reliability issues. There will be times for any such app—likely both during development and after shipping—when issues are reported and either users or testers become unable to use the app or developers become unable to make development progress. When either happens, someone needs to figure out what's going on.

If the server component of your app is a third-party service, this might simply involve finding the web page for that third party that shows the service's current availability status. It may involve opening a ticket with the third-party vendor to get your problem resolved. It may involve proving to that vendor that the problem is on their end and not on your end.

If you are hosting your own server, then you will need to have someone track down the problem and fix it so that your users, testers, and/or developers can start working again.

Either way, you need to have access to someone who has the requisite skills. Many mobile developers have, or at least claim to have, such experience. However, if you are relying on your mobile developer for this skill, it is important to specify that upfront and make sure it's in the developer's contract so there won't be any confusion or surprises later.

Many app creators drastically underestimate the amount of effort required in supporting and maintaining these services over the long term.

Often, some sort of server or service is required in order to bring an app idea to fruition. Many, many apps use or incorporate such services. Make sure you understand what you are signing up for when you choose to incorporate such functionality.

User Experience Design

User experience design is less about what the interface looks like (that's the realm of graphic design, discussed next) than how it functions. It's about workflows and transitions and control placement. It's about creating an app that enables users to interact with it efficiently and without confusion. Figure 6.2 shows an example of user experience design. Compare it to Figure 6.1, which is the code that the programmer generates to make this vision happen, and Figure 6.3, which is the output of the graphic designer.

The good news is that each mobile platform vendor has created a number of controls and layouts that are common to the platform and are already familiar, well designed, and useful from a user experience standpoint. To the extent that your app uses these built-in controls and layouts, you may not need dedicated user experience design resources. Unfortunately, most users are bored by apps that have only platform-supplied user interface elements. On the other hand, depending on the app, boring might not be as important to your users as functionality. The bottom line is that if you want an interesting app that's not overly expensive, the trick is to use custom user interface elements sparingly.

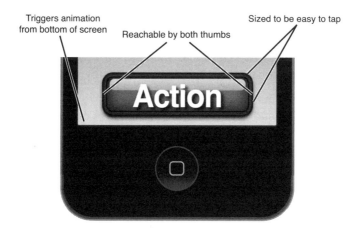

Triggers animation from bottom of screen   Reachable by both thumbs   Sized to be easy to tap

Figure 6.2
A piece of a wireframe showing a button that triggers an animation in a sample iPhone app. This is the kind of output that user experience designers create.

As discussed previously, user testing can tell you when you have poor or confusing user experiences. User testing also tells you whether the changes that you've made to your app have made the user experience better or worse. However, relying solely on user testing is a hit-or-miss prospect. A good user experience designer can tell you how to go from an interface that users find confusing to one that's straightforward and efficient, yet still attractive, without many iterations of trial and error.

With programmers, it might take you quite a while to figure out whether they've done a good job. But evaluating the work of a user experience designer can be much more straightforward. If you can incorporate the user experience designer's input into an interactive prototype, as discussed in Chapter 3, "Prototyping and Wireframing Your App," then putting that prototype in front of real users should tell you whether the work you're getting is worth the cost and effort.

As with programming, the demand for mobile apps has created a plethora of resources intended to teach people about mobile development. Although I haven't seen as many user experience design classes at educational institutions as I have for programming, they do exist. And many books and web tutorials talk about the various points of user experience design. (When searching the Internet for user experience design resources, note that it's often abbreviated *UX*.)

User experience design is a relatively new phrase that is being used to differentiate this field from graphic design. As a consequence, there's still some ambiguity about exactly what is meant by the phrase. So let's discuss some examples of user experience design, as I use the term.

It's important for users to be able to see, understand, and interact with the various controls in an app. In mobile apps especially, it's common for controls to be too small or to be clustered too close together for users to reliably touch only the control they are attempting to interact with. It's also common for controls to be placed such that the user must obstruct a control with his or her fingers while trying to interact with it.

A good user experience designer can take a look at a wireframe and immediately point out the areas where controls are likely to be hard to hit or hard to see.

Another thing that happens is that as users move from screen to screen in a mobile app, the buttons under their fingers remain in the same position on the screen but take on drastically different behaviors. For example, imagine an app that pops up two Yes or No dialog boxes in a row. Imagine that the first dialog box contains an innocuous question, and if the user chooses Yes, another dialog box immediately pops up, asking if he or she wants to delete all the app's data. In that case, because the user's finger is already on top of where the Yes button goes, it's easy for him or her to accidentally tap the Yes button on the second dialog box, thus inadvertently destroying all the data. A good user experience designer makes sure the buttons are switched or offset so that it's not trivially easy for a user to take such detrimental actions by accident.

Although they are becoming far more common, smartphones are still relatively new to most people. The modern smartphone era didn't start until 2008, and while it's been a few years, if you compare that to, say, how long people have been reading books, you'll see how new smartphones really are. If you're reading a book and it accidentally falls closed, it's clear to you what happened and what you need to do to get back to the page you were on. But if you accidentally tap something in an app, it's often not at all clear how to get back to where you were.

This is where animations can come in. By animating a glow on the button that was tapped, or by showing the new screen animating in from the right, you give users some indication of what they touched or where they went and what direction they need to go to get back. Any good mobile developer ought to be able to program a large number of different animations, but the trick is knowing which ones are appropriate in a given situation and which situations really need them. That is the realm of the user experience designer.

Great Artists Steal

The simplest and cheapest way for you to get a user experience that you like is to find an app that behaves the way you want yours to behave and copy it. This is a common practice that's done—within reason—all the time. Copying the entirety of someone else's app is inconsiderate and rude at the very least, and it could get you sued or get your app removed from the store. But it's common to take individual pieces, behaviors, and interfaces of different apps and put them together to make a new one.

When this technique is applied judiciously, it allows new and useful interface paradigms to spread throughout a given platform and makes things better for everyone.

That having been said, you should make sure the interface paradigms you are copying are appropriate for your app and make sense in context. If you take an icon or a behavior that users are used to meaning one thing and try to make it mean something else in your app, you are likely to end up with a mess. And just because a design works well in a popular app doesn't mean that it will work well in yours.

Here's a case in point. One iteration of the Facebook app had several buttons identified by little icons across the top of the screen. Some apps took this to mean that having buttons along the top of the screen made sense. But normally, the top of the screen contains text that indicates which screen you are on. Users are familiar enough with the various functions in Facebook that they can tell which screen they're on without needing such indication. This did not turn out to be the case in many apps that tried to copy this design style, and it led to a lot of user confusion. Many apps that used this design style failed. Whether they would have failed anyway is anyone's guess, but I'm sure it didn't help.

So try to be careful to emulate only those user experience elements that are a good fit with your app's functionality.

Finding and Hiring a Professional

Unfortunately, freelance user experience design professionals can be kind of hard to find. There are some, but often, they are either attached to a creative firm or do mobile programming or graphic design in addition to their user experience design work. It can be difficult to get someone to do just user experience design for you.

Your best bet is likely to select either your graphic designer or your programmer first and then see if either he or she also does UX work or has worked with someone who does. Failing that, a valid strategy would be to keep your app's user experience design simple for the first release and then branch out into a more complex design for the second release. This has the advantage of keeping your first release less expensive. User experience designers are expensive by themselves. In addition, you need to spend even more time and money to have the designs they generate implemented.

Graphic Design

An attractive app has a large advantage when users are looking for the right app to fit their needs. Making apps attractive is the purview of graphic designers. The downside of graphic design, as you might guess, is the expense. Figure 6.3 shows an example of graphic design work. Compare it to Figure 6.2, which is how the user experience designer puts this button graphic in context, and Figure 6.1, which is the code that the programmer generates.

Figure 6.3
A graphic of a button from a sample iPhone app. This is the kind of output that graphic designers create.

Built-In Art Assets

Every mobile platform development environment ships with a number of art assets. Whether they are buttons or icons or glyphs or fonts, they were professionally designed and are free for you to use. Besides their price, another benefit of these assets is that users of your app will be familiar with them and how to use them (as long as you don't deviate from their documented uses).

In addition, keeping at least some standard art assets in your app makes the app feel like it belongs on that platform. Making every single button, icon, and control in your app custom can alienate users of a particular platform if it's not done carefully.

Using built-in graphics has another advantage in that when the platform vendor makes major changes to the look and feel of the platform, you get those changes for at most a little bit of work. Apps that make heavy use of custom graphics can end up needing to be restyled more or less from scratch in the event of a paradigm shift in the prevalent style of the mobile platform, as occurred in the Apple development community with the release of the significantly redesigned iOS 7.

There is another advantage to primarily using built-in look and feel: When looking at screenshots of your app, it's much easier for your potential users to focus on the content of your app than to be distracted by the style. The downside, of course, is that it will be much harder to differentiate your app from all the others that are using the same built-in components.

Stock Photos

When you need specific graphics for your app, often a stock photo site is the cheapest and most convenient way to go. Whether you need examples of avatars or photographs to show off to your users the functionality of your app, or a particular kind of vector art that you want to turn into a button, stock photo sites can be your best friends.

Of course, the downside of stock photos is their rigid nature. You may not be able to find exactly the piece of art you're looking for. This can be both frustrating and disappointing. Unfortunately, it's the downside of the convenience and inexpensive nature of stock photography. But if you can be flexible and can work around the differences between what you had envisioned and what you can find, you may be greatly rewarded.

Stock photo sites can also be a source of inspiration for features you might want or directions you might go that you might not have thought of otherwise. Several times I have been perusing stock photo sites and stumbled across one item that made me think about my project in a whole new way.

Vector Icon Packages

A number of sites sell groups or packages of lots of little icons that can be used in various places throughout your app. You might want to put these vector icons on toolbars and on buttons. Things like trashcans, Bluetooth icons, silhouettes, and the like can inexpensively make your app look somewhat custom.

Another benefit of using vector icons in toolbars or as buttons instead of text is that those icons have a much better chance of being recognized in foreign markets than the corresponding English words.

These collections can be extensive, with hundreds if not thousands of little icons in various file formats for less than $50 or maybe $100. When it comes to bang for your buck, it's hard to go wrong with these.

Your App's Icon

When it comes to the visual design of your app, many would argue that nothing is more important than the icon. First and foremost, your icon is the item that your potential users see first. When users are on their device, looking for an app to download in the app store, the icon is one of the few pieces of information they have in a list of apps to influence their decision about whether they should examine your app. If they don't like or understand your icon, they are far less likely to tap the list item for your app to read the full description. Correspondingly, your icon is often the major component in the user's decision about whether to buy or download your app. Apps with ugly, amateurish, or confusing icons generally get far fewer downloads than apps whose icons are attractive and professionally designed.

Once a user has decided to download your app, you want your app to actually get used. Some surveys have shown that as much as 95% of all apps are only ever opened once. If your icon doesn't tell users which app is yours and what it does, they may never open your app again. And if they don't use it, they won't recommend to their friends.

A well-designed icon can actually make your users want to show your app to other people. It can also be the cornerstone of a well-done marketing campaign. We will talk about marketing a bit later, but for now, consider that every web page and review that mentions your app will display your icon. So if you do a good job with your icon, you have a head start on doing a good job on your marketing.

Getting a Professional

There are two primary issues with getting a professional graphic designer. The first one is subjective and arbitrary and difficult and can be summed up in the word *taste*. Finding a graphic designer whose work you like and whose taste matches your own can be quite a trick. The only advice I can give, since your taste is unlikely to be exactly the same as mine, is to look at portfolios, sites, and apps whose designs you already like and try to find the designers responsible.

Also, make sure that your designer can interact well with developers. In large graphic design shops, there are often two tiers of designers. The lower tier is called *production design*. Production design in this vernacular is the set of tasks involved with taking high-level design art, such as a design file from Photoshop that contains comps (or compositions) for all the screens in an app, and chopping it up into a number of small graphic elements like JPEGs or PNGs suitable for being incorporated into an app by a developer. These small graphic elements have to be in very specific formats appropriate for the targeted mobile platform or platforms so that they can look attractive on a variety of devices with different screen sizes and resolutions.

Some designers either don't have any experience with this kind of production design work or consider it beneath them. A decade or so ago, most graphic design was for print. Even today, a lot of graphic designers make their living from print work. When designing for print, there is no need to chop up your design into a bunch of little pieces.

When interviewing or selecting designers, make sure to have a conversation about how their designs are going to be converted into art assets to be consumed by the developers. If they're not sure what you're talking about, walk away. Then with future designers, either specify that they must give their work to you in a format appropriate for the specified mobile platform or platforms or make sure you have a developer who is capable of taking their Photoshop files and slicing and art assets themselves.

Sound Design and Music

Not every app incorporates sound design, and not every app needs to. In fact, many apps are used only with the silent switch turned on or the volume of the device turned all the way down, in which case adding sounds would be a waste.

But some apps have user experiences that lend themselves to making extensive use of sound. Many of the apps that use a lot of sound and music are games, which have different sets of issues. (You'll learn a little more about games later in this chapter.) The rest of this section is about non-game apps.

Stock Sounds and Music

Several websites offer stock sound effects for sale. As long as you're careful about understanding the licensing involved with the effects you pick, these can be a great option. These sites can be hard to navigate, with many different sounds in many different categories. It can take a while to find a sound that fits what you're looking for. After a while, you might even start hearing weird sound effects in your sleep. But hopefully, eventually, your patience will be rewarded.

You can attempt to shorten your search by writing down all the different actions in your app for which you want sound effects, along with some idea about the kind of sounds you're looking for. But keep in mind that most sounds in apps are arbitrary. The *swoosh* sound that an iPhone's Mail app makes when a message is sent makes perfect sense in hindsight, but keep in mind that no movement of air is required for an email to be received by a server. Any noise could be used there, and users would eventually get used to it.

So you might find at a stock site that if you are flexible in what you are looking for and put in the time, you might end up with a much better set of sound effects than you expected or envisioned.

Some stock sites have music that's appropriate to be played in-app, but music in a non-game app is fairly unusual, so see the section "About Games" for a music discussion.

Synthesizing Your Own

Because the sounds played in an app are arbitrary and don't correspond to real-world sounds, one option is to make your own. Once upon a time, this would've been quite difficult, but with tools like Apple's GarageBand, it's much simpler to do now than ever before.

In one of my early apps, I used a music program I had licensed to generate mp3 files of small snippets of themes from Tchaikovsky's *Peter and the Wolf*. It's unlikely that many people would have recognized the music from the two, three, or four notes that I actually used. But I found that Tchaikovsky's choice of key for the themes of each of the characters gave the emotional impression that I was looking for, even when the theme was so short as to be unrecognizable.

If you choose this route, make sure you understand the licensing arrangements of the music you choose and the software you use to synthesize it.

Hiring a Professional

In my experience, professional sound designers tend to work for large studios. Although it's possible that some of them might do freelance work, I haven't seen much of that. What I have seen is indie game composers who, in addition to scoring games, generate custom sound effects. Tracking down one of these folks through their website is a good strategy for finding them. Alternatively, finding a community of music students at a nearby university can be a way to find someone skilled enough to generate sound effects for you.

Copywriting

For this book, I'll define *copywriting* as the art of writing short passages of text to inform app users or potential users either in the app or in the marketing for the app. Copywriting is far more of a skill than many people think. It seems that it would be easy to write the language to go in your app or onto your website to explain your app. Once they've tried it a few times, though, most people realize that there's more to it than they thought.

Give Yourself a Trial Run

One way to decide whether you might want or need help with creating copy for your app is to write up a simple web page to describe what your app will be like after you get it built. You don't have to actually make a web page; you can just do it in a word processor. The point here isn't the HTML; it's the verbiage.

You need to make sure to give your page all the elements of a web page—at least a headline, a subtitle, a picture with a caption, and a call to action that tries to entice users to download your app. Each of these types of copy has unique subtleties and requirements. The individual doing the copywriting for your app will need to be familiar with them all.

You can use your sample web page as a prop when discussing your app with people, whether they are friends, potential contractors, or potential customers. Once you start getting feedback from people about whether your sample web page makes them want to pay money for and use your app, you should have a much better idea of both how difficult copywriting will be for you and how much help you might want or need.

Once you've done this exercise, if you still want to do your own copywriting, the next thing to do is to see how effective your copywriting is in the real world. There are a number of ways to do this, but they all involve putting words on a page that is exposed to potential users of your app and seeing if your words strike a chord with them.

Although it's not strictly a one-to-one comparison, the way a lot of people hone these skills today is to create a blog and measure success by how many readers come to it.

You can of course start a blog about the app you want to build. That would be my recommendation. Many app creators are hesitant to talk about their app ideas for fear that someone might steal them. As discussed in the next section, on marketing, many people (including me) believe that you are far, far more likely to have an app die in obscurity than be stolen by someone else. In this app market, there are more apps released each day than a diligent user or reviewer could hope to download and examine in a 24-hour period. Going unnoticed is far more likely than being plagiarized.

However, if you still don't want to make a blog about your new app, make a blog about something. And once you've created it, write on it often, even daily. You also need to pay attention to what articles and blog posts are more popular or less popular than yours. Work on your writing skills as a way to attract a larger and larger audience over time.

Learning Copywriting

As with user testing your app, improving your writing by responding to the traffic your blog gets will eventually make you a good copywriter. But the trial-and-error approach can take a long time.

The Internet has a vast number of resources that can help you learn to be a better copywriter in less time. However, these resources are subject to the standard Internet problem: It's really hard to tell the good ones from the bad ones. You might try a few and see which ones seem to work for you, or you might get lucky on the first one you come across.

Alternatively, you could examine curated resources, such as books from reputable publishers. In general, when I am looking for useful resources to teach me new skills, the success rate that I've had with professionally published books has been quite a bit higher than the success rate with content I've found on the Internet via a web search.

Marketing

Marketing may be the most difficult thing about making your app successful. Gone are the days when the good, or even excellent, apps rose to the top of the app stores. With such a high volume of published apps being released every day, getting noticed is more difficult than ever before. The only apps sure to be seen in this environment are those from established brands with a lot of built-in name recognition or large advertising budgets.

Of course, you have to have built a good app even to have a chance in the first place. To paraphrase David Ogilvy, "Nothing will kill a bad app faster than good marketing" (see www.zagstudios.com/ZagStudios/famous_quotes_on_advertising.html). But building a good app is just the price of admission, a chance to compete. Then your app has to be found.

One school of thought believes that being featured in an app store is an app's ticket to success. There are arguments on both sides of this assertion, but there's a catch: Before your app can be featured, it has to be noticed by the relevant people who make the decisions about what apps will be featured. And that requires some sort of marketing.

Marketing takes time (unless you have a lot of money to spend on advertising). Waiting until you ship your app is almost certainly way too late to start marketing. I subscribe to the belief that you should start marketing as soon as you start coding (see www.softwarebyrob.com/2010/10/14/startup-marketing-part-6-why-you-should-start-marketing-the-day-you-start-coding/). Many people don't want to do this because they think their idea might be stolen. It's possible, although *extremely* unlikely, that you've come up with an app idea that no one has ever thought of before. But it is far, far more likely for your app to die in obscurity. A recent survey (see http://app-promo.com/wake-up-call-infographic/) showed that almost 60% of apps that are released fail to make back their development costs, much less turn a profit. So think honestly about which is a higher risk to you: having your idea stolen or not making your money back?

Marketing Resources

The best resource I have seen when it comes to marketing apps is the book *Pitch Perfect* by Erica Sadun and Steven Sande. In their positions working for one of the most popular app review blogs, they are in an ideal position to see the differences between the apps that do well and the ones that don't.

Marketing Services

When it comes to paying someone to market your app for you, I advise extreme caution. I have seen money spent both by myself for my own apps and by some of my clients for theirs, and I have never seen any evidence that the money spent resulted in any increase to sales whatsoever, much less enough increased revenue to cover the costs paid to the marketing service.

Keep in mind that this is anecdotal evidence, not a statistically significant study, but treat it as a cautionary tale. Make sure you know what you're getting before you spend any money on app marketing services.

Monetization and Pricing

Monetization is loosely defined as the act of turning free users into money. In the app world, this is usually done either via displaying advertisements, in-app purchases, or both. *Pricing* here means deciding how much money to charge in order to maximize revenue. There is a lot of overlap between the skillsets involved, so in this section we're going to discuss them together.

Pricing and monetization are still works in progress when it comes to apps. There are no hard-and-fast rules about how much you should charge or how you should go about doing it.

But for any app, someone has to make the pricing decisions. That person needs to do market research and be up on the current trends. Comparable apps need to be found and understood. Estimates need to be made about what the market will bear. Pricing needs to be adjusted over time, and often sales or other experiments need to be run.

You could roll dice to determine what to charge for your app. Many apps might as well have done so, for as little thought as was put into it. But if you choose not to take pricing and monetization seriously, you could be leaving a lot of money on the table.

About Games

Games have a unique set of challenges not present in productivity-oriented apps. This means that a number of skills or skill variants are needed in game building that aren't needed for other apps.

Game Platform Experience

Most game apps are based on some sort of game engine at their core. You need a programmer who has experience with that engine, whether it's Cocos2D on iOS, AndEngine on Android, Unity 3D, which runs on both iOS and Android, or some other engine.

These game engines are different enough from native programming and from each other that using them might as well be considered a completely different programming environment. They're not extraordinarily difficult for a programmer experienced on other platforms to learn. But before you hire a programmer who doesn't already know them, you have to ask yourself if you want to be the one paying for that learning time.

Game Design

Games need to be fun and engaging, not just functional. Game design is the art of making games fun, and in my opinion, it's much more of an art than a science. I haven't really heard of any full-time freelance game designers, as the ones that I've heard about or met are all either hard at work on their own games or in the employ of a game studio. That being said, I do know that some exist who will take some freelance work on the side.

However, virtually all the potential app creators I have met who want to do games intend to do the game design themselves. I think that people who really want to do games consider designing the game play the fun part.

Keep in mind that making games fun is a real skill that requires experience. A study (see www.streamingcolour.com/blog/2011/09/28/results-ios-game-revenue-survey/) looked at revenue made by game developers on the Apple App Store. It found that in general, the more games you have made, the more money each of your games makes. So if you want to learn to be a game designer, consider that, to be a success, you might need to make a commitment for the long haul.

Game Assets

As a category, games tend to use far more graphics than do non-game apps. In addition, the art style of a game tends to be a signature and has a great influence on how well the game sells. So you are far less likely to be able to get away with stock graphics when making a game than when making a productivity app.

When it comes to preparing the graphics to be incorporated into an app, it's especially complicated in the game world. Games tend to use packed textures or sprite sheets, where many different individual graphic items are packed or tiled into one file. This makes memory and file access much faster while the game is going on than if the graphics were individually placed on disk. But this memory savings comes at the price of making life more complicated for both the production graphic designer and programmer.

Sound effects in games can also be a game's signature. Many of us who grew up in arcades have immediate emotional reactions to the sound effects of the games we played as kids. Many game sound effects are so familiar that they are still heard as ring tones and text message alerts even 20 or more years later. If you want your game to really stand out, hiring an experienced sound designer may well be worth the expense.

Games are some of the few apps where music in the background is often expected. As with sound effects, many iconic themes from old games can still be heard as alerts on modern smartphones. Luckily, indie game music composers are far easier to find than full-time freelance game designers. You can often get started by locating the composers of indie games that you like on the Internet. Quite often they will have contact information on their websites, so you can start a discussion with them about scoring your game. Many of these game composers can also act as sound designers and create sound effects for your game.

Although I said earlier that game creators are less likely to be able to get away with stock graphics than other app creators, there are times when this isn't true at all. Many games make heavy use of textures or ancillary graphics for walls, ceilings, floors, or screen backgrounds. For these kinds of assets, purchasing stock graphics works really well. Some game engines, such as Unity 3D, even have their own stores where you can purchase such stock assets.

Wrapping Up

This chapter discusses the skills required to successfully build an app. You can acquire these skills by hiring or contracting professionals, learning the skills yourself, or purchasing stock artwork, sounds, or app components. Here are some key points to take away:

- Programming usually takes the bulk of the time and expense for an app. You can reduce the expense by learning to do some programming yourself, but it will take longer, and the output won't be as robust. You can also buy app templates or engines, which can save you both time and money, but your app won't be as flexible, and you'll likely find yourself wishing you could do something that isn't possible or supported inside the framework you purchased.

- If your app relies on a server or service, make sure you understand what you are signing up for. When something goes wrong (and it will), you might end up waiting a long time for your issue to get resolved unless there is someone on your side who can troubleshoot the issue.

- User experience design becomes more important as your app's interactions become more complicated. Either keep your app simple, use well-known design patterns that apply to your app's functionality, or expect to need to find a good UX designer or spend a lot of time on user testing (or both).

· Making your app, and especially your icon, visually attractive can greatly increase your sales or downloads. Stock photo sites can help give your app personality at a lower cost than hiring a graphic designer to produce every element. When you hire a graphic designer, make sure everyone is clear on what format his or her output should be in when it's given to you.

· You may be able to find stock sound effects that will work if you are flexible and keep an open mind. Custom effects can get expensive.

· Copywriting is more difficult than most people think. You can hire a copywriter or learn copywriting. To see if you want to do it yourself, start with blogging.

· Marketing may be the most difficult part of making your app successful. Many for-hire app marketing services are rip-offs, though, so be wary.

· Mistakes with monetization and pricing can leave a lot of money on the table.

· Games have their own unique challenges. They make heavy use of sounds, music, and graphics. Also, making games fun is far more art than science.

7

Finding a Developer

After you decide to hire a mobile developer, how do you go about doing it? It's not as simple as running a web search for "contract app developer." The hard part of finding a developer is not getting a list of potential developers (Google can give you 20 million results in 0.27 seconds) but narrowing that list to a handful of developers who are worth your time.

Do you really need one? Do you want an independent developer or a *creative agency* (a.k.a. an ad agency)? What are the pros and cons of each type? Does it matter if the developer is local or overseas? Could a bright college student with a couple of apps in the store do just as well as an established firm but for a lot less?

This chapter discusses these and many other questions. Although there are a lot of variables and no 100% scenarios, this chapter talks through the issues and will hopefully leave you with a much better grasp of your options and the potential trade-offs.

Template App Sites

It's possible that, under specific circumstances, you won't actually have to hire a developer to build things for you. Instead, you may be able to purchase work from a developer who has already built something that you can use. Many sites can generate an app for you from a template that's already been built, requiring no development skills from you. Template sites offer low cost, little risk, and a quick time to market, but the lack of options for features and appearance mean that such sites often are not worth it. Code quality is highly variable. See Figure 7.1.

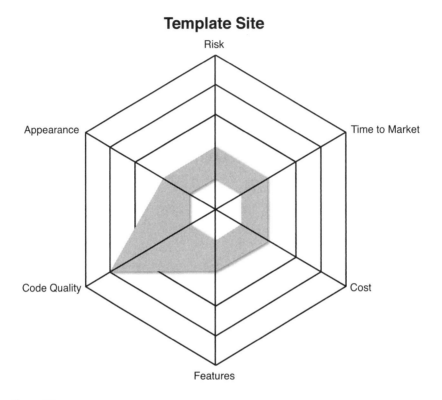

Figure 7.1
Template sites.

There are a few different variations on this theme, but with the same kinds of restrictions and limitations. In the unlikely event that you can live with the downside, a template site could be a potential solution for you. I say *unlikely* because the people who can live with the restrictions are unlikely to be reading this book.

Still, these sites have a place in this book, for two reasons. First, these sites relieve some of the demand for simple apps that would otherwise be flooding the app development marketplace. Second, these sites often make grandiose claims about what their technology can do that don't hold up to scrutiny. This exaggeration makes some people who use these services feel ripped off, which is unfortunate, but it also causes confusion in the marketplace about the value of an app. If you have a web service that tells you that you can get the same product for one-tenth the price of what a custom mobile development company might charge, it makes you wonder about the price discrepancy. Either the web service is overselling what it can do, or the developer is overcharging (or possibly both).

The Fill-Out-This-Form App

The first category of template apps is those specific to a focused vertical industry (think lawyer or real estate agent). You just enter your contact information, pick some colors, and out pops an app. Once upon a time, there were a bunch of these in the Apple App Store, but Apple removed many of them. They still exist in other stores, and occasionally Apple still approves them.

You can find a spectrum of these template apps. At the simple end, they're what some people derisively call *glorified business card apps*. They get progressively more complicated, but fundamentally, they're all about picking from pre-generated screens, filling out form fields, and answering questions.

They're not exciting, but some people find template apps useful. If your platform's app store allows them, and if that's all you need from an app, then it might be a choice for you.

The Package-Your-Website App

This category of templates builds a submission-ready app out of your website. One variant makes an app that's mostly static, incorporating and packaging your existing content. Another variant pulls your website's content dynamically, via links, and RSS or Atom feed. This way, when you publish a new blog post, it shows up in your app.

Apple has also discouraged the creation of these apps. Apple has alternately said that these apps should be submitted as eBooks to its iBooks store or simply be mobile websites, but some of these apps do get approved by Apple, and, of course, many of the other app stores don't have the same restrictions.

This kind of app can be an inexpensive path to an app store in the event that all you want to do is showcase your existing content.

The Drag-This-and-Drop-That App

This is the most complicated category of template apps, and it can run the gamut from a simple app with a couple screens to a fairly sophisticated game app. These template app vendors present to the app creator an *app builder tool* that contains a number of preexisting controls that can be arranged onscreen via some sort of graphical interface. The builder tool usually has a palette of user interface elements (text forms, buttons, toolbars, and the like) on one side of the screen and a picture of a smartphone screen on the other side. The app creator uses a mouse to drag the user interface element—let's say a button for purposes of discussion—and drop it on the place on the smartphone screen where he or she wants the button to be. Then there's some mechanism for describing what the button will do, like maybe creating a new screen for the app.

Most of these builder tools have websites written in JavaScript, but a few have downloadable Windows or Mac applications that are used as their interfaces. For the most part, whether the builder is a website or a full application doesn't really affect the functionality of the app being created.

The fundamental limitations on apps built from this type of service all relate to the number and flexibility of the controls or widgets available to the app creator. In short, if the person creating the tool didn't build a widget that does exactly what you want, then you can't have what you want. That leads to the next problem: How do you know whether one of these services will be able to produce the app you want to build?

This is where the limitations of such services really become apparent: Typically it takes quite an investment in time, money, or both before you really know whether the service is capable of building the app you're looking for. You also typically have to spend quite a bit of time learning the tool, and that's time that isn't spent improving your app.

What doesn't help is that these services typically market their capabilities as being far more powerful and flexible than I have found to be the case so far. Their documentation is also generally lacking. That combination makes it very difficult to decide whether a given service will meet your needs without spending a lot of time and effort—and potentially money—with it.

Also keep in mind that each of these services does things differently. Any time you spend working with one service isn't transferable to any of the other services. So if you pick one service, and then after some experimentation discover that it's not right for you, that work isn't going to be applicable to whatever you try next.

And if you do end up finding a service that works for you, and you build your app on it, you generally become locked into that platform for future versions. If, as is common, you discover after your initial release that there are new features that your users really want you to add, unless those features happen to be available or become available from the service you have chosen, you'll likely end up needing to rewrite your whole app from scratch to get the new functionality.

But if you have a relatively simple app idea, and your goal is to get it to market in as little time and with as little effort as possible, and you're not concerned about needing to rewrite it in the future if it takes off, then a template app site or service may be a valid option for your needs.

App Developer Matchmaker Sites

The next option in order of expense is usually to post a developer request at one of the many app developer matchmaker sites. On these sites, app creators post short descriptions of the apps they want to build, and developers bid on what they would charge to build an app with that description. The app creator then chooses a bidder to build the app. Matchmaker sites are very high risk. Features and appearance are about average. Code quality is low to average. And time to market is all over the map. See Figure 7.2.

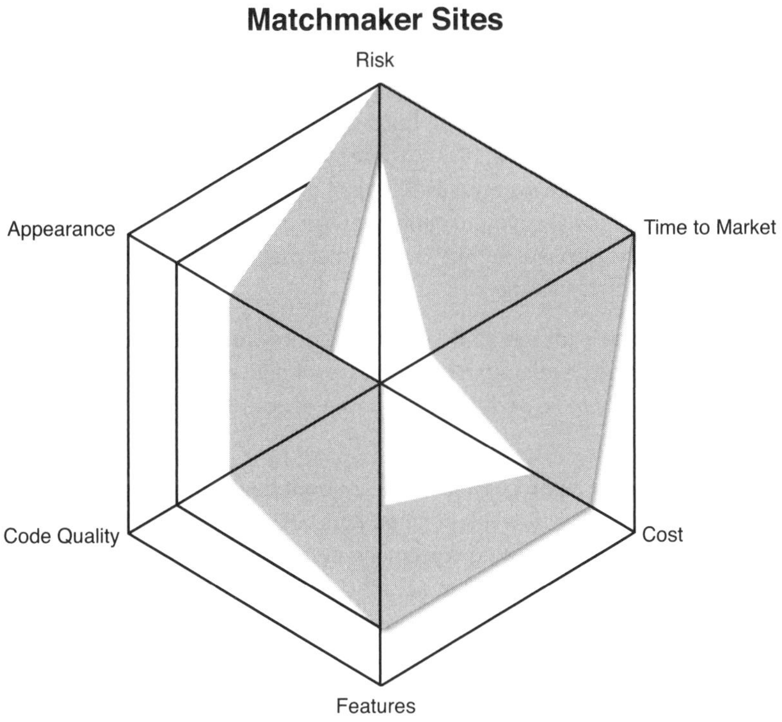

Figure 7.2
Matchmaker sites.

What is not immediately obvious from looking at these sites is that after the bidder is chosen, an entirely new set of negotiations takes place. Typically a nondisclosure agreement (NDA) is prepared and signed, the app creator gives a set of wireframes to the selected bidder, and then the bidder tells the app creator how much it's *really* going to cost. At that point, they generally either enter into a contract or the app creator selects one of the other bidders.

I've worked with several app creators who have used this kind of site with disastrous results. But one app creator who is a friend of mine has had some real successes with this method. The difference is likely that this successful app creator is very technical. He is a former programmer who has started and built and sold several successful software companies. He is therefore able to closely manage these development arrangements to make sure he gets when he's paying for. With proper oversight, it is possible to be successful working with this kind of developer.

It's Not What You Know but Who Knows You

The downside of working with the kinds of developers who use matchmaker sites is that these developers have little at stake. If your engagement goes badly, and you leave a bad review for a developer, it's trivial for them to delete their account and switch to another one and then get some friends (or their own dummy accounts) to build up the new account's good reviews. Remember that the vast majority of these sites do no useful vetting or verification that there was actually a project before reviews can be posted. It can also be difficult for you to verify that the developer you are talking to actually built the apps he says he built or that the references he gives you are actually his former customers.

The primary issue with this kind of site is the anonymity (or at least effective anonymity) of the developers. As is the case with Internet comments, people are far more likely to lie or defraud or ignore people they don't know and who don't know them.

By far the most common complaint I hear about developers at matchmaker sites is that the contract developers "go dark." They stop answering emails, answering calls, and returning voicemails, either for an extended period of time or permanently. They can do this quite easily with little or no consequences if the app creator paying them has no links to their home or family or other customers.

A couple failed projects that I was asked to consult on after the fact had suffered this developer-going-dark fate. After being unresponsive for weeks at a time, the developer would return with some sort of excuse about health problems with family members or the like. They may have been true, but it's not unreasonable to insist on being notified fairly quickly in those sorts of situations rather than days or weeks after the fact.

It's possible in those kinds of cases that the developer used the unresponsive time to do someone else's project. It's also possible that the developer was lousy at managing his business, had poor time-management skills, and let the project get away from him. There's no way to know, and knowing doesn't help put a derailed project back on track.

One thing to understand about this kind of quasi-anonymous developer (although, as we'll discuss in Chapter 8, "Interviewing and Selecting a Developer," it's not limited to them) is that they are often in a position to decide whether they are better off cutting their losses and walking away from a project. This kind of project is usually fixed price. So if they set the price too low for the work they are going to have to do and the project goes astray, they may just walk away and find a different project.

It's not necessarily that these developers are evil, or that they set out with the intention of scamming app creators (although some do). Remember from Chapter 1, "What Could Possibly Go Wrong?" that most software projects, even well-funded enterprise software projects with professional project managers, are late or over budget or fail completely. This is especially the case when there are relatively inexperienced individuals on either or both sides and the parties are separated by a long distance. It doesn't take an app developer (or a potential app developer) long to realize that many app projects fail, too. Generally in the matchmaker site world, when a project fails, the developers don't get their last payment. If it appears to developers that a project they've been partially paid for is likely to fail, then their time suddenly becomes better spent looking for their next project than in finishing yours.

I don't mean to imply that every single developer you might find on one of these sites is crooked or incompetent, but many are, and it can be hard to tell if a given one is—at least not until you've wasted a lot of time (and perhaps a lot of money). The friend I mentioned earlier tells me that he had to terminate relationships with several developers that didn't work out for each one who managed to complete a successful project. The odds might not be in your favor, but if you play your cards right, the budget could certainly be.

Local Versus Remote Developers

Certainly, many or most of the issues with matchmaker site developers is that they are often remote (many even overseas). However, that doesn't mean all remote developers (or remote development relationships) are bad. Many are quite successful, but even they have their share of challenges.

One of the biggest obstacles in successful software development is communication. It's critical that you explain your vision to the developer, it's critical that the developer keeps you informed about the project status, and it's critical that you have an opportunity to provide input often as things are built so that what could be a small course correction doesn't become a major overhaul because of all the additional layers of code that have been piled on top of it. All this is a lot easier to do when you are both in the same room. But it's not impossible to do if you aren't. It is, however, a lot harder.

There are no two ways around it: If you engage a developer who isn't local, it's more work for both of you to communicate adequately to ensure that the project gets started and stays on track. It also requires you both to depend on more technology of the partnership.

The vast majority of the time (unless you are working on an app for visually impaired users, which has its own issues), most conversations that take place about the development of an app involve visual information. Screenshots with annotations (superimposed arrows, boxes, and text) are generally far more effective in conveying the idea of what you need than are any several paragraphs you're likely to write. Often the easiest way to communicate animations or motion is to record and send a screencast video. This also needs to go the other way. You need to make sure that any potential remote developer you hire is willing and able to make annotated screenshots and videos to send to you when he or she has questions.

It's important that you have regularly scheduled times for you and your developer to sync up on the status of the project and any open issues or questions. (I talk more about this later in the chapter.) This is especially important when the developer is remote. You learn a surprising number of things about a person when you speak face-to-face a few times. The social interactions that people are expected to perform when they meet in person—greetings, small talk, transitioning to the topic at hand, navigating changing subjects, transitioning to ending the conversation, and saying goodbye (among others)—provide a lot of information about the other person. Is the person verbose or terse? Does he or she seem generally happy or anxious? There are lots of cues that are easy to take for granted until you don't have them anymore. It is far, far easier to tell whether a developer has run into an unexpected difficulty when speaking in person than over the phone or even via a video call. And in the event that your developer has run into a problem (and usually there's at least one), it's important for you to know as soon as possible, so you can adjust your plans. Developers, however, are likely to want to try to keep that information to themselves as long as possible. This is especially true when you and your developer have not yet had an opportunity to generate trust.

Trust is fundamentally what it's all about. In order for you to get the app you're paying for with a minimum of hassle for everyone involved, you and your developer need to trust each other. Of course, that begs the question of whether you and your developer are able to trust each other, but let's assume for the moment that you can. Let's assume for the moment that both of you want nothing more than to build the best app that you can together. In that case, when one of you has a problem, both of you have a problem; and if both of you have a problem, the best course for both of you is to handle it together as soon as you can.

If your developer is trustworthy, then in order to get the best app, you both have to establish a relationship that allows you to trust each other. It is simply harder to engender trust when you're in different cities, talk only infrequently, and usually communicate over email. (If your developer isn't trustworthy, see Chapters 9, "Managing to Milestones," 10, "Understanding What You're Getting," and 11, "Pulling the Plug Early," which discuss how to find out and what to do about it.)

I'm not trying to scare you. It is perfectly possible to hire a good developer, build a good relationship, and create a good app when the developer is remote, and often, it's cheaper that way. Just understand that this is one of those cases where there is no such thing as a free lunch. Dealing with a remote developer can be hard.

If it makes sense to you to choose a remote developer, just keep a few things in mind. First, get to know the developer and his or her friends (on Twitter or LinkedIn or someplace public) and make sure they are not anonymous to you. This probably means that your developer will know how to find you as well. Try to see this as a good thing, as it will help to build trust between you. It's hard to remain anonymous to someone while preventing that someone from being anonymous to you. Good business partnerships are rarely built on partners not being transparent with each other.

Second, have frequent regularly scheduled meeting times, and have as many of those meetings as possible via video or voice. The developer needs to know that you will notice if he or she gets behind or disappears for a while.

Finally, do what you can to establish reciprocal trust. It's easier for your developer to hide problems if he or she is remote, so you need to make the person feel like it's okay to bring small problems to you before they become much larger problems.

Creative Agencies

Another kind of developer you're likely to run across are those who work for so-called creative agencies (what we used to call ad agencies). Generally speaking, these folks are expensive, and they're not the kind of developer to choose if you're a solo entrepreneur or an early-stage startup. However, if you're a manager at a marketing department of a large company, as many app creators these days are, a creative agency might be exactly who you're used to working with. Creative agencies tend to offer beautiful but expensive apps. Risk tends to be high, and many of these groups have little (or very little) mobile experience. See Figure 7.3.

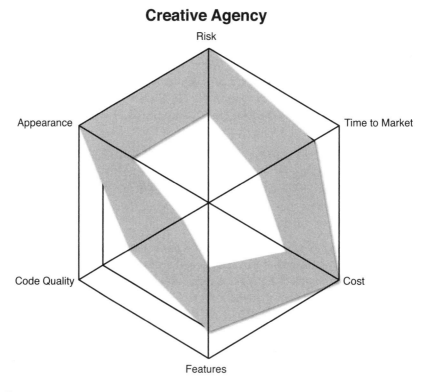

Figure 7.3
Creative agencies.

The good news about creative agencies is that they're creative. While that sounds like a tautology, I really mean it. What creative agencies generally do well is design. Their app designs are well branded, usually well focused on the target demographic, and generally anything but dull and boring. They are the kind of app designs that are likely to go viral because they often contain the elements that cause people to want to show the app to their friends.

There is one thing that their designs have in common that often isn't so great: They often design apps that upset users by collecting too much personal information from them. This is often the kind of design that appeals to marketing managers of large companies. There is likely a correlation there, but I'm not here to judge your app idea, so I'll just leave it at that.

The thing that creative agencies often don't do well is development. Although a handful of them are getting better, as a general rule, their in-house app development staff are inexperienced or nonexistent. In my experience, most creative agencies build apps by using subcontractors. Now this isn't always a bad thing, as a lot of those subcontractors likely have significant experience. (Full disclosure: I've been subcontracted to creative houses several times.) The trick, however, is that often these projects have a hard time keeping a balance between what the designers think looks cool and what the developers believe can be done within the allotted time, budget, or both. Often the designer falls in love with an idea without having an understanding of what's possible on the device. Then the client (that's you) gets sold on the idea (and the budget and schedule). And only then does the agency let staff developers look at the design, who often say, "it can't be done (at least not within that budget or schedule)."

From your point of view, this conflict is often invisible. What you see is a project that's running long and costing more than you expected, and then when it gets delivered, it doesn't live up to the idea you were sold.

I recommend trying to mitigate that risk by insisting early on that the agency produce a technical design document as a deliverable that explains the architecture of the app they want to build, specifically call out any risks, and enumerate possible challenges. This will hopefully cause the agency to engage the developers earlier in the process and keep them engaged throughout. Try to have the things that are risky scheduled as early in the project as possible (this is good advice for any project) and make sure they know that you will be unhappy if it turns out that a problem arises from an aspect of the app that wasn't considered to be a risk. This will hopefully temper their enthusiasm for fancy designs with a healthy dose of risk management.

Also, before signing a contract, while the agency is regaling you with stories of all the apps they have already built, ask specifically whether the individual contributors responsible for those apps will be working on your app. If the firm was responsible for a number-one-selling app, but none of the programmers who worked on that app will be working on yours, then you're not benefitting much from those individuals being at the agency.

In an environment where the designers and the developers might not have worked together before, it's especially important that you follow along with the development. You want frequent milestones (I recommend weekly), and you want to see how those milestones track with the overall plan. Keep in mind that they likely have more than one project going at once, and you want to make sure yours is not the one they might lose track of.

That being said, some good creative agencies can build really good apps. And there are agencies that have done a good job of staffing app development talent. So, hopefully, you'll find one of those. But just in case, be mindful of the potential risks.

App Development Companies

Many app development companies, like creative agencies, are usually one-stop shops that have design talent and development talent under one roof. The difference here is that these companies are usually much younger and were started by programmers instead of print designers or advertising designers. App development companies generally are your best bet for features and code quality, but they tend to be expensive. See Figure 7.4.

These companies aren't cheap. Like creative agencies, they often have office space with an accounting department and project managers on staff (all of which you pay for indirectly). If you're looking for a low-cost option, look elsewhere.

But if you are willing to pay for it, a reputable app development company is probably your best bet at getting the app you want (although it's not a sure thing, as you'll soon learn). Figuring out the good ones isn't hard. Just remember that companies are made of people, and then look at the employees. I have a tendency to start by searching for the company on LinkedIn and then looking at the employees listed there—where else they've worked, how long they've been in app development, etc. Then I search for a few of the employees. I find their blogs, articles, books, and/or speaking engagements and then the open source utilities and libraries that they've published. It becomes pretty clear pretty quickly which companies have developers who have good track records.

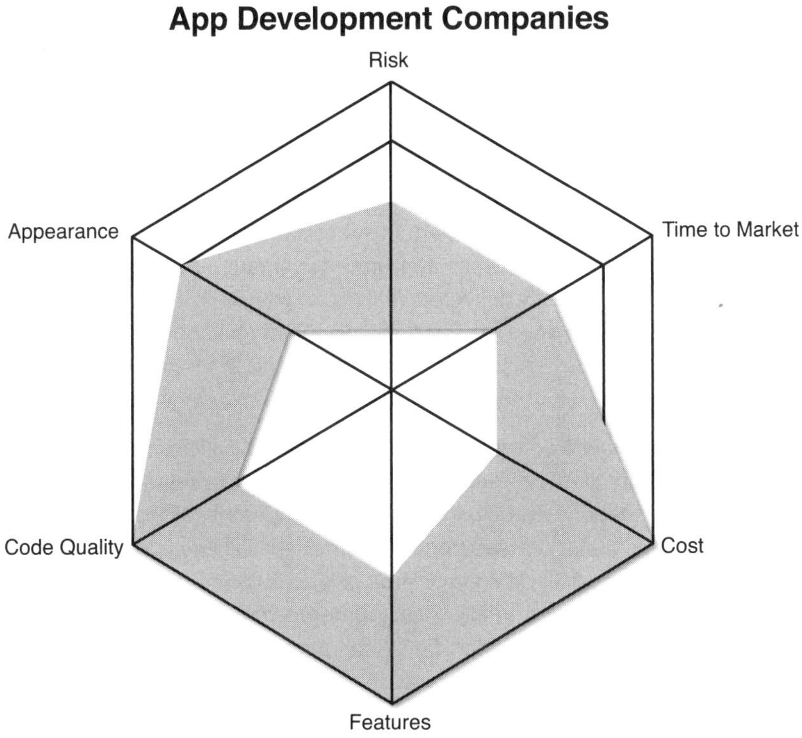

App Development Companies

Figure 7.4
App development companies.

If you do your homework, the app company you select should be perfectly capable of building the app you want. However, just because the company is capable of it doesn't mean it's going to happen. Again, remember from Chapter 1 that most software projects fail or go over time or budget, even those with experienced developers. As discussed many other places in this book, communication is key here.

The trick with app development companies is making sure they are staffed appropriately for your project and that either they don't get overloaded, or if they do, they give *your* project priority. Although it's not cheap, you want to make sure that your project is the first one that comes up at the company status meetings—or at least that it's not the last one.

I don't know how long it will be the case, but barring some drastic, sudden event, the reputable app building companies are likely to have more work than they can do for the next several years. However, that work is sporadic, and there are periods of high demand and periods of low demand that are often obvious only in retrospect. Everyone is afraid of turning away work and then ending up with idle developers for a period of time because the next job they expected to close took longer than they hoped to materialize.

If an app development company gets overloaded, it will likely do the same thing the creative agencies do: bring on subcontractors. Many of the same rules apply here. Ask which of the apps in the company's portfolio the team you are paying for actually delivered. Make sure you are in a position to know when new developers are added to the project and make sure you ask about who they are, why they are joining the project at this time, and who, if anyone, they are replacing.

You shouldn't throw a fit just because one developer leaves or joins your project. That's one of the reasons to go to an app development company instead of an independent developer. App development companies generally have a bench so that if one developer becomes unavailable (say, due to illness), it won't endanger the entire project (as would more likely happen with indie developers and smaller development teams). But make it clear that you don't want a bait-and-switch. Some companies, especially remote ones, have the unethical habit of selling you on an experienced development team and then swapping for a group of cheap first-timers as soon as the ink is dry. Don't let this happen to your project.

The Case of the Third Time's a Charm

I have a friend who is a decent iOS programmer in his own right who was a principal in a startup that wanted an app to try to attract customers to its product. Given that it was a different kind of app than any my friend had worked on before and that the startup was trying to get to market in a short time frame, he decided to outsource the development of the app. The startup contracted with one of the more well-known app development shops and figured all would go well.

The result was a disaster. The app took much more time and money than expected and launched with obvious shortcomings, resulting in poor reviews and far fewer downloads than expected. There were multiple causes, but the primary issue was basically poor communication. The person the app development shop assigned to be the liaison with the startup was by all accounts a good programmer, but the individual had previously always been teamed with a project manager and had never been solely responsible for client communications before. In addition, the development team and the startup were remote, separated by several time zones, so they didn't communicate as well or as often as they should have.

When it was time to do the updated version of the app, which the startup hoped would fix the initial issues, it went to a different well-known app development shop (although not as well known as the first). This development shop was in the same city as the startup, and there was an existing relationship with the new project manager, so it was expected that things would be better this time.

Instead, they were worse. It turned out the app development shop was overloaded and had subcontracted the programming of the app to a much smaller development shop that had never worked on an app of that type before. Again, the project ran over time and budget, and the app was poorly received. (My friend's company did finally get it right on the third attempt.)

Even reputable shops have projects go bad. You need to know who is working on your project and make sure your ideas are communicated to those people clearly and regularly. You can't trust the development shop to do that for you, even if you're paying it to. It has different incentives than you and can't read your mind. Only you can prevent your app from having this kind of poor outcome.

Independent Developers

Independent developers, for purposes of this book, are small development shops with a small number of developers (usually only one, but sometimes two or more) that have low overhead and no additional staff. They have no big, grand offices, no salespeople, no accounting departments, and no project managers. The person who answers the phone is likely to be writing and checking in code. Independent developers are the most variable option. Some are really good, and some shouldn't be allowed near a paying customer. Working with these developers requires the utmost vigilance on your part. See Figure 7.5.

There are benefits to working with an independent developer. First and foremost, lower overhead means the total project cost should be quite a bit lower. Also, with fewer people involved, you're less likely to have communication problems happening within and among your development shop. I've seen many cases in large shops where information was not communicated between the individual who talked to the customer and the person doing the work.

There is a downside to having a small development staff. In the event that someone gets sick or has something else happen that makes him or her unable to work, your project's schedule will suffer. However, this is not as different from what will happen with a larger shop as you might think. Rarely are developers completely interchangeable, and the information and experience about your specific project already gained by one developer is certainly not easily transferable in the event of an absence. Chances are that even with a larger development shop, if one of your developers has a long illness, your schedule will suffer. But in a large shop with managers and project managers, your app is far more likely to get done following the loss of a developer, although it might be late. In a shop with only one employee, if that one employee becomes unavailable, you are back to having to find another development shop.

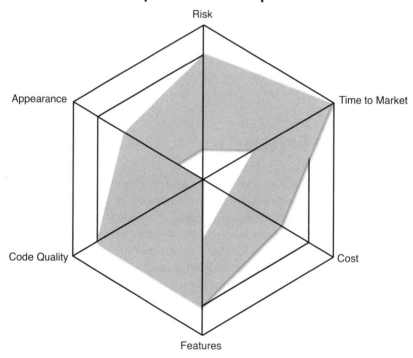

Figure 7.5
Independent developers.

But by far the biggest struggle with independent developers is vetting them. Hopefully, you find them directly, via their blogs or people who know them rather than a matchmaker site, and hopefully they're local, or if not, at least will be easy for you to communicate with. I use the same kind of technique here as when checking out the employees of larger shops. I start with LinkedIn and see if I can find someone I know who has worked with the person before and might be able to vouch for him or her. Then I move on to GitHub,

Bitbucket, and/or other open source sites, and I see if I can find and read his or her blog.

But all that research still doesn't tell you if a developer is a good fit for your app. Honestly, he or she might not even know if it's a good fit. If you were to pick a development shop with 20 app developers who have all been developing apps full time since 2008 or 2009, you can be pretty sure that whatever your app is, the shop can deal with it. With one guy, he might not realize immediately what your app idea is going to entail, and he might not realize how far out of his experience scope your idea is. It's unfortunately easy and common for a programmer to believe that something is within his capabilities and just be flat out wrong. In fact, it's so common that programmers erroneously think that their way is obviously superior that we have a phrase for it: the Blub Paradox (see http://c2.com/cgi/wiki?BlubParadox). Note that when this phrase was coined, it was about programming languages, but now it's often used in the context of programming techniques within a single language or platform, which is how I'm using it here.

In programming, there are often times when the techniques that you've used to solve a problem before turn out to be unexpectedly inadequate for a new task. Once you learn how to adjust for that and know what resources you have at your disposal to acquire new techniques to solve new problems, it's no longer traumatic (although it can still throw off a schedule). But before a programmer learns how to adjust for that, it can mean the difference between a project being profitable for the person or not. After all, programmers have to eat and pay their rent. If someone's expected income from a project will no longer cover those expenses, the developer will likely stop working on the project. At that point, the best outcome for you is that he or she will call you and tell you that, and you can try to work something out. The worst outcome for you is the person takes another project and starts avoiding you (because people tend not to like admitting failure).

The unfortunate truth is that right up to the point that developers realize that a feature won't work the way they had been planning to code it, they absolutely believed that they were capable of fulfilling your project requirements. So even if you were a perfect judge of character, there wouldn't be any way that you could catch them lying beforehand, because they truthfully believe that they could do the job.

Having a project suddenly switch from being profitable to being a financial failure can happen with more experienced developers as well—only with a twist. In this case, it's not that the developers didn't know how to program the feature, it's that they misunderstood you and thought the feature was more basic than you meant it to be. They gave you a price, expecting the feature to be rudimentary, and later came to understand that building the feature you actually wanted would be a lot more work than they initially understood it to be.

For example, let's say that you wanted an app for a classroom teacher to record grades for each student and display the average. It will be a fairly simple app. You provide the developer with a mockup, and the two of you settle on a price. Then he brings you his first iteration of the app for your feedback, and you ask "Why hasn't the app filled in the grades for this student from the server at the school?" At this point, the project is a failure. Your developer thought he was building an app that tracked numbers on your phone—a simple spreadsheet app. But you wanted a network-aware app that knew how to talk to the servers at the school. The app you wanted was far more expensive than the app that the developer thought he was building, and the developer will not be able to give you what you want for the price that you had agreed upon; it's just not financially possible. A large app development shop might go ahead and do the project anyway and take a loss on it, relying on its higher prices and other projects to stay in business. But a lone developer will either have to work out a new arrangement with you or declare financial bankruptcy; he or she won't have the financial resources to absorb that mistake.

To avoid this fate, it's important to make sure that your potential independent developer both understands what components your app requires (which is the point of Chapter 4, "Determining Your App's Components") and has done enough work with each of those components to be able to give you a reliable estimate of how much work each feature will be. This is the part where being a good judge of character can help because "How much work have you done with apps that send and receive this kind of data with this kind of server?" is much harder for the developer to be naively overconfident about than "Are you sure you could build an app that sends and receives data with a server?"

As with creative agencies, you should ask what challenges the independent developer foresees, and you should have him or her enumerate the pieces of your app that are like apps that he or she has done before (and how) and what parts will be new. You both need to be confident that the gaps in the developer's experience are surmountable in your time frame and within your budget.

It's All About Timing

The other trick with independent developers is timing. Unlike larger shops, the number of projects an independent developer can do at the same time is limited (often to one). If you catch developers in the middle of a project, they might not be able to help you at all. If you catch them when it's been a while since their last project ended, they may be desperate and give you a discount.

In many ways, timing is the bane of an indie developer's life. In general, there's an abundance of mobile app work out there. But getting the leads to the projects when you need them is hard. I've often had to turn down great projects because I was already fully engaged, and I have virtually always taken more time to find my next project than I've intended.

So if you can plan ahead and be flexible about the start date for your project, you'll have much better luck with finding an independent developer who can work with you. If you need someone to start quickly, that makes it much harder to find an independent developer who can be ready when you are.

Grow Your Own Developer (Maybe Even You)

Of course, all app developers have to start somewhere. It's possible to find someone who hasn't done app development before, or who hasn't done much of it, and get him or her to write your app for you. I know of many people who have tried this, and none of them have gotten the app they wanted from their first developer. But that doesn't mean you won't. Even the apps I was writing for myself when I was first starting out ended up being less than what I had envisioned when I'd conceived them.

But if you're willing to compromise on functionality, willing to let the process go a long time, or both, you might be able to get an app done on the cheap by growing your own developer.

The primary thing you're going to sacrifice is planning and predictability, and perhaps refinement. The primary theme of this book is using planning and tracking to make your app development process as predictable as possible. If you're going with someone who has never done this before, then almost by definition the person is not going to be able to plan it accurately and won't be very predictable.

Planning is still important in this case, though. Doing the best you can to break an app into smaller, manageable tasks will go a long way toward keeping the project from becoming overwhelming to a novice, and it will increase the odds that the app gets finished. In this case, though, it won't help you predict when you might be done, and you won't be able to use how the developer tracks against his or her plan to determine whether your developer is unreliable or incompetent.

Portions of Chapters 9, 10, and 11 may not be helpful to you. Those chapters presuppose that you attempted to hire an experienced developer, and you want to get your money's worth. Attempting to apply those chapters (especially Chapter 11) after hiring an inexperienced developer would be unfair to that developer.

If you're determined to get an app built in the cheapest way possible, or if your app's vision can be compromised in the interest of providing a sandbox that someone can use to learn, then this might be the right option for your situation.

Wrapping Up

This chapter discusses several different categories of developers that you are likely to run across while searching for a developer for your app idea, as well as some of the pros and cons of each. This chapter is about narrowing your search criteria to decide who is worth interviewing (which is the subject of the next chapter). Here are some key points to take away:

- Sites and companies will offer to generate an app for you without your having to write any code. If your app is simple enough, this might work for you. Just look past the marketing claims and make very sure that the service has all the functionality your app idea requires before you hand over your money. (Hint: If you're reading this book, the service probably doesn't have all the functionality you need.)

- Matchmaker sites will connect you with a developer's email address, profile, portfolio, and reviews. Succeeding with this kind of developer requires a lot of micromanagement. Expect to fire a lot of developers before you find one worth keeping.

- Creative agencies are expensive but can produce well-branded apps. Just make sure you know the experience levels of the specific developers on your project and require technical plans to make sure the developers are involved early in the process so you don't get an app design that's gorgeous but unachievable.

- App development companies are your best bet if you have the money. Just do your homework, make sure your project is staffed with individuals experienced in your app's required components, and stay on top of their progress.

- Independent developers are a good lower-cost option, although working out the timing can be tricky. Verify his or her experience as best you can and don't hesitate to change providers if things start to go wrong.
- If you absolutely, positively have to spend the least amount of money possible, you can try to grow your own developer. Just expect it to take longer than you planned (even after adjusting your expectations for this statement).

Interviewing and Selecting a Developer

It's often difficult for a non-programmer to determine solely from an interview whether a programmer actually knows what he or she is talking about. I'll let you in on a little secret: It's often difficult for one programmer to determine from an interview whether another programmer knows what he or she is talking about. This has led to a number of common interviewing strategies involving brain teasers and stupid questions about why manhole covers are round or how many of a certain *thing* can be fit inside a certain *structure*. Google, a company started by programmers, used these kinds of questions to hire programmers for years, and now it's "found that brainteasers are a complete waste of time" (see www.nytimes.com/2013/06/20/business/in-head-hunting-big-data-may-not-be-such-a-big-deal.html).

This chapter talks about useful things you can ask in interviews. The answers to those questions won't, however, give you any unshakeable proof about whether the person will be able to program. But they're useful things to ask that correlate well with the kind of mobile developers you're likely to want to hire.

But remember that interviewing is a two-way street. It's important for you and your interviewee to get to know each other and to understand how each of you expects to do business with the other. If the developer wants to get paid hourly but you want a firm total app price, then it doesn't matter whether they're a good technical fit; you're not going to be able to work together.

This chapter walks you through conversations to have with the developers who made it onto your short list as a result of Chapter 7, "Finding a Developer." It should help facilitate the process of selecting a developer and arriving at an agreement with a developer that will be a good fit for you and your app.

Mandatory disclosure: This chapter speaks some about legal agreements, non-disclosures, noncompetes, and the like. I am not a lawyer. I do not play one on TV, and I don't pretend to be one on the Internet (or in print). I am not giving or attempting to give you legal advice. I am simply relating my perspective and experiences. If you have in any doubt at all, you should consult a qualified legal professional.

Nondisclosure Agreements

The first thing that many potential app creators want to do is to get a prospective developer to sign a nondisclosure agreement (NDA). I am not going to tell you not to do this (especially since that would potentially be legal advice). What I *am* going to tell you is that if you insist on this, a number of good developers will refuse to talk to you at all. Why?

First of all, most of the potential app creators developers speak with don't end up shipping any products at all. Second, developers speak with many potential app creators for each project they actually do. If we were to sign NDAs with every app creator with whom we spoke, we would be opening ourselves up to nearly constant legal litigation. I have found that there are actually very few original app ideas. Most of them are variations on one theme or another. If a developer signs an NDA with you and then later another potential app creator comes to him or her with a similar idea, that developer is now in a quandary. Choosing to work with the second app creator might open the developer up to being sued, even though he or she had nothing to do with the second app creator's idea.

It's certainly possible that your idea is truly unique, or that you represent an established brand (in which case you probably have your own legal department already). I'm simply asking you to consider whether you think that protecting your idea or getting the best developer is more important before you require a signed NDA at a first meeting.

Setting Up an Interview

An important early step in interviewing a developer is setting up an interview. If you've been a hiring manager before, feel free to skip this section, but I've found that a surprising (to me) number of people haven't done this before, so I thought I'd spend a little time going through setting up and framing the interview.

Remember that setting up an interview is not itself an interview. Don't call a developer out of the blue and start asking technical questions. For an interview to happen, both parties must have a block of free time and need to be in the same mental context. This is important because the interview is where the initial expectations are generally set, and if your expectations are out of sync at the beginning of the relationship, the relationship is unlikely to go well.

You want to contact the developers, usually by email or phone, and you want to say that you are looking to contract a developer for your app project and that you would like to know if you could set up a time to discuss the project with them or with someone from their company. You might include a short description of your app as well. You don't have to call it an interview (that word seems to be used fairly rarely in this context, although that's largely what the meeting is).

At that point, just wait and see what the developers say. They might tell you that they don't have time to take on a new project right now. Or they might ask you for more information about your app (which can be a good sign). Have the initial conversation and see where it goes.

Sometimes you end up scheduling a meeting. If so, face-to-face is best, but a phone call or video call will work; I recommend not trying to do the whole thing via email. Sometimes, you may be told that the developer isn't available or isn't interested. In that kind of situation, feel free to ask if there is another developer he or she might recommend. It can't hurt to ask, and it might be useful to you.

Hopefully, it won't take too much effort to get at least one meeting scheduled with a developer (or a representative of a development shop). Scheduling two or three different meetings with different developers is ideal so you can compare and contrast them, but that might be hard to do, depending on your location and the time of the year you are interviewing.

You might be meeting with the developer who would actually be doing the work for you, or you might be meeting with a salesperson or an account representative, depending on the size and kind of development team you are interviewing. Either way, the process and questions will largely be the same. If you're contacting a large firm, be sure to say up front that when you meet, you are going to have some technical questions. That way, the firm will know to send someone who can speak to the firm's technical history and experiences and answer those questions without needing to have a second meeting with a technical person. If you've worked through Chapters 3, "Prototyping and Wireframing Your App," and 4, "Determining Your App's Components," of this book, you should be more prepared than most of the app creators they are used to talking to.

The Case of the Empty Bullpen

I once talked to some people at a company about building an app. Although they would have been paying me, I wouldn't have been building the app for them. Rather, I'd have been building it for one of the company's customers. (The company was primarily a user interface design firm that had recently moved into the app space.) Of course, as is often the case in such arrangements, I wouldn't have been able to work with the end client directly, but only through the company, and I was to act as one of the company's employees during the project.

It seems that the company had gotten a contract to build this app for a client but didn't have the ability to do the work (either because it didn't have the expertise in-house or because all the in-house developers were overbooked, I'm not sure which). The company offered it to me, but we couldn't come to an agreement on the contract language, so I passed.

Several months later, I was talking to a friend at the iOS programmer meetup I'm currently organizing. He said that he had just been approached by the same design firm to build an app for the same client. I asked how far along the project was by that time. He expressed surprise and said the project hadn't started yet. The design firm had been looking for a resource to do the development for months, apparently without success.

To avoid this, before you make your final selection, make sure you've had an interview (or at least a conversation) with at least one of the developers who will be doing the actual work. Hopefully that way you'll avoid the multiple-month delay that this poor end client got stuck with.

Previous Work

The single most relevant factor in whether app developers are a good fit for your app is whether they have done a good job developing an app like yours before. However, you are unlikely to find developers who have done an app *exactly* like yours. (And if you do, it's quite possible that they might be contractually prohibited from dealing with your app and/or you might need to reconsider how common your app idea is.)

It's likely that the question you really want to ask is how close they have come to making an app like yours. It could well be the case that if you took the bits and pieces of three or four apps the developer has already done, you could put those components together to get something very close to yours. However, even if that's the case, those pieces will still have to be rewritten by that developer. The actual code a person wrote for someone else is unlikely to be available to you under normal circumstances, for legal reasons. The good news is that most of the time developers write components similar to what they have written before, and the new iteration ends up being better than the last one, based on more recent experience.

You should go into each interview with a list of the components you expect your app to need. You should have a pretty good idea what this list looks like after getting through Chapter 4. Go down the list and ask, for each component, how they have worked with apps including that requirement in the past and what went well and what might not have gone well. Try to get a feel for how quickly the information comes to them and how much detail they can provide when you have specific questions about their experience or how they would address one of your requirements for the app. The "what might not have gone well" question there is important. No engagement ever goes perfectly, and if they can't (or won't) tell you about mistakes that they've made or lessons they've learned, it's going to be difficult to judge if they're being honest with you. If they say that they don't want to or can't discuss old clients, then ask them to tell you about the kind of things that could go wrong on a hypothetical client engagement, using that technology or component. Make sure they know you aren't looking for blackmail material or anything. You just want to feel confident that they know what kinds of problems might arise and how to handle them.

Do not try to get them to write code for you during your interview, or ask them to walk you through source code. That's not how code is written in the real world, and it will likely just frustrate both of you.

Note that at this point, it's not necessary to have shown them your prototype or have gotten into much detail about your app idea. App creators often have a tendency to try to sell the developer on the idea of the app, as if the developer were a potential customer or an investor. I'm not saying you should hide your app idea or anything, just that you need to remember that the purpose of this meeting or phone call is for you to decide if you are going to give a lot of time and money to this developer. You can't do that if you spend most of the interview time talking about how great you think your app idea is. Figure 8.1 shows the factors you want to look for.

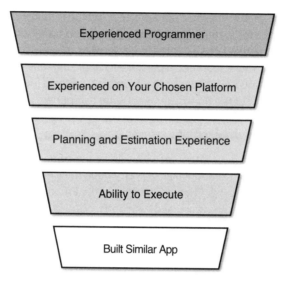

Figure 8.1
This is a rough visual about what you're looking for. Not only do you need an experienced programmer who has worked on your chosen platform, but you need someone who can build a plan and an estimate for you, as well as execute that plan. After all that, you want someone who has worked on an app using the same kinds of components that your app will have (or as many of those components as you can find).

Gap Analysis

Once you've been through your list of components, it's time to ask about any potential issues the developers see with them in your project. Ask what areas you have discussed might be the most challenging.

The developers might need more details about your app to answer this question. If so, that's fine. It's okay to open up to a larger discussion at this point. Just make sure not to let them off the hook about telling you what challenges they would expect.

Once you get them to tell you what might go wrong, ask them what they might do to help prevent that. Generally, these problems fall into one of two areas: either technical (large volumes of data, data synchronization, or similar issues) or business (short time frames, cost, or something similar). Hopefully they will come up with an approach that sounds reasonable to you. If it's a technical challenge, then the resources discussed in Chapter 6, "Skill Gap Analysis," might be an appropriate response. If it's a business challenge, then maybe one of the project management techniques discussed in Chapter 9, "Managing to Milestones," might help. Either way, if they aren't able to come up with something that might go wrong as well as a suggestion about how to prevent or resolve it, they're probably not a fit for your project.

Contingency Plans

You want to make sure to discuss contingency plans with your potential developers. What happens if your lead developer gets sick for an extended period of time? What would happen? How much work would be lost? Has this happened to them before? What was the result?

If you're talking to a solo developer, this can be a hard question to get answered. Most solo developers try not to think about such things, and often, if something serious happened to them, they would be unable to do anything about it. The way I deal with this issue when I'm a solo developer is by turning over all my code and notes (usually via source control and/or bug reporting systems) every time I submit an invoice (which is usually every one or two weeks). That way, if something happened to me, my client could pick up my planning documents, project plan, source code, and bug list and give them to another developer, who could then pick up where I left off. Hopefully no more than a week or two of my work would be lost (just whatever I hadn't finished in the current one- or two-week development cycle), and my work would be comprehensible enough that another developer would be able to come up to speed relatively quickly. The client would have to find another developer, but at least the new person wouldn't have to start over the entire project from scratch.

If you're talking to a development firm, this seems like it ought to be an easy question, but in practice it isn't. Having a number of developers who could theoretically take over for one another is a selling point for many of these firms. Often, though, making it a selling point is as much thought as it was ever given.

Absent some requirement from the customer (that is, you), most firms don't produce documentation about how the app is designed, how the pieces fit together, what technical choices were made, what alternatives were considered but discarded, etc. And in the event that you get such documentation, it's likely to be a buzzword-laced, slightly altered version of the same boilerplate-based document that was given to the many previous customers about their own apps. But as a general rule, different developers have different skills and experiences, and those differences cause the developers to take different approaches. Without having access to documentation explaining why certain choices were made, and without an understanding of where the developers thought they were going, it can be very difficult to pick up where someone else left off without major impact to the schedule or budget.

In many (if not most) development projects, any documentation to be written is left until near the completion of the project. While that might be good enough to help you maintain the app and plan for the next version, it is of no use if the developer who would have written the documentation leaves the project before the documentation gets written; in that case, all the information that exists only in that person's head leaves the project, too. Leaving documentation for last can also lead to challenges when it comes to testing, as internal testers or external beta testers may not have any guidance to help them test the finished project.

Estimating and Planning

At this point in the interview, you've talked to the developers about their experience building apps and app components, and you've asked how they have worked with the different pieces that will comprise your app. You've also asked about some risk management strategies, either for skills they may need to learn or for people leaving the project. Hopefully by now you have a feeling about them working on your app. If it feels to you like they're out of their depth, it's time to end the interview. If not, it's time to talk about planning.

Obviously, you know that not all developers are of equal experience or capability. But of all the variations of expertise and proficiency, the single most important *to you* is the ability to make (and keep) accurate plans.

Some programmers are task workers. This is a useful trait, and almost all programmers have it to some degree. With more junior programmers, or programmers who are new to a given platform, task work is their primary contribution. The problem with task workers is that in order for them to be useful, someone has to break the whole project down into tasks that are to be completed. That person is the planner, and that skill is the lynchpin of getting an app build completed on time and within budget.

If you were a software development manager with a decade or more of programming experience and a couple successful app projects in your rearview mirror, that planner could be you, and programmers to complete the tasks that you will explicitly define might be exactly who you would be looking for. But chances are, you aren't that person, and if you're not going to plan out your app's development into easily accomplished task-sized chunks, someone else will need to do that step for you.

There are easily 10 times as many developers who can build apps as there are developers who can break an app idea down into a plan with tasks suitable for more junior programmers to execute. The task workers are cheaper— or at least they seem to be. The problem is that there's no way to have any confidence that they're going to get finished on time. Someone who's cheaper by one-third doesn't turn out to be much of a bargain if he takes twice as long (or longer).

The other advantage of developers who are planners is that they are much less likely to end up painting themselves into a corner. When you plan all the tasks in an app, you spend time thinking about what all the pieces are and how they're going to hook together and interact with each other. When you work through this process, you are far less likely to run into a situation where when you start building thing B, you figure out that it's incompatible with the way you already built thing A, and you now have to go do A over again.

Now just because programmers have experience making accurate plans doesn't make them perfect. Everyone makes mistakes and is susceptible to misunderstanding your intent and planning something simpler or cheaper than you had in mind (see the "Independent Developers" section of Chapter 7). But programmers who have experience making accurate plans are far, far more likely to get it right, and if they're wrong, they're still likely to get far, far closer than someone who can't do an initial plan in the first place.

Planning has another great advantage where an app creator is concerned: It can be measured. Developers love to make claims that their code is "better" or "more maintainable" or something like that. You're not going to know if that's true until it's too late (usually when you hire your next developer). Even claims like "faster" are largely useless terms. (Faster than what? Measured how?) But if someone tells you that this tab will contain a scrollable list of content pulled from a certain website by next Tuesday, you'll know next Tuesday if he or she pulled it off. It's rare for a non-programmer to have a clear measurement of programmer quality, and planning is as close as you're likely to get.

And that, in a nutshell, is the secret. It's not completely foolproof, but if your developer can break your app idea into a plan with frequent milestones, and he or she hits milestone after milestone on time, that goes a long way toward giving you confidence that you're getting your money's worth and that the project will be done on time. The next several chapters are devoted to this idea, the techniques it unlocks, and how to use them. But for now, we're still talking about interviewing.

Ask Them About Planning Experience

So now it's time to ask about project planning. How do the developers estimate? At what level of detail can they provide an estimate? How do they track their progress as an app is being built? If you were to sign a contract with them, what kinds of plans would you get? What kinds of tracking documents would you receive as their client, and how often? Do they produce weekly reports to give to their clients, showing whether they are on track? Do they have plans, estimates, and tracking documents from previous projects that they could show you (after potentially removing identifying information such as the previous client and app names)?

At this point in the interview, a lot of app developers are going to be dumbfounded. Most of them don't produce Gantt charts or other planning documents before they start. Of the ones who say they do produce planning documents, most are usually talking about proposals. This is the level of detail I usually see in these proposals:

- Design: 60 hours
- Development: 320 hours
- Testing: 120 hours

This is a cost estimate, not a plan. There's no good way to use this information for tracking purposes. You want a plan with tasks and dates and durations—ideally with tasks broken down into day-sized chunks or less. You want that plan updated frequently during the project, and you want to be able to see at a glance whether you are on target or how much you are off from your goal. You want the output of a schedule tracking tool, as discussed in Chapter 5, "Finding the Right Tools." Make sure the developers understand this and ask how they are going to meet this requirement.

Some developers at this point in the interview will try to convince you that you either don't want or don't need project tracking, or they'll tell you that they don't work that way. That's fine. Thank them politely and walk away.

Some developers will try to discourage you by telling you that project management is expensive. To some extent they're correct. But it's not as expensive as a failed project. When good developers say it's expensive, they are referring to the fact that a lot of customers don't want to pay for it. Assure them that you're willing to pay for it. When other developers say project management is expensive, they mean that they don't want to do it. Make sure they understand that if they want to work with you, project management is not optional.

Some developers will tell you that project management isn't worth it and that projects change too much for project plans to be tracked successfully. We talked about this back in Chapter 2, "The App Development Life Cycle." Plans change. Features get added and dropped. That's okay. Planning doesn't magically make everything perfect, and it doesn't mean that you can't change your mind. It means that you always have an idea where you stand, how you are doing, and how close you are to done. It's not a panacea, and it's not a silver bullet. The further away in time an item is on the plan, the more likely it is to be incorrect, but as you get closer to the item and the plan gets refined, the more accurate your estimate for it should get. And the alternative is not tracking your progress at all, and that's worse.

Tell the developers that you want a full project plan (with a cost estimate) for the whole app before the project begins. Tell them that you want demonstrable milestones every week or so for the whole project. Tell them that for the first two to four milestones, you want tasks broken down to no longer than half a day (a day at the most). If they tell you they won't build such a plan for free, that's okay. Ask them how much it would cost you. I usually charge between a few hundred and a couple thousand dollars, depending on the size of the project (and thus the size of the plan). Sometimes I build the plan for them for free if it sounds like an interesting project that I want to do.

While planning should be nonnegotiable, the details of the plan can be. If they only ever break things down to day-long tasks, that's not the end of the world. If they only want to do milestones every two or three weeks, that can be okay, especially later in the project. Beware of month-long milestones, though, especially early on. You want to minimize your risk if they turn out not to be the developers you'd hoped for.

Ideally, you want to get and compare plans from two or three different developers before you make your decision. Yes, you might be paying a developer or two to produce a plan that you're not going to end up using, but that's a small price to pay to make a better-informed decision.

Working Relationship

At this point, if you've decided that the developers you are talking to have a clue, and they've agreed to create a plan for you, you might as well get a few things straight about how you will be working together.

Financial Arrangements

Your developers are going to want to talk about money at some point. After all, this is what they do for a living. You're going to want them to submit a cost estimate and breakdown when they give you the project plan, but you don't need to negotiate price now (except for the price of the estimate and planning document).

What you do need to talk about now is the form you want that price estimate to take.

Revenue Sharing

Revenue sharing seems the ideal situation from the app creator's point of view. If the app sucks and no one wants to buy it, then the developer doesn't get paid, and you aren't out any money. In practice, few if any developers will take that kind of a contract these days. The exception is when you have something truly extraordinary to bring to the table—an established brand or a marketing channel. But even if you are sure your app idea is surely going to generate millions of dollars, don't expect to find a developer to work only for a portion of the future revenue.

You may get them to take some revenue sharing in lieu of some current compensation, but expect that to be a small part of their expected price to build the app.

Fixed-Price Project Work

After revenue sharing, one fixed price for an entire project is the next most desired payment method in app creators' eyes. But I think it's a bad deal, both for the developer and for you.

The problem with trying to agree on one fixed price for all your work before the project even starts is that it puts you and your developer in an adversarial position. You want the most for your money, but if the money is fixed, the thing for the developer to do is to hold you to the letter of the contract. Expect lots of disagreements about whether something is a bug (and, therefore, the developers need to fix it for no additional cost) or a change (in which case either you need to pay them more or something else needs to get thrown out).

Those disagreements do two things. First, they aggravate both of you, and you will get a better app if you're both motivated and working well together. Second, they waste time and effort that doesn't improve the app in any way.

Fixed-price contracts also put the developers in a spot where, if they mistakenly underestimate some portion of the project, they might not be able to afford to complete the project. If it turns out that it's going to take them two months longer than they expected, then they're likely to just walk away from the project and leave you hanging. And that's not what's best for you.

Today's app developers aren't likely to be publicly traded multinational conglomerates with enormous margins that can absorb a huge loss on a project without declaring bankruptcy and dissolving. And the cost and effort of litigation if you were to sue your developer is likely to be greater than any settlement you might actually receive. The reality is that in this business climate, a fixed-price deal is likely to be completed only if it continues to make business sense for both parties all the way until the end of the project.

By insisting on a fixed-price deal, you are making the developer guess at how much work your app will take, setting up an adversarial relationship where you and the developer will argue constantly about whether each issue you bring up is within the original scope of the project, and running the risk of the developer walking away and declaring bankruptcy if the original guess turns out to be wrong.

To sum it up, fixed-price arrangements are inflexible and a poor fit for the uncertain nature of the app development world.

Time-and-Materials Work

The most common pricing option is hourly pricing. In my opinion, this is not the best deal for you or the developer, either.

The good thing about using an hour as a unit of measure is that it's something that everyone can understand—or so it seems. But let's think about that for a minute. Assume that a developer is working on your project and gets a notification that a new email has arrived. After switching to look at the email, the developer determines the email was spam, clicks Delete, and switches back to your project. The total time elapsed was 30 seconds. Should the developer deduct that 30 seconds from time billed to your project? You don't want to pay for that 30 seconds, but on the other hand, you don't want your developer distracted by having to keep track of every spam email he or she receives, either. In practice, uncertainties about whether your developer is billing you for time spent deleting spam email rarely turn into contentious issues.

There's also the matter of time taken to accomplish a task. How do you know whether a given feature really took 43.5 hours? Couldn't it have taken 41.5? How would you know? Even if you made the developers punch a time clock, you don't know what they're really working on. Even if you were looking over their shoulder at what was on their screen, you don't know what they're actually thinking about.

I think we choose an hour as a unit of measurement because that's what we're used to doing. And for some jobs, it makes sense. A lot of people start their first job in a customer service industry. If you're staffing a customer service business (a restaurant, a computer help desk, a retail store), the most important thing is making sure you have employees there while the establishment is open. You pay people by the hour because hours are what you need from them.

I think when it comes to knowledge work, that model breaks down. You want your app to get done, and toward that end, you want your next milestone completed on time. The only time you care if that takes 38 hours of effort or 44 hours of effort is when you're forced to care by the billing arrangement you've chosen.

But hourly pricing has advantages. Hourly projects can run over budget, but they have much less risk of developer default than do fixed-price deals. Conversely, they can bring much more risk for the customer if the project is not well defined or understood before the project starts.

So I don't think it's ideal, but hourly pay is the most common arrangement, and it's serviceable. Everyone knows what to do with an hourly invoice, and every piece of accounting or payroll software in the world has that as an option. Even when there is potential confusion about what should or shouldn't be billed as part of an hour, it usually manages to work itself out.

Milestone-Based Pricing

My favorite way of pricing projects is what I call *milestone-based pricing*. Think of it like a series of fixed-price deals, each deal being one to two weeks long. They all end up being roughly the same price. Some might be 20% or so over the most common price, and some might be under, but it usually works out so that the average price (the mean) ends up being right about the same as the most common price (the median). You can almost think of it as setting a weekly price, with the exception that if the developer misses his or her estimate of what can get done that week, the developer, not the app creator, is responsible for the overage.

This is a much lower-risk scenario than a fully fixed-price project, because if there's a discrepancy in an estimate for a task that was supposed to take only a week to do, it's much less likely that the developer will miss by so much that declaring financial bankruptcy becomes a viable alternative. But it has the advantage of taking a lot of paperwork off the table. Now neither party has to track hours, and you're paying for the delivered milestone, not the time spent in front of the keyboard.

Here's how it works: You and the developer get together in person or on the phone and agree on what the next milestone will be. It's usually the next milestone listed on the project plan, but it doesn't have to be. (If the project just kicked off and there's no plan yet, the first milestone for me is normally writing and delivering the project plan.) You agree on a tentative date when you're going to get back together (often that same time the next week). As the developer works on the milestone before the next meeting, if the developer feels that he needs more time, he can push the meeting back a day or two. Then, when the appointed meeting time arrives, you get back together, the developer demos the newly completed milestone, and you decide (in that meeting or in a discussion soon after) what the next milestone will be. The process repeats until you're done.

Note that this fits in nicely with the iterative approach discussed in Chapter 2. You can have a milestone that a certain feature will be implemented and functional and then come back later in the project with a different milestone that enhances that feature to be faster or prettier, with fancier animations or whatever.

You can also have multiple smaller milestones in a time period. You might want to pick several items that are shorter than a week and bundle them all into a single milestone (or agree that each is a milestone with its own smaller price but that you won't get back together until they are all completed).

The primary downside of this method is that it's still quite uncommon. People don't really understand it, and invoicing software doesn't know what to do with it. A lot of explanation has to take place before everyone feels comfortable with it. But I find it makes it easier to focus on the things I care about in projects and not worry about the trivial stuff like time tracking.

Figure 8.2 shows a summary of the various pricing options.

Invoicing and Timing

Regardless of what kind of financial arrangement you agree on (assuming that you've been able to agree on one), you should also spend some time here discussing invoicing and the timing of invoices and payments. If your developer wants to be paid a considerable portion of the project cost in advance, and you (wisely) don't want to pay much until after work is delivered, then you are at an impasse, and you shouldn't be doing business together.

Figure 8.2
The relative risks to you and your developer of the various pricing strategies. The lower-left corner of the graph represents the least risk for both of you, and the upper-right corner represents the maximum risk.

One of the things I like about pricing based on milestones is that it makes the invoicing arrangement a lot cleaner (at least in my mind). A milestone gets completed, the code and notes get turned over, and the invoice gets submitted. It makes a very natural synchronization point between the financial part of the transaction and the deliverable part of the transaction, but it's not required. You can agree that invoices for hourly work will be submitted weekly or monthly, or twice a month, or whatever makes sense to the two of you. Some developers care deeply about invoicing and payment on a regimented schedule, others less so.

Remember, though, that there is always a concern in the back of the developer's mind about whether he or she is going to get paid. I've been stiffed for payment by a few clients over the years, although thankfully never for huge amounts of money. But I did once have a $20,000 invoice go more than 90 days late. That was a very uncomfortable time for my family and me.

It's often uncomfortable to discuss money, but it is a critical part of this type of partnership. It's unfortunate, but money creates many misunderstandings and leads to resentments that could be easily avoided if the subject could be more openly discussed by all parties involved. If you choose to do so, you can establish a lot of trust with developers by bringing up the subject first. Ask them how often they need to be paid and how they'd like to get payments (by mail, by hand, etc.). I love clients who write me a check on the spot after I've completed the demo of a milestone for them. That goes a long way toward smoothing out any future disagreements about whether something might or might not be in scope.

Many contracts are written as net-30, which means the check is due to the developer 30 days after the invoice is received. If the developer submits an invoice after 2 weeks of work, the developer has done 6 full weeks of work on the project before he receives a dime in compensation. Keep in mind that such a long wait can be a very stressful situation for the developer.

Meetings/Status Reports

Another thing to establish in the interview is the reporting and meeting arrangements. If you want to speak on the phone or in person at least once a week, and your developer doesn't want to spend time talking to you more than once a month, then this is the time to work that out or agree to disagree and go your separate ways. I've seen too many arguments about this kind of thing because it was never discussed and the contract was signed and only then did the difference of opinion become apparent.

Also talk about notes and status reports. Make clear to the developer what you want. When I'm leading a project, I generally keep daily notes of what is being worked on, and I update the project plan at least once a week to show progress. Now is the best time to see if you and the developer can work with each other's expectations.

Tools

Chapter 5 discusses tools extensively. If you have questions or concerns or requirements with respect to the tools you want your developer to use (or not use), now is the time to bring them up—not after a contract is signed. I recommend that you prepare your wish list (or a list of concerns) before you sit down for the interview.

Technical Support

Technical support is another area that generates friction between developers and clients, especially when it's a smaller client that doesn't have an IT department. Discuss with your potential developer what needs and expectations you have with regard to tools and the use thereof. Think about all the things you want to ask about—getting the project to build or source control or bug tracking or whatever. Make sure all those things come up and you reach an agreement before any contract is signed.

For example, if I were an app creator, I would tell a developer that I wanted access to a source control repository for the project that was updated with the current code at the end of each milestone. I would tell the developer that I expect that source repository to contain all the code and libraries that I would need to build the project, and that if at any time the project didn't build for me, I would be calling to ask what was wrong and expecting his or her help.

Service After Release

The interview is the time to talk to your developer about your relationship after your app gets released. If bugs are found only after the app has been downloaded and is being used by your customers, whose responsibility is it? Who will fix it, and who will pay for it? Getting that information in writing can be critical later on.

Wrapping Up

This chapter discusses how to interview and select your developer, including a list of topics to bring up and things to make sure are agreed before you enter into a contract. Here are some key points to take away:

- There are some valid reasons to require NDAs to be signed, but attempting to get them in place prematurely can chase off good developers.
- Make a point of setting up the interview. Don't just call the developer and start asking questions.
- Your biggest clue about whether a developer can build your app is how well he or she has done with other apps like yours. Ask about that early on.
- Ask about the challenges the developer might expect to have with your app and what strategies he or she intends to vuse to mitigate them.
- Ask what he or she does when things go wrong and ask for some examples.
- Make sure you explain that project planning is not optional and that you expect a plan (with cost estimates) to be the developer's first deliverable, potentially even before you make a decision about whether to use him or her. But don't expect him or her to spend days making a plan for you for free.

- Agree on what kind of financial arrangement you are going to have: revenue split, fixed price, hourly, milestone based, or some combination. (Specific numbers can wait until you get the plan with the estimated costs.)

- Discuss your expectations for meetings, status reports, tools, and technical support.

- Make sure you bring up and discuss invoicing and billing cycles and timing early on. You'll earn a lot of trust by recognizing that developers worry about not being paid for their work and discussing how you can make them feel comfortable that they will be paid.

Managing to Milestones

At this point, I would like nothing better than to give you the formula to ensure that all your app projects are successful. Even though I'd like to, I can't—because there is no such formula. The state of the art in software development has not yet reached the point where success can be guaranteed—or even assured. Based on the advances of the past 20 years, I would not expect software development to reach that level of maturity in my lifetime. The closest I think we can come to a formula for successful software projects is to set and work toward short, frequent milestones.

Never Agree to "30% Down, and I'll Talk to You in Three Months"

One of the easiest ways for a project to go wrong is to let it go a long time without checking in. The most obvious reason this happens is procrastination on the part of those involved in the project. Like a term paper that isn't due for months, development projects with no deadlines have a tendency to get put off until later. It's human nature, and things happen, and before long, a project can be so far behind that it can't be completed on time. At that point, the common result is that the developer starts avoiding emails and phone calls. Everyone loses. Reputable, professional developers generally know better than to fall into this trap, but it happens more often in the app space than you might imagine.

One insufficient approach that is often taken to get around the procrastination problem is forcing developers involved in a project to provide frequent status reports. This isn't exactly useless, but it doesn't solve many real problems. Besides, do you really want to pay developer rates for time spent writing status reports? Status reports only give you an indication that the developer did something but don't actually give you any indication of the quality of work or whether the work performed is actually what you want performed.

Even with good developers, an even more likely problem than procrastination is miscommunication. The longer you go without giving feedback to the development team, the more work has been done that might not meet your expectations. We humans communicate imperfectly. Even if the developers on a team think they are clear on the requirements, it's really easy for them to be mistaken. It's surprisingly common for something to go unmentioned because one party thought it was obvious.

Protecting against communication problems requires a feedback loop. It's not enough to look at trouble tickets/bug reports or project plans or read status reports. You have to actually look at the functionality that the team is producing and give feedback on that. Many times I've seen a customer's simple question about what he or she was looking at lead to a discussion that resolved a misunderstanding. (We'll talk more about this in Chapter 10, "Understanding What You're Getting.")

Minimizing Risk with Frequent Milestones

In many human endeavors, we intuitively know how to measure our progress. We know that books have chapters, and we can tell easily how far into a book we've read by comparing the number of chapters we've completed with the number of chapters that remain. We know how many miles or kilometers or turns or hours it should take us to drive from point A to point B, and we can relatively easily tell how much further we have to go. Even when creating things in the tangible world, we often have obvious checkpoints. Houses are normally built according to blueprints and designed to comply with building codes, with permits and inspections required at different stages. Books are usually written according to an outline that is approved before the contract is signed .

But in the software industry, we're just not there yet. There aren't any obvious or intuitive or proscribed metrics that are in any way useful for software development. The metric most discussed is "number of lines of code," which could arguably be an effective measure of software complexity. But since there's no way to know how many lines of code any given project should take, there's no way to use the number of lines of code written so far as a measure of completeness.

Because there are no easy or obvious metrics in software, most app developers (and most app projects) don't even try. Or worse, they use fake metrics, like "number of hours billed" or "percentage of budget spent," which don't actually tell you anything about what has been produced or how close to completion the project actually is.

We've discussed how bad it is to let a project go without checking in on it and providing feedback. But we need some metric to decide when to provide feedback and to know how to tell how far along we are when we do. We are fundamentally unable to manage a project unless we can measure progress.

The best solution to this quandary I know of is to structure a project such that there are frequent milestones. I tend to attempt to create milestones of about a week in length to make planning and communication easier. Scheduling checkpoint meetings for the same time every week is convenient and encourages a regular pattern. The exact frequency isn't important, though. It's a trade-off: If you make checkpoints too frequent, you spend more time with the administrative work of checking off milestones than you need to. If you make them too infrequent, then you risk too much work being wasted if it turns out that the work performed for that milestone was based on misunderstood expectations.

Note that I said "*structure* a project such that there are frequent milestones." Milestones don't just happen. Someone has to think about what needs to be done on the project and figure out what tasks can be grouped together in such a way as to produce a useful and verifiable milestone. Doing this well actually requires thought and effort, but most development teams don't bother to do a good job of it.

How I Learned to Stop Grumbling and Love Milestones

In the unusual event that a project does have milestones, they're generally perfunctory, paid only lip service, and the developers think of them as unnecessary administrative overhead, like timesheets or status reports. Most developers resent milestones and work with them only grudgingly.

For much of my career, I was like most other developers: I hated milestones and thought of them as useless busywork performed for someone else's benefit. And then, one day, I realized I was looking at it all wrong.

What changed was that I was going through a period where all my development projects were billed on a fixed-price basis. For reasons that made sense at the time, I was taking on all the risk; if I completed a project on time, I would get paid. If not, I wouldn't. I was (and still am) the sole income source for my family of three. So if I managed to meet the terms of the contract, I would have money to pay our mortgage and pay for the living expenses for myself, my wife, and my daughter; if not, I wouldn't. I had done fixed-price work in the past, before my daughter was born, when my wife was still working. But with a family and without a safety net, it was different.

During that period, I came to embrace the milestone as the tool that would keep me on track. It worked—even better than I had expected. It allowed me the confidence even to overlap projects when I needed to, working on more than one at a time. This can be very lucrative, albeit exhausting. But when you're a one-developer shop, there are times when you have more work than you really want, and you have to deal with that somehow.

These days I always build milestones into my projects, even the hourly ones. Because even though I could let a project run long, I'd rather wrap it up and move on to whatever the next project might be.

Milestones Are Not Sprints

We've talked about sprints previously, primarily in Chapter 2, "The App Development Life Cycle." Sprints are short (usually one- to two-week) time periods during which developers perform a sequence of tasks and then demo or deliver the code (or designs, documentation, or whatever) to the client. Sprints are often placed on a calendar or a project plan and treated as if they are milestones, but they aren't.

A *milestone* is, according to my dictionary "an action or event marking a significant change or stage in development." When a milestone is complete, the project is in a different stage than it was before; there is something significant and measurable that exists now that didn't before—a new feature, a new interface, new functionality, or the like. When a *sprint* is completed, you're one sprint closer to the end of the project. These are not equivalent. Whereas a completed sprint indicates *motion*, a completed milestone indicates *meaningful motion, in the direction the project needs to go, that is necessary in order to reach the project's goal.*

I've been on projects where multiple sprints were completed without a single piece of new functionality being completed. I've seen development teams go months without anything more than generic "bug fixes and performance improvements" to show for it. If that development team is a group of salaried employees that you're paying for anyway, and those "bug fixes and performance improvements" incrementally improve the product, then this might not be a bad approach. But if you're paying contractors to build an app that needs to be released to the world, you need to make sure the project is progressing in the right direction.

Let me be explicit about one thing, though: Milestones and sprints are *not* mutually exclusive. It *is* possible for a development team to use both. It's extra work, and it's rare. In fact, I don't remember the last time I saw it done. But it is possible. It is possible for a milestone to be achieved during a sprint, and even to coincide with the end of a sprint, but don't confuse the milestone and the sprint and, more importantly, don't let your developer convince you that "completing sprint number 1" counts as a milestone.

The Case of the Hurdles in the Sprints

I did an Agile sprint-based project once in which the project manager insisted that we, the programmers, stayed 100% utilized. So for each 2-week (10-working-day) sprint, he would have each developer schedule 7 or 8 days' worth of work. Then, as each of us finished our work for that sprint, he would assign us arbitrary tasks from later in the project that filled up the time until the sprint's end.

So if I finished my primary task for the sprint on Wednesday, I'd get handed a 2-day task or a couple of 1-day tasks or a combination of two half-day tasks and a 1-day task, or the like. This was to keep each of us busy.

The problem was that those short-duration tasks had nothing whatsoever to do with what was currently going on with the project; they were eventually supposed to hook up to other parts of the app that hadn't yet been built. Unsurprisingly (at least to me), it turned out to have been wasted work. Almost without fail, once the app reached the stage where we could hook up those isolated chunks of work, the integration failed. It turned out that the assumptions that were made when trying to do 1 day of work on an inaccessible screen rarely lined up with later reality, and the small stand-alone chucks of code were effectively rewritten under the guise of integration. We'd end up taking 12 to 16 hours to integrate a feature that had only taken 8 hours to write in the first place.

The customer would have been much better off if, once a developer had finished his or her primary work for the sprint, that developer had then gone on to work on the next important task. As it was, since the client was paying by the hour, the client ended up paying for work that wasn't useful, and the developers ended up frustrated and annoyed.

Organization, Sequencing, and Focus

There is more than one way to build any given app, and two different development teams might approach the problem, and develop a solution for it, in different ways but still end up in the same place. It's perfectly possible for one group to move through a sequence of milestones to get to a completed app and another to build the same app without any milestones at all. Some developers might tell you that milestones aren't necessary; strictly speaking, that's a true statement. Milestones aren't strictly necessary, but they do reduce risk tremendously.

The differences between development teams that use milestones to plan and ones that don't can be summed up in three words: organization, sequencing, and focus.

Organization

Milestones, unlike sprints, have to be conceived ahead of time, and they have to be planned and written down. To create a set of milestones, you need to break down the end goal of the project—in our case the app—into required pieces of significant, measurable functionality. Each piece of functionality has to be broken down into the individual tasks required to build it, and then those tasks have to be grouped together in an intelligent, logical way. Each task in each functional grouping needs to be specified to the point that it can be understood by the person who is assigned to perform the task, and the time required to do the task needs to be estimated accurately. This requires a degree of organization that many development groups are either incapable of or are unwilling to expend the effort to produce.

This degree of organization is important because, without it, project teams often discover more and more tasks that still need to be done the closer they get to the schedule's end. It's not unusual for new requirements to be discovered over the course of a project, but if task after task is still being defined when you're past the planned halfway point, something is wrong. And if your project team's organization skills are that poor, you'd really rather know it long before you get to the halfway point in your schedule (and likely also your budget).

Having all the tasks for a project planned, organized, and estimated allows your team to create a useful schedule, and a schedule makes it possible to approximate progress in the project—both where you are in a project and how much remains to be done. Not all schedules are useful, though. For any given piece of functionality, if you can't tell from the schedule what tasks have been completed, what tasks are in progress, what tasks remain, and when a particular piece of functionality is expected to be delivered, the schedule is unlikely to be accurate. Be especially wary of schedules claiming that you're some percentage of the way toward being done with something without explaining where the percentage came from, what's been done, and what's left to do. Schedules without that level of detail are rarely anything but wishful thinking.

Sequencing

The difference between a list of milestones (with estimates) and a schedule is that a schedule puts the milestones in an appropriate logical order. While there may be many different sequences that can lead to a successful project, the good ones tend to have a few attributes in common. First of all, the schedule needs to reflect the technical dependencies within the application. For example, if your developer attempts to parse a large amount of data from the network before the data storage component has been completed, there will be no place for the data to go, and someone will have to come back later and hook the data-parsing routines up to the storage. Unless the developers were planning on this, wasted effort and frustration are likely to result. And often when this kind of missed sequencing occurs, there turn out to be differences between the way the developer writing the parser expected the data to be stored and the way the storage code eventually ended up written. This kind of development process usually results in bugs, wasted time, and wasted money.

Once the dependencies are identified, there are still usually a lot of decisions to be made about the order in which tasks should be completed. There are some rules that I find helpful in keeping problems on track:

- **Schedule the tasks with the highest uncertainty or the highest risk as early in the project as feasible.** This is especially true of items that depend on resources or factors outside the development team's direct control. Many times I have seen projects come apart with the finish line in sight because problems arose with an unfamiliar component toward the end of the project, and features that were already complete had to be torn apart and reengineered to accommodate the solution.

- **Components that have performance implications should be scheduled before components that don't.** If a piece of your app's functionality runs the risk of being slow (like search, or data storage, or a piece of code that performs complicated complex calculations), try to get that piece done as soon as you can. In general, the more components that are involved, the slower the app will go. You don't want to integrate the slowest one last and then discover that the app is too slow to be usable and major refactoring is required.

- **Group dependent and related tasks together.** One of the errors naive teams make is that they keep revisiting and adding on to or modifying features and components throughout the life of the project. This increases the risk that one of the changes later in the process will break something in that region of code that was built previously in the project and had been working fine. Finishing all the tasks related to one feature or component and then leaving it alone greatly reduces (though never completely eliminates) the risk of introducing regression bugs.

- **Integrate early and often.** One of the biggest mistakes people make is to build screens or components individually and try to combine them all at the end. Imagine that you were having four different people each build a wall of a house by themselves and then you tried to prop up all four walls and hook them together to make the house. The walls would be far more likely to fall apart than to fit together seamlessly. Similarly, with an app, the bigger and more complicated the individual pieces, the harder it is to find the issue when things don't hook up right.

- **Schedule checkpoints for correctness and performance as you go.** The right time to figure out that something is slow or doesn't work correctly is immediately after it's built, not after all the pieces are assembled. There's a reason that electrical and plumbing inspections are usually required before the walls of a house are finished: It's far easier to fix leaks and shorts when you can still see the pipes and wires. Similarly, once an app's user interface is complete and polished, it's harder to fix performance problems without breaking parts of the UI and causing duplicated labor and wasted time and money.

- **Don't put all the testing time at the end of the schedule.** The end of the schedule is far too late to find out you have major performance problems. Make sure the schedule is arranged so that meaningful things can be tested along the way.

Focus

The remaining attribute of a good milestone-driven development team is focus. Unlike groups working from unrelated buckets, a good project team spends most of its effort on one area of an app at a time, and it hooks that area into the rest of the app and tests it before it goes on to the next thing. The team is confident that as it moves from component to component that it's building a working app that will continue to work as more pieces are added and that it's moving the project in the right direction.

The biggest killer of focus is throwing more people at a project to try to complete the project earlier. This causes people to try to build pieces independently in parallel with each other as much as possible so that more people can seem productive. But this method usually leads to integration problems at the end of the schedule, which often pushes things out even more. It happens so often in software that it's cliché. "Nine women can't make a baby in a month" is one saying that programmers love to quote to each other behind the project managers' backs. Another is Brooks's law from *The Mythical Man-Month* by Fred Brooks, which is often stated as "adding more programmers to a late software project makes it later" (see http://en.wikipedia.org/wiki/Brooks's_law).

Let Conway's Law Be Your Guide

Conway's law (see http://en.wikipedia.org/wiki/Conway's_law), which, like Brooks's law, is another rule of thumb about software project management, states: "Organizations which design systems…are constrained to produce designs which are copies of the communication structures of these organizations." Now that's a mouthful and not immediately obvious, so let me explain by example. Conway's law implies that if you have three different groups of programmers working on a project, and they're reporting to three different managers, and those three groups build an app together, if you look closely at the structure of the app, you'll find that it's in three different groups of components and that each group of components was largely programmed by only one of those groups of programmers. Likewise, five groups of programmers would mostly likely create a system with five logical sections of code.

If you think about it, this makes some degree of sense. In order for two people to write a piece of software that behaves as if only one person wrote it, a lot of communication between those two people is required. The more communication that occurs between people, the more integrated and seamless the interactions between their programming code can be. But when two people (or groups of people) don't communicate much, their code doesn't interact very much, either.

Conway's law seems to have been intended to be an observation on the sociology of programming, but personally I tend to treat it as a roadmap when architecting software.

As the person ultimately responsible for the creation of an app, you might find yourself coordinating between various groups. I've often been involved in projects that involved many different contract programmers or contracting companies. The cases where there was a strong coordinating presence overseeing the interactions between these groups of people generally have tended to fare far better than those where the different groups were left to their own devices.

Many projects, even app projects, have multiple groups of programmers at work. The most common division of labor is that programmers who write the code that runs on the server are a different group of people from the programmers who write the code that runs on the smartphone. Conway's law says that these two groups of people will produce two different bodies of code. That's okay; you can work with that.

You know that these groups won't communicate with each other nearly as much as the members of each group will communicate among themselves. You also know that the better the groups communicate, the better their code will interact. So, if you're responsible for seeing that these groups write good solid code, it's time to take matters into your own hands. You need to make sure that this communication actually happens reliably.

You need to require that each group create a document that explains exactly what it needs from each of the other groups. You need to create and consolidate those documents, and then you need to create a list of deliverables that each group is responsible for producing. You need to make sure that each group gets what it needs and that the interactions between the code produced by each group are spelled out.

In the previous section, we discussed the fact that items that depend on resources or factors outside the development team's control should be scheduled as early in a project as possible. That is definitely true of this document and these deliverables. If there are misunderstandings between the groups—and there almost certainly will be—they need to be understood and get resolved as soon as possible.

Left to their own devices, development teams tend to focus on the things they are directly responsible for, and they downplay things that are wholly or partially outside their control or their responsibilities, leaving them for later and hoping the other group will take care of it. Many times I've seen each group on a project claim that its part is done and that the integration failure is the other group's problem. Way too much time has been wasted on such blaming activities while deadlines are missed and costs pile up. It is crucial to get the list of deliverables to each group as early as possible and make sure they know what is expected of them before concerns become problems.

The next thing that is needed is clear explanations of the places that software components being developed by different groups will be interacting. For each interaction, the responsibilities of each component should be defined, and examples of interactions should be spelled out. Examples here are better than voluminous explanations in English. This is good practice for any components that interact in your project, regardless of who is writing them, but it's especially critical when there are multiple groups involved.

So, for example, when one group is writing the iPhone code and another group is writing the server code, someone should create sample data that shows how the interactions between the two components should be performed. First, decide what the data interchange format is going to be and ensure that it's supported by the software on both sides of the transaction. Two popular data interchange formats these days are XML and JSON. Then, for each individual request made or piece of data that gets moved in either direction between the client (app) and the server or vice versa, there needs to be a defined standard of what URLs and characters get moved between the two pieces of software, with sample JSON or XML payloads that should be sent as part of the transaction.

I recommend using a source control repository with individual JSON or XML files. This is a better way to share the information between teams than a Microsoft Word document, but if Word is your tool of choice, using that is far better than doing nothing. The important thing is to get the information captured in writing, shared, and agreed upon and to ensure that any confusion is cleared up as soon as possible.

Scheduling Software: Strongly Suggested

Although technically you can create milestones without creating a project plan, you'll miss most of the point of having them in the first place. Milestones are valuable because they give you a metric by which to judge the progress of your project and the quality of your team. You desperately need these particulars in order to make informed decisions. Figure 9.1 shows an example of a project plan with milestones.

Chapters 10, "Understanding What You're Getting," and 11, "Pulling the Plug Early," talk more about these decisions. For now, let's talk about scheduling and trade-offs.

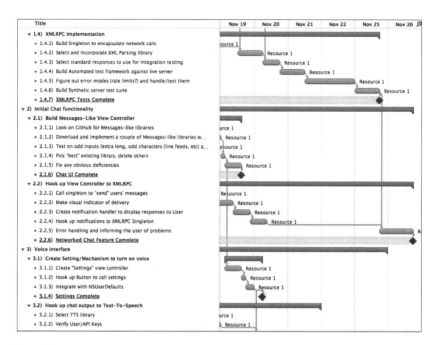

Title	Nov 19	Nov 20	Nov 21	Nov 22	Nov 25	Nov 26
▼ 1.4) XMLRPC Implementation						
• 1.4.1) Build Singleton to encapsulate network calls	ource 1					
• 1.4.2) Select and Incorporate XML Parsing library		Resource 1				
• 1.4.3) Select standard responses to use for Integration testing			Resource 1			
• 1.4.4) Build Automated test framework against live server				Resource 1		
• 1.4.5) Figure out error modes (rate limits?) and handle/test them					Resource 1	
• 1.4.6) Build Synthetic server test suite						Resource 1
♦ 1.4.7) XMLRPC Tests Complete						♦
▼ 2) Initial Chat functionality						
▼ 2.1) Build Messages-Like View Controller						
• 2.1.1) Look on GitHub for Messages-like libraries	urce 1					
• 2.1.2) Download and implement a couple of Messages-like libraries w...		Resource 1				
• 2.1.3) Test on odd inputs (extra long, odd characters (line feeds, etc) a...	source 1					
• 2.1.4) Pick "best" existing library, delete others		Resource 1				
• 2.1.5) Fix any obvious deficiencies		Resource 1				
♦ 2.1.6) Chat UI Complete		♦				
▼ 2.2) Hook up View Controller to XMLRPC						
• 2.2.1) Call singleton to "send" users' messages	Resource 1					
• 2.2.2) Make visual indicator of delivery		Resource 1				
• 2.2.3) Create notification handler to display responses to User			Resource 1			
• 2.2.4) Hook up notifications to XMLRPC Singleton			Resource 1			
• 2.2.5) Error handling and informing the user of problems						R
♦ 2.2.6) Networked Chat Feature Complete						♦
▼ 3) Voice Interface						
▼ 3.1) Create Setting/Mechanism to turn on voice						
• 3.1.1) Create "Settings" view controller		Resource 1				
• 3.1.2) Hook up Button to call settings		Resource 1				
• 3.1.3) Integrate with NSUserDefaults		Resource 1				
♦ 3.1.4) Settings Complete		♦				
▼ 3.2) Hook up chat output to Text-To-Speech						
• 3.2.1) Select TTS library	urce 1					
• 3.2.2) Verify User/API Keys		Resource 1				

Figure 9.1

An example of a Gantt chart from a recent app proposal. The diamond-shaped markers are conventional notation for milestones.

As your project progresses, you will want to keep track of how much of the project's schedule and budget have been exhausted and how much of each remains. It is virtually inevitable that somewhere during the project, something unexpected will happen. Maybe one of the developers will get sick or become otherwise unavailable. Maybe an unexpected bug will arise and take so long to fix that it throws off your schedule. Maybe you'll have a great idea for a fantastic new feature. Maybe your testing with normal users will uncover something confusing that will hamper your app's adoption. Whatever the reason, when the unexpected happens, you will need to make a decision.

Maybe the decision will be to extend the schedule and the budget. Maybe the right decision is to cut or reduce the scope of one of the other features to make up the difference. Maybe, if you're lucky, you'll even be able to rearrange things so that there is no measurable impact. For example, if the developer working on a particular feature becomes ill, you might be able to postpone milestones that depend on the feature whose developer is now missing and move up milestones from later in the project that have no such dependency. Perhaps you can replace some customized UI with an off-the-shelf component that, while not exactly what you wanted, is close enough, given the new circumstances.

The important thing to note here is that, without a thorough and current schedule in some tool that lets you examine trade-offs, you're pretty much stuck. There are all kinds of alternatives, both straightforward and creative, available to an informed project manager. Without the tools and information on hand to help you guide decisions, you are at the mercy of any random events that occur.

Remember That Estimates Are Only Estimates

With all this talk of schedules and estimates and plans, it's important to remember that estimates are, at best, educated guesses, and all carry a degree of uncertainty and risk. If estimates were certain, there would be no need for project planning or scheduling or trade-offs—or even this book.

Software estimates, when well done, are still accurate only in aggregate. Some tasks take longer than expected and some take less time, but hopefully over the course of a project, you end up close to the date that you had originally projected.

The accuracy of estimates depends on several factors, including familiarity, uncertainty, and isolation.

Familiarity

Familiarity is how well the person creating an estimate understands the specifics and details of the task to be accomplished. In general, as discussed in Chapter 8, "Interviewing and Selecting a Developer," someone who has already built an app just like yours will have the best chance of building your app. Likewise, that person will also have the best chance of creating an accurate estimate for building your app. The closer the estimator's experience is to the project being estimated, the more accurate that estimate will likely be. Details and minutiae are important here, as very small differences in expectations can unfortunately balloon into large blocks of time.

There is an issue with self-reported familiarity that I have seen often: Familiarity is greatly reduced in the absence of accurate feedback. Often, especially at established companies, the person or individual(s) responsible for creating the project estimate are only peripherally involved in the delivery of that project (and sometimes they aren't involved at all). This can happen for a number of valid reasons. Some firms have dedicated technical sales staff whose job is to assist in getting a sale and then move on to the next sale. Sometimes there is a delay between the estimate being created and the project starting, during which the developer who built the estimate gets assigned to another project.

The problem is that if a person estimates a project but isn't intimately involved with it afterward, it's very hard for that person to judge the accuracy of the estimates made for that project. It's easy for an estimator to fall into the trap of believing his or her estimate must have been correct. This makes the estimator tend to believe that he or she is far more familiar with a project and its associated tasks than is actually the case. This can lead to the same mistakes being made over and over.

So when you're judging the quality of an estimate or beginning to use an estimate to track a project, make sure you ask not only how familiar the person making the estimate is with the details of the project in question but to what extent that familiarity has been informed by the actual results from the previous projects.

Uncertainty

Uncertainty is the amount of information missing during the estimation process but that the estimator needs in order to make an accurate estimate. These gaps in information end up being filled in by making assumptions (guesses) about what that information is likely to be.

One element of uncertainty in estimation, especially at larger firms, is the question of who is actually going to be doing the work. Estimates are often created with one set of programmers in mind, often led by (or at least including) the person doing the estimate, and if a different group of programmers actually ends up on the project, the difference between the knowledge, skills, and experience of the assumed and actual groups can be the difference between success and failure.

Another factor in uncertainty is the amount of communication the project will require. It depends on team size, customer requirements, project management overhead, and tools.

If I estimate the number of development hours it will take me to build a feature by myself, that estimate will be wildly different if that feature is divided up among six people and those six people have to spend time coordinating among themselves who is going to be doing what part and how each part is going to connect to and communicate with the other parts. The total number of calendar days it takes to build that feature may well be reduced with a team of six, but I guarantee you that the number of person-hours spent will be greatly reduced if one developer with the equivalent experience builds the whole feature alone.

Likewise, if each developer has to create and submit a daily report of what he or she has completed at the end of each day, roughly 3% to 6% of your developers' programming time is devoted to daily reports, not programming (and likely a higher percentage, if they resent it and grouse about it). A daily scrum or stand-up meeting reduces effective time on task by a like amount. Note that I am not saying here that you should never have stand-up meetings or daily reports. The communication occurring there might have value to you. The problem arises when that communication time is not assumed in the estimates you are working from. If you have 100% perfect estimates but institute a daily scrum that was not anticipated by the estimator, you've guaranteed that your project will run 5% or so over time and budget.

Isolation

Isolation is the degree to which each task is independent of anything else. This means both how distinct it is from other tasks in the project and how factors external to the project may affect the duration, difficulty, or developers of each task.

If a task is dependent on other tasks in the project, then problems with the first task can cascade into the dependent task and cause it to be more difficult or take longer. For example, say that you planned a screen in your app that was to contain a custom control (like a complicated dial), and the control ended up being a lot harder to build than expected. That added complexity might mean that the amount of time estimated to connect the control to the screen of the app was insufficient, and it will take much longer to get information relevant to that screen into the control.

The place I see this happen most often is with interactions between server-side code and client-side (app) code. Often the number of methods needed for communication between the server and client ends up growing as the project progresses and more and more use cases are added. (Often this is driven by the need to get more information from the server in fewer trips so the user doesn't end up having to wait as frequently.) Adding use cases causes an increase in both the work the server team needs to do and the amount of work that needs to happen in the networking portion of the app. It often even requires additional logic to be placed in each screen of the app so that app's network layer can determine the correct combination of requests to get the right set of information from the server at the right time.

The other part of isolation is understanding how a task can be affected by issues outside the project itself. This can be a huge unknown and a huge risk. Imagine, for example, your lead developer's computer dying. Even if good software engineering practices are being followed and all the developer's data is backed up and recoverable, it's still going to take some time for that developer to become productive again. Some amount of time will be spent making sure the machine is, in fact, dead, and then a new machine will have to be acquired, and then the backups (hopefully they exist) will have to be restored. When considered in the context of a six-month project, this is hardly noticeable. But if you're looking at a week-long milestone, an event like that can cause a 20% or even 40% delay.

Other problems are new software releases of the development tools the developers are using for the project, environmental factors such as severe weather and power outages, and illness or other life events. For the most part, these externalities can't be prevented and often can't even be mitigated against. These are some of the most difficult issues to plan for and recover from.

Padding

The way that estimators deal with the vagaries of tasks is by *padding*—adding more time than they think something will take, just in case something goes wrong. If I know that I'm uncertain about who will be performing the work, I might add an additional 20% or 50% to my guess of how long it would take me. If this task is something I'm not familiar with, I might double or triple my guess at how long it will take (and even then, I might still be too low).

Sometimes padding occurs at more than one level. Sometimes the person doing estimates pads his or her guesses, and then the person putting together the proposal multiplies all the numbers by yet another padding factor. This seems like overkill, but it often produces accurate estimates. Software estimators are fond of quoting a maxim that explains this. It's called Hofstadter's law: "It always takes longer than you expect, even when you take into account Hofstadter's law" (see http://en.wikipedia.org/wiki/Hofstadter's_law).

Padding is an unavoidable reaction to uncertainty, and it's the generally accepted way to estimate in the face of the unknown. It can cause some details to look a little off if you look too closely. Often I end up with project plans that have items like "create view controller for [a particular feature]: 2 hours." Now, the actual act of creating a view controller in Xcode takes about 1 minute (File > New File > Cocoa Touch Class > UIViewController > Type in a name > click OK). However, a lot more actually has to happen than that. First of all, I have to decide what kind of view controller to use (there are many), I have to decide where the data is going to come from, and I have to decide how that view controller is going to be reached in the view hierarchy. And there are many other decisions that have to be made that I lump into that same "create view controller" task. So try not to nitpick small individual durations, as there's often a method behind the apparent madness.

Granularity

One of the ways to judge the quality of an estimate is its granularity. In general, the more detail an estimate has, the more accurate it will be. One schedule item called "build user interface for list view" that is estimated to take 2 weeks is much more likely to be wrong than a corresponding collection of 40 or 50 tasks that are estimated to take between 1 and 3 hours each. This is because you know that the person who broke down the user interface into dozens of individual components spent time thinking about what was involved; also, a task simple enough that it can be done in an hour is much more likely to be estimated correctly than one so complicated that it will take a week, according to the plan.

If you get a proposal in which each tasks is estimated to take days or even weeks (or the equivalent number of hours), ask where those numbers came from and whether there's more detail behind the estimates. Hopefully there is, but if this is as much detail as they have to give you, then take the estimates with a grain of salt; they could easily be off by a factor of four or five or more.

Estimated Tasks Aren't Final Tasks

Another thing to keep in mind about estimations is that the tasks created for purposes of estimation are, in fact, estimates. The actual tasks done by the developers on your project may be different—although they will hopefully cover the same functionality and take about the same amount of time. As your project progresses, the tasks for a given milestone will likely morph from a simple set into a more detailed list, with specific resources assigned and specific dates added. This doesn't indicate a failure in the estimation process but is a natural evolution that is nothing to be concerned about. (Again, individual tasks may vary wildly in duration from the estimate, but hopefully the aggregate is close.)

Renovation Versus New Construction

When discussing uncertainty in estimation, it's important to consider one of the largest sources of uncertainty: unfamiliar code bases. There is inherent risk in trying to build something on top of someone else's code. I can say with no hesitation that, of the estimates I've gotten wrong, the ones that have been the furthest from reality have all involved updating, changing, or adding features to apps that someone else had built. And never in my career in estimating and building apps have I completed a task noticeably sooner than estimated because the previous developer's code turned out to be of better quality than I had feared.

There are several reasons it takes longer to work with unfamiliar code bases. One is that, even if the code is of good quality, it's not *my code*, so I don't understand it as well as I would if I had I written it to begin with. This means that when I rely on it to act the way I expect in the face of new use cases, I often turn out to be wrong. Of course, the code is there (usually), so it's possible for me to read it and eventually understand exactly what it will do in any given situation. Although it's possible, it's often not practical. Reading and making sure I understand every line of code at that level of detail would take me close to as long as it would take me to write such code myself. Few customers (understandably) want to pay for that. On rare occasions, I don't even have access to the old code but just to the binary built from it. (This can be the case with third-party libraries, for example.) Not being able to read through the code (even cursorily) increases risk even more.

Another reason it takes longer to work with unfamiliar code bases is that usually app creators move up the experience ladder when changing developers rather than down it. It's far, far more likely for an app to be built first by the lowest bidding developer and then switched to a more experienced (and therefore more expensive) developer than the other way around. Usually this happens because the first developer fails to deliver a satisfactory product. I don't know that I've ever seen an app built by an experienced, expensive development company given to a much cheaper group to do the second version. (It's probably happened sometime in the past few years, but I don't think I've seen it.)

This is akin to the difference between building a new house and adding a room on to an existing house. When you're building a new house, many more of the variables are under control. You know exactly what materials are being used, and you know the skill levels of the people putting them together. But that's not the case when renovating. If the builder creating a new house knows he is building the house with this additional room, he will make sure that the beam supporting the room will be strong enough to handle it, and he will make sure the foundation extends under the new room. When renovating, the new foundation has to be attached to the old foundation, and the beam may have to be given extra reinforcement so that it can hold the new load.

But worse than that, when adding on, you have to make sure the rest of the house stays intact. A half-finished room exposed to the elements is no big deal in new construction because the floors are concrete, and water will run right off. But when renovating, you have to protect the existing carpet from rain that comes in through the hole (or replace the carpet at added expense). In a worse case, lead paint or asbestos may be found, which will require additional expenses.

Adding on to an existing program is actually quite similar to adding on to a physical structure. You're not sure how each section of code was intended to be used or what use cases the original programmer considered and which he or she didn't. And you don't know what changes you make over here can unexpectedly break that part of the program over there, since you didn't even realize it depended on this part of the code.

Working with an unfamiliar code base makes for such uncertainty that you may not be able to figure out reasonable milestones or anything more granular than "maybe it will take a couple weeks." And often, you end up being wrong, and almost always it takes longer than you feared. It's unfortunate, but that's just the way renovating existing code bases goes.

Estimates and Entomology

Entomology is the study of insects, or bugs. Bugs in code are numerous and prevalent. Bugs in code, by definition, are things that the code is doing that the programmer didn't intend or expect for it to do. And if the programmer didn't intend it or expect it, then the uncertainty is almost assuredly quite high. Therefore, estimating how long it will take to fix a bug can be a Sisyphean effort. If you don't know enough about a bug to fix it, then you probably don't know enough to estimate it either. And by the time you do know enough to estimate it, you're probably close to getting it fixed. This makes the estimation process for bugs particularly unhelpful.

Usually soon after a nontrivial bug has been discovered, the best estimate that can be made is a lower bound (for example, "I know it's going to take me at least a couple days just to figure out what's really going on"). Rarely does a bug that will take more than a couple hours to fix have enough information to estimate accurately. This is especially frustrating toward the end of a project, when the only things left to do before declaring victory are fixing the last remaining bugs.

I'd love to give you a magic formula for estimating bug fixes, but even more than that, I'd love to *know* a magic formula for estimating bug fixes, and I have never seen evidence that such a formula exists or could exist.

So what do you do when trying to plan for bugs you don't know enough to estimate accurately? You guess, you add padding, and you hope that the code exhibiting the bug was written well enough that the bug will be easily discovered and can be fixed without side effects rippling through the rest of the code base.

Plan Reevaluation and Project Feedback Loops

One thing that I see very few project managers do is reevaluate an existing plan in the face of completed tasks. I don't know why this is because it seems to me an obvious thing to do.

I recommend that, at the end of each milestone (or sprint, if you must), you should look at how long each task and subtask took compared to what it was estimated to take. Once you have that information, look through the remaining parts of the project for similar tasks and then try to guess how likely it is for each of those tasks to take as much or longer to do as the ones just completed.

For example, imagine that your developer estimated that it would take 4 hours to get a particularly complicated view in an app to rotate correctly from portrait to landscape and back, but it actually took 12 hours. At that point, it would make sense to see if there are other views that are also going to need to rotate and, if so, whether it will take longer to get them working correctly than estimated as well. It's possible that you learned enough getting the first view to rotate that you now know enough to fix the other ones as estimated. But even if that's the case, it's definitely worth asking the question. Surprisingly few people do, and many of them end up with task after task running "unexpectedly late" for the same reasons.

Wrapping Up

This chapter discusses how you can use milestones to reduce the risk of a failing project. Here are some key points to take away:

- Having frequent checkpoints with your developer reduces the risks of procrastination and communication issues.
- Using milestones is the most effective means for keeping a project on track.
- Milestones are significant pieces of functionality, unlike sprints, which are just buckets of tasks.

- Not all development organizations can or will create and work from milestones. Doing so takes organization, sequencing, and focus that many organization aren't capable of or aren't willing to expend the effort for.

- For milestones to be truly effective, they need to be tracked in some kind of scheduling or project management software.

- The accuracy of estimates depends on a number of factors, including familiarity, uncertainty, and isolation.

- No estimates are 100% accurate, and the trick of project management is to compensate for inaccuracies in estimates.

- Some tasks are harder to estimate than others. Bugs and unknown code bases are the most difficult of the lot.

- When taking stock at the completion of a milestone, use the difference between the estimated effort and actual effort to adjust the estimates of any similar future tasks.

Understanding What You're Getting

You have now officially reached the point in this book where you learn how to determine whether your project is coming together or falling completely apart. We've talked about common project issues to watch out for, what you want your app to become, who you want to build it for you, and how much time and money the developer estimates it's going to take. By this point, you ought to know that development shouldn't begin until you have a plan for your app's development and a set of milestones that you and your developer can use to track progress.

Now it's time to watch the development happen, evaluate your developer's output and communications, and decide whether the project is going smoothly and whether your needs are being met. This is where the rubber meets the road.

This chapter discusses how you can try to infer what's going on with your developer and use that information to work with him or her to maximize your project's chance of success. In Chapter 11, "Pulling the Plug Early," you'll learn what to do if everything else has failed and you need to cut your losses and move on.

There is no way to be 100% certain that any app project will succeed. This chapter is filled with warning signs that you should look out for. Each such issue you encounter indicates that your chance of getting a quality app developed is diminished, at least somewhat, and the more issues that present themselves in what you get from your developer, the more risk your project is incurring.

Living Within Your Means

It is important to keep a sense of perspective when evaluating the software you are paying for. Nitpicking and second-guessing your developer are unlikely to make for a healthy working relationship and are unlikely to lead to a successful project or product.

You have to walk a tightrope here. It's vitally important that you maintain control of your development project: You can't delegate responsibility for your app idea to your developer and take your eye off the ball without drastically reducing your odds of success. On the other hand, micromanaging your developer will also make things worse. The good news is that this is not a unique problem; every parent or manager has faced a variant of it at one point or another.

The difficulty for many app creators arises not because they don't understand this dichotomy but because they aren't familiar enough with development (and app development in particular) to know where the line is. As a general rule, I see app creators having too little involvement in their projects, and so that's what this book (and especially this chapter) covers in the most detail. But I would be remiss if I didn't warn you that too much involvement usually also leads to bad outcomes.

The good news for you (hopefully) is that you had a good idea of what you wanted your app to do and what components it needed to have before you engaged your developer in the first place. If you worked through the first few chapters of this book (especially Chapters 3, "Prototyping and Wireframing Your App," and 4, "Determining Your App's Components"), you and your potential developer had a strong idea of what your project involved at the beginning of your engagement. If you did a good job of communicating what features and functionality your app needed to have, and if your developer gave you a plan for how to deliver that functionality, with a time frame and a budget, your odds of success are much better than those of the average app creator. As long as you try to stay within the plan and the functionality expectations you set up front, you aren't very likely to put your project at risk by micromanaging.

I say often, when asked whether a given budget is reasonable, that there is a version of an app that meets those requirements that can be done in that amount of time and money. It's not necessarily the best version, the most full-featured version, or the ideal version, but there is at least one version that can be created while satisfying those constraints. Try to keep in mind that there may be better, fancier, slicker, faster, or prettier versions of the app you are building, but they might be more expensive or take longer than you can live with. You and your developer (hopefully) agreed on a specific version of the app and documented that agreement well early on. If you try to expand the scope beyond that agreement later in the project, friction is bound to arise.

If it becomes necessary to add new functionality to your project, for whatever reason, something else is going to have to give. Either some other piece of functionality will need to be reduced, or the time and expense will need to be increased. You can't get something for nothing. Think about it this way: If your developer could build your app and add new functionality for the same time and money as the initial estimate, then it stands to reason that the developer must have padded the initial estimate by at least as much as the new feature. Is that something you would want your developer to be doing?

You and your developer can have a discussion about who should shoulder the cost of the new functionality, depending on why it turned out to be necessary in the first place. It might be reasonable that some or all of the cost should be paid by the developer because he or she failed to recognize and estimate functionality that he or she agreed to build for you, but that's not the same thing as getting the new functionality for nothing. There's still no such thing as a free lunch.

The Ticking Clock

Now that I've reminded you that you shouldn't try to expand the scope you agreed on, I want to stress the urgency of understanding what is going on with your project contemporaneously. As software development projects go, app projects tend to be relatively short. Because of this limited time frame, there isn't a lot of extra slack in the schedule to compensate for even small mistakes. A common 90-day project schedule has fewer than 65 working days. If a misunderstanding, illness, or hardware problem causes a week of work to be lost, that's nearly 8% of your total project time, which is really hard to make up. A friend of mine analogizes it this way: "You can't hide a body under a throw rug."

More Meetings Is Not the Answer

One way people commonly try to deal with the ticking clock is by having more frequent meetings, but this doesn't ever seem to have the desired effect.

Meetings cause productivity loss far beyond the time they actually take. Time before meetings is often lost as well because people think there is no point in starting something in the hour or so before the meeting because there wouldn't be enough time to actually get anything done. Paul Graham has a great essay explaining this called "Maker's Schedule, Manager's Schedule" that you can (and should) find and read online; see www.paulgraham.com/makersschedule.html. It does the best job of explaining it that I've seen.

Agile methodology requires a daily stand-up or scrum meeting, which attempts to get around this timing problem by happening first thing in the morning, so that less of the day is lost. If everyone on the team comes in at the same time in the morning, this can work to some extent. The problem is that different people naturally have different inherent schedules; some people are morning people, and some people do their best work after their kids go to bed at night. By forcing everyone to come in at the same time, some members of the development team are virtually guaranteed to be working outside their peak hours.

The most important thing, however, is that what you want to measure is the work that is being done: the code that is being developed, the documentation that is being written, and so on. Meetings aren't indicative of real work; meetings are additional time spent not doing real work.

It's About the Work

What I do, and what I recommend you do, is focus on the artifacts of the work being created. Get the source code to your project, and get whatever documentation is available about what your developers are working on. (This documentation is often captured in a source control tool, as discussed later in this chapter, or a bug-tracking tool, as introduced in Chapter 5, "Finding the Right Tools," and discussed at length in Chapter 12, "Communicating Using Bugs"). Read through these artifacts on a periodic basis. Then, ask questions about any parts of how the project is progressing that you don't understand.

I'm not trying to encourage you to audit the actual code that is being written (with a couple of exceptions, discussed later); rather, I'm trying to encourage you to understand what features and milestones are being actively worked on, what issues the team is experiencing, and how what you are seeing fits into the overall project plan. You ought to be able to understand these things from reading the comments in the code, the log messages in the source control system, and the descriptions and updates in the bug tracker (and/or other task-tracking tool). If you can't, you need to ask. I recommend asking these questions in email because you will get an answer you can reference later, if needed, and so you don't interrupt what might be productive development time, as you would with a phone call.

If code is being checked in that doesn't seem to be associated with an item in the bug- or task-tracking tool, that's unacceptable, and you need to either get clarification about which bug or task that code is for. Either you'll discover that a task was omitted from the plan (which is bad, and the task needs to be added and tracked) or that there was insufficient explanation about the purpose of the code (in which case, by having asked the question, you will have encouraged the developer to do a better job of referencing the relevant task or bug in his or her comments).

Justifying Effort for Your Project Size

Not all projects require the same amount of effort from the app creator. As I mentioned back at the beginning of Chapter 5, some app projects are self-funded or of very short duration. In such a case, it might not be worth the effort, for example, to try to understand the structure of the code base your developer is building or to check each build for compiler warnings. Projects with less at stake might be fine with more risk than the following recommendations assume. As always, your mileage may vary.

Get the Code, Even if There's Nothing to See in the UI

To be able to use the artifacts of a team's work to understand the status of a project, you need to get access to those artifacts. This means, at a minimum, getting access to the source control system and the bug tracker that the team is using (and the task tracker, if the team is using one of those as well). If at all possible, you need to own these (for example, your company needs to host the server on which these services reside, or you need to be the owner of record at the third-party vendor that provides the service). Chapter 5 discusses these services.

Your developer may be hesitant about giving you access to the source code because if you decide not to pay, withholding the source code is the only real leverage a developer has. As discussed earlier, this is the kind of conversation that needs to happen when the contract is being negotiated and not after it is signed. Explain to the developer that access to the source control system means that you won't have to take as much of his or her time for meetings (which is a good thing, as most developers hate meetings). Talk to the developer about whatever concerns he or she might have and work out whatever arrangement you need to. Without access to source control, you will have a much harder time assessing code quality or switching developers, if needed. Virtually all reputable developers will give you at least read-only access to the source control system as the project goes on, although they might have some contractual hurdles for you first.

Once a project has started and you get access to the source control system (ideally, a reputable third-party service, as discussed in Chapter 5), and you get a tool that will let you copy and examine the source code on your system (your service should have a list of tools you can use; see Chapter 5 for that as well), you should make sure you can get a copy of the code from the service and also see the comments, log messages, and the history of the project as it is being built. You want to do this as early as you can. The time to figure out how to get the source code is at the beginning of the project, when things are going well and everyone still likes each other. If the project starts to go badly, your developer will no longer have any desire to help you with any source control issues that crop up.

Once you have access, grab a copy of the code, the history, and the log messages on a frequent basis. I would recommend doing it once each workday, but at least once a week. Think of this as a backup. If something goes wrong and your developer decides to withhold the code, then anything you haven't already retrieved will be lost to you.

The expected process here is that there are normally a number of *commits* in the source control system. A *commit* (sometimes called a *check-in*) is a collection of code changes, often spread across multiple code files (and sometimes affecting non-code files like configuration files and graphics files), that together constitute a particular piece of functionality added to the code base. Normally each task in the project plan is accomplished when a number of these *commits* are aggregated together to complete a specified feature.

As you see commits coming in from your development team, you are also seeing progress being made for some number of tasks in the project plan. You don't necessarily have any way to determine how many more commits are required in order to complete the relevant task, but at least you can see progress. (And it's appropriate to ask periodically how much time and effort the team estimates to remain before each task is completed.)

Comments in Source Control

As you grab source code and the history from the source control system, you'll want to look at the commit logs that the developers enter. These aren't actually part of the code itself, but rather messages the developer enters to give information about or indicate the purpose of the collection of code changes being committed to the source control system.

You should be able to find these by using your source control tool. Figure 10.1 shows an example of a source control tool. The commit log for the selected code change is the part that says "Save every pass through the loop. It's simpler to explain. Premature optimization is the root of all evil." Right underneath that is "SeismicJSON/EarthquakeFetchOperation.m" which is the name of the file that was changed on that commit, and below that is the changes to the code that were made.

Figure 10.1
A source control tool looking at an open source project I wrote for a class I was teaching.

On a client project, there should always be some way to understand, for any given code change, what piece or task of the overall project plan that change is a part of. There isn't such an indication in Figure 10.1 because that wasn't a client-facing project. (Sorry about that, but I can't put client-facing code into this book due to intellectual property issues.) Exactly how this is indicated varies from project to project and from development team to development team. Sometimes it's a string with a particular format in the commit log, sometimes it's a function of the branch the change is on, sometimes the bug-tracking tool references the commit identifier instead of the other way around, and sometimes it's something else entirely. It's perfectly appropriate at the beginning of a project to ask your team how they intend to tie commit information into the bug and project trackers. It's also perfectly appropriate to hold them to whatever they say. It's important for that to happen, and it should happen consistently.

Once you can understand what task on the project plan that code change was a part of, the next question is "What was that change intended to do?" Hopefully, the comment explains the purpose of that commit in a way that you can understand. If not, it's appropriate for you to request clarification. This is important for a number of reasons, not the least of which is that hopefully at some point in the future you will want to have a new version of this app written, with updated features that your users want. Your hypothetical future developer will have a much easier time if the comments made by your current developers are clear and understandable.

Some developers might have trouble getting started on this. Not a lot of non-programmers look at commit messages (which is a shame), and therefore many developers aren't used to having to care about what they write there. However, once you've asked for clarification a couple times, the developers should get the message and start producing informative and comprehensible information that ties into the overall plan. If that doesn't happen within a week or two into the project, that's a real concern and indicates that your developer might not be up to the professional standards you need or deserve.

Next, you are going to want an acknowledgment of what is left to do in order to complete the portion of the project plan that contains this commit. You're more likely to find that information in the bug- or task-tracking tool, and we discuss this more thoroughly in Chapter 12.

Over time, you may see patterns in the commit logs. Hopefully, a pattern shows a progression of comprehensible information being added commit after commit, and hopefully you see the features being mentioned and described in the commit messages coming to fruition as you run and test the app yourself. If that isn't the case—if the commit messages don't become and stay comprehensible and if the functionality the commit messages say should have been added to the app doesn't materialize when tested—you might have a problem. (In case you face this, we discuss what to do in Chapter 11.)

Comments in Code

In addition to seeing commit logs in your source control tool, you should also be able to see the actual code changes in a commit. If you look at the right side of Figure 10.1, you'll see the code changes, which also include changes to the comments made in the code.

A code comment in most languages used in app development for mobile devices starts with either two slashes in a row, like this:

```
// This is a Comment
```

or is enclosed inside slashes and asterisks, like this:

```
/* This is a Comment */
```

or at least this is true of native development in iOS, Android, and Windows, which all use programming languages with syntax that derives from a language called C.

Figure 10.2 shows the right side of Figure 10.1 increased and scrolled so you can pick out the comment:

```
//Keep track of if we need to save or not
```

and the comment:

```
//Now remember that we are going to need to save
```

among others.

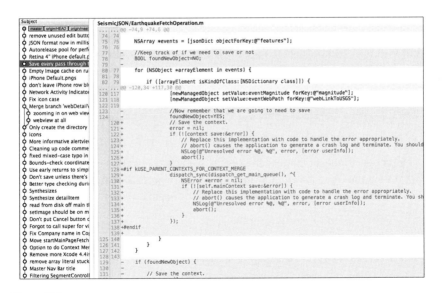

Figure 10.2
This is the same output shown in Figure 10.1 but resized and scrolled to emphasize the code changes.

Now in this particular case, those two comments are being removed. You can tell by the minus signs (-) preceding those lines. The lines preceded by plus signs (+) are being added in this particular change.

If you were you to scroll through the whole of this particular commit, you'd see that a variable that kept track of whether a save was required was removed from the code, and the code that actually causes the data to be saved (which is preceded by the comment `//Save the context.`) has been added. That is consistent with the commit log shown earlier that said, "Save every pass through the loop. It's simpler to explain." (If you care, previously I was making this sample code run faster by calling `save` less frequently. After writing up my slides for the associated class, I decided that I was trying to pack too much into the slides already, and I didn't want to have to explain that, too, so I went with a simpler implementation that always called `save`.)

The ability to pick out comments from the code changes can help you figure out what's going on without having to ask your developers. (Or, if you want to ask, it's easier and better for everyone if you can say "It looks from the code like you are doing *X*. Am I understanding that correctly?" than if you have to ask "So, what are you working on?") Don't worry if you can't figure this out at first; your skills will get better at over time.

Not all developers comment their code well (or at all). It would be really nice if we could all mandate that developers were required to comment their code, but it's just unlikely to happen. If you see your developers checking in a bunch of code that doesn't have any comments, you can try to suggest that you would prefer that they added more, but that doesn't mean they will, and it doesn't mean that you should switch developers just because they don't. It does, however, mean that you need to be extra wary and that you might be somewhat more likely to have a poor developer.

If your developers document their code in a way that makes sense to you, that's a bonus, and it's an indication that they're professional, and that they care, and that they're trying. Professional is good, and trying and caring can take a project a long way.

Build and Run the App Yourself

Chapter 5 discusses the risk involved in taking the developer's word that you are getting all the code that is needed to build the project you're paying for. If you're thinking as you read this that you don't want to build the app yourself, go back and read the sidebar in the "The Development Environment" section of Chapter 5 and think long and hard about whether you want to risk ending up like that poor app creator.

The easiest way to build and run the app yourself is to ask your developer for documented instructions on how to do it. If you get the same set of developer tools that your developer has and use the same set of processes as the developer, you should have an easy time of it.

Failing that, you should be able to do a web search and find an introductory tutorial on building code for your platform. You should be able to get things building from those instructions. If you can't, then you need to ask.

Note that when it comes to getting code actually running on a device, life gets a little complicated because code generally won't run on a smartphone or tablet unless the code is signed or the device is configured in a particular way. There are many tutorials about how to get code running on a device on your platform, but doing so is not always easy. If you can't get it working, you might ask your developer to help with this, or you might go to a local developer meet-up group and see if you can get someone there to help you. The good news is that most development environments have a simulator or emulator that will let you run your developer's code without having to get it running on the device, and that should be good enough for most purposes.

Please, whatever you do, don't trust that you have all the code that you need without verifying it yourself. Keep in mind that even if your developer is meticulous, he or she might still make a mistake and forget to check a necessary component into source control. (I've done it accidentally myself.) If your relationship with your developer takes a turn for the worse, you won't be able to ask for help then.

Also, in general, the earlier in your project it is, the simpler the code base will be (if for no other reason than your developer hasn't had time to write enough code to make it complicated). If you get building early, you're likely have an easier time of it.

Remember, though, that just because you built the project and got it running once doesn't mean you will always be able to. Over time, projects get more complicated, and new steps get added to the build process. Don't assume that just because it worked for you last week, it will also work next week. You should always verify, and if something doesn't work, ask about it. My rule of thumb is that you should never write a check to pay an invoice without first verifying that you can build the project from the code you have.

The most common reason that code which used to build correctly stops building is that a third-party library is added. Often, these libraries are included in such a way that they need to be retrieved separately. There are several different ways that this can happen, and your developer picked one.

If it's not obvious to you how you should retrieve that third-party component yourself, you should ask.

Third-Party Libraries

As third-party libraries and components get added to your project, you must consider a number of things. First, understand that third-party components can be a good thing. They can save your project a lot of time and money. Often, they have been tested more widely and for longer than your budget or schedule would allow. This can be advantageous.

Third-party libraries are not a panacea, though. They have the disadvantage of trying to be more generally useful and widely applicable than code written specifically for your project is likely to be. This makes them more complex and therefore more error prone.

There are also legal and copyright issues, and some components require that you give their authors credit and/or make source code available. I'm not a lawyer, and I don't even play one on TV, so I'm going to leave that up to you. I just want to make sure that you're aware to look out for such issues.

Most importantly, though, by incorporating a third-party component, you are tying yourself and your app's future to the ongoing maintenance of the component's author(s). We discussed this at length back in the "Dealing with Third-Party Frameworks" section of Chapter 4, "Determining Your App's Components," so I won't rehash that here. The good news on that front is that the more contained the component is, the easier it would be to swap out with another component in future versions of your app, and therefore the less ongoing risk that component will pose to future iterations of your project.

The easiest way to tell how invasive the component is in your app is to remove that component from your source tree temporarily and try to build the app. As a rule, the more errors that are generated when the component is missing, the more work it's going to be to replace it with something else.

You may or may not want to insist on being notified (or having to give your approval) before a new third-party component is added. That's up to you. Either way, though, you're going to have to make a decision to either trust your developer's recommendation; keep in mind that deciding not to might damage your relationship.

You can always do a web search for the component in question and see what other people are saying about it. The trick, though, is that this is inherently attempting to predict the future; the risk is more about what is going to happen to the component's code base in the future than whether it meets your needs at the moment.

Whether a component is good or bad, though, it needs to be identifiable. It's not appropriate for a third-party component to be copied to your source code project without some documentation of where it came from, where new versions of it might be found in the future, and what its license requirements are. The preferred and ideal method is to have all your third-party components included by reference so that, as part of your source code repository, you have links embedded to pull the correct version of the third-party component from its home out on the Internet. Failing that, part of the build process for your app might be constructed to grab the correct component. But at the very least, you need to make sure there is some kind of document that explains where the component was acquired and where new versions of it (and bug fixes for it) may be found and where its maintainers are expected to be reachable in the future.

Source Code Project Organization

This section talks about how your source code is organized and what you should look for there. First, though, we need to disambiguate the word *project* here. In the majority of this book, the word *project* refers to the overall set of tasks that culminate in an app being completed. However, many developer tools use the word *project* to mean the set of source code and other files (like graphics) that together get compiled into a particular version of a machine-runnable application file. When we're talking about that collection of files in the remainder of this chapter, I'm going to use the term *source code project* so you can differentiate the two different uses of the word *project*.

There are no completely unambiguous rules about source code project structure. Ugly, messy code can still be serviceable, working code. But, like many of the other things in this chapter, ugly code is an indication that things are less likely to go well.

Think of the code files in a source code project as chapters (or sections) of a book or as supports of a structure. If you see one really, really long file and the rest of the files are fairly small, this is an indication that the code isn't organized well. The files shouldn't all be exactly the same size or anything, but there should be a few longer ones, a bunch of medium-sized ones, and some small ones.

And it's certainly true that there's an upper limit on the reasonable size of a source code file. The exact value of the size limit is debatable, but 1,000 lines seems to be a popular choice. Certainly if you have files longer than that, you're likely working with either an unprofessional developer or one who isn't being particularly diligent.

Inside a file, the rules are similar. In the programming languages we're talking about here, the files contain blocks of code called *methods*. A *method* is a group of commands put together in a routine that can be called from another place in the code. They make code modular and better organized. Like with file sizes, if there are one or two methods that are way bigger than the rest of them, this is an indication of poor coding hygiene, and it's another indication that you may need to say goodbye to your developer before the project is complete.

Ideally, all the code in a single method should fit on a single screen of your monitor. Realistically, they often grow bigger than that, but they shouldn't grow too much bigger than that, or they need to be *refactored*. (You can think of refactoring as dividing code up into smaller parts.) Any method of more than a couple hundred lines is definitely a cause for concern.

Automated Test Coverage

In my professional opinion, the best indication of the quality of a code base is the amount of code with functionality that is verified with automated tests (often called unit tests). This is a metric we call *code coverage*, or *test coverage*. It's the first measurement of code quality in the TIOBE Code Quality Indicator (see www.tiobe.com/content/paperinfo/TIOBEQualityIndicator.pdf), which is one—although by no means the only—attempt to objectively measure code quality.

Unfortunately, this is a mostly useless metric for your purposes. Automated testing has never really caught on in the mobile space, and very few developers here use it (unlike in other software disciplines). If you find one who does, that's great, but if I were to tell you to insist on a developer who wrote automated testing, I'd narrow the field of developers that you would accept to an unacceptably small fraction.

Please ask your developer about this, though. As more customers request automated tests, more developers will start using them, and that will be better for the entire mobile industry.

Detecting Plagiarism

One unscrupulous technique that I have seen used by poor developers in the past is stealing code. I've seen this more than once, and it's frightening—for more than one reason.

First, it opens you up to legal liability; second, it's a rip-off because you're paying for development that you aren't getting. But it also means that your development team is pretending to have written (and therefore pretending to understand) code that is being presented to you. The odds that they are actually going to understand plagiarized code (and therefore be able to fix bugs in it) are fairly small.

This, in my mind, is one exception to the "nothing is 100% certain" mantra we started the chapter with. In my professional opinion, if you find plagiarism in your code, you should fire your team and never look back. To me, if they're willing to lie to you about that, then they're willing to lie to you about how many hours were worked, or any one of dozens of other things, and you shouldn't trust them at all. But that's a decision only you can make.

You might suspect plagiarism when whole files are checked in at once, and when the style of the new code doesn't seem to match what you've seen so far (either spacing is all different, or the filenames look different, or the variable names don't seem similar, or things like that).

The procedure for detecting plagiarism is fairly straightforward in this day and age. Take small sections of code and paste them into a Google or GitHub search window and see what hits results you get. In order for this to be useful, you need to pick sections with meaningful content and meaningful variable names. And then if you find an identical section of code out on the Internet, you need to examine larger sections of the code before you can be sure that it's actually plagiarism. In practice, though, it isn't very hard to determine. Usually people stupid enough to plagiarize code aren't smart enough to hide it well. When I've found plagiarism, I've generally found a file that's more than 90% identical—just a couple lines changed here or there and the copyright statement at the top of the file changed or removed.

The Case of the Copy/Paste Subcontractor

Once I was working with a company that had contracted a firm to do its primary app development. The actual programming was being done by a subcontractor somewhere in Eastern Europe. The project was behind schedule, and a number of issues had previously arisen before I had become involved with the project.

The subcontractor had claimed that a number of issues that he had been having were due to bugs in a third-party library he was using called RestKit (mentioned in Chapter 4). I'm not sure why the subcontractor was using RestKit (whether he had chosen it himself or if it had been in the code base previously), but the contractor had determined that RestKit was going to need to be removed from the project and had estimated a considerable amount of time to do that, as well as to write code to replace its functionality.

After time had passed and a considerable amount of money had changed hands, I was asked to look into the issue. It turned out that the contractor had simply lifted large chunks of RestKit, changed a few names, and removed all the copyright statements and comments (making it much harder to understand what was going on) and then checked that in as the new version. It was very obvious that this is what had happened because there was so much similarity between the new code and the old RestKit code that the source control system in one case considered the change to be a renamed file rather than a new one. I was quite surprised that the subcontractor had made such a brazen attempt to plagiarize code, and I recommended that the developer (or at least the subcontractor) be removed.

There were many discussions about copyright laws and the cultural and legal differences between the United States and the country where the subcontractor was located. The company decided that it had too much history with the development firm and the subcontractor and that it was too close to the desired ship date to change developers now. The company decided to just get the development firm to restore the copyright statements and return some of the money. Later, long after my part of the project was finished and I had moved on, I ran into one of the employees of that company and inquired about the end result. He told me that after keeping and continuing to pay that development firm for months without anything being shipped, they eventually had to fire the developer, and the entire code base had to be scrapped, at great expense. Turns out not only had the subcontractor been dishonest but incompetent as well.

Compiler Warnings

Virtually all modern development environments have mechanisms by which that tell you about issues that might exist in your code. There are errors that generally stop the compilation and build process, and then there are less serious issues, usually called *warnings*.

Warnings indicate that something may be wrong—that performance might be impacted, or crashes might be possible, or the code is using a development approach that has been changed since older versions of the development environment. Whatever the specific warning, it indicates that good coding practices were violated, and they shouldn't have been.

If you find warning messages in your code base, you should ask your developer to fix them, and if the developer gives you excuses, you should insist.

Duplicated Code

Code duplication is another metric that the TIOBE Code Quality Indicator uses. Beginning programmers often grab sections of code from one part of an app and copy that code to a different place and then make small changes to adjust the functionality to match the new need. The problem with this technique is that when it turns out later that there was a bug in the original code, it now has to be fixed in multiple places.

There's an easy fix for this, called *refactoring* (mentioned earlier), but refactoring takes diligence and effort. By leaving the same (or almost the same) code in multiple places, a developer is taking the easy way out—a way that leads to more bugs and more difficult maintenance in the future.

There is a type of code called *boilerplate* code—code that necessarily has to be the same or close to the same by virtue of the way it needs to be used. For example, any time in iOS programming that you need a table view, there are a number of methods that you are required to implement, and much of what those methods do is the same (and much of it is default code that is put in the file by the development environment at the point where you create a new table view file). It might not be the easiest thing for you to understand what duplication is boilerplate and what isn't, but in general, the more lines are duplicated in multiple locations of the code, the more likely it is to be a real problem.

Standard boilerplate code also turns up a lot in web searches (as described previously, in the "Detecting Plagiarism," section of this chapter), so that's another way that you can predict how big a problem duplicated code might be. And if it comes down to it, you can always ask.

Commented Out Code

As code changes over time, code that was formerly used may become useless. When this happens, the old code is often commented out (that is, turned into comments, as described earlier in this chapter). That's okay—at least in the short term.

As soon as the new code is working, however, the old code should be cleaned up. If not, it creates confusion down the road; code that's not cleaned up indicates a lack of confidence (and professionalism) in the developer. Code that has been left commented out for more than a few days (or more than the length of one milestone) is a red flag that your developer isn't doing good work for you.

Magic Numbers

Another bad coding practice is so-called magic numbers. *Magic numbers* is a phrase developers use to indicate a number that pops up in a formula or calculation somewhere in code with no explanation about what that number means.

For example, if the designer decided that there should be a 20-pixel margin between the left edge of the screen and the left side of a particular UI element, then when calculating where the button should be placed, the number 20 will end up needing to be used in that calculation. The problem is that, next year, it won't be at all clear where that number 20 came from. The correct programming practice in a case like this is to create a variable with a meaningful name, like `leftButtonMargin`, and set that variable to have the value `20`. At that point, when the calculation happens to determine the placement for the button, the name `leftButtonMargin` is used. This way, a year from now, when developers working on the next version of the app look at the calculation to try to figure out what's going on, they will know that someone decided that the left margin should be `20`, and they'll know whether they need to change that value. For more information, you can look up "unnamed numerical constants" on Wikipedia.

Huge Combinatorial Complexity

It's inevitable in programming to have sections of code that do either one thing or a different thing, depending on some value. The most common uses of this are if statements or switch statements. The issue comes when there are many if statements in a row.

There are many better coding practices than to have dozens of consecutive lines in a group of if statements, and your developer should be using one of them. If you find a giant switch statement or a bunch of if statements one right after the other, that is a red flag that the code you are getting might not be particularly maintainable.

Useless, Ambiguous, or Confusing Naming

It's been said that there are only two hard problems in computer science and that one of them is naming things (see http://martinfowler.com/bliki/TwoHardThings.html). There is definitely some truth to that, and the names of classes, methods, and variables are certainly subjective.

However, the naming of things is important, and it's something that you hope your developer will put a sufficient amount of effort into. Ideally, even a nontechnical person should be able to understand names, although programming terms do tend to creep into programmers' vocabularies.

At the very least, the naming of things should be consistent, by which I mean that if there is an object in your code base called a `Score`, and there's a method in the code base called `getScore`, then those things should be related to each other. If you find that the same word is being used to refer to different things, that's an issue and will likely cause problems down the road.

When asking clarifying questions of your developer when you don't understand something, feel free to reference the names of things that you don't understand. Let the developer know that the easier it is for you to understand what is going on by looking at the variable names, the less you have to bother him or her with questions. Hopefully the developer will get the message before too long.

The "UI Thread" or "Main Thread"

Most modern mobile platforms (at least iOS, Android, and Windows Phone) include the concept of a *UI thread*, or *main thread*. Without getting too technical, this is the mechanism the platform uses to update the screen that the user is seeing. If too much other processing happens on this thread, then the user experience suffers.

On the other hand, when processing is happening on another thread (often referred to as a *background thread*) and that processing needs to update the user interface, the background threads needs to cause that update to happen on the UI thread.

Each platform has at least one (and usually more than one) mechanism for pushing tasks between threads (and each platform documents these quite well). If you can find such a mechanism being used in your code base, that's great. If not, then as development progresses, ask your developer to show you some examples of where their code is using different threads and then look for other places that mechanism is used (by looking for other occurrences of that string). If the developer can't tell you how he or she is using multiple threads, or if the developer isn't using other threads except in one or two places, he or she probably is not knowledgeable or diligent enough to take full advantage of the platform, and you might have performance problems show up in your app later.

Wrapping Up

This chapter discusses how to use access to your source code to work with your developer, determine what intelligent questions to ask, and reduce the need for lots of meetings. It also discusses things you might find in your code base in the process and what they might tell you about the quality of your developer. Here are some key points to take away:

- Live within your means and within your agreed-upon scope, or project contention will almost certainly result.

- It is vitally important that you look in on your project frequently. The shorter the project, the faster it can go wrong and the harder it will be to recover.

- You should get access to the source control system as soon as possible, and you should build the code yourself to make sure you are actually getting what you are being told you are getting.

- Commit messages in source control should tie each code addition to some bug or task so that you can tell where in the project plan it belongs.

- Third-party components are usually helpful in small doses, but they're problematic if they're too invasive.

- Source code files that are too long are warning signs.

- Automated testing is a great indicator that you have a good developer, but chances are your developer won't use it much, if at all. It doesn't hurt to ask, though.

- Developers who steal code and present it as their own should probably be fired outright. The good news is that plagiarized code is fairly easy to find these days.

- The code you get (including third-party libraries your developer selects) should be free of compiler warnings.

- Code should not be duplicated or commented out for very long, if at all.

- Numeric and string constants should be given meaningful names so that future developers know what they are for.

- Large blocks of chained if statements or switch statements should be avoided in favor of more preferable techniques.

- Variable and method names should have a consistent scheme and make at least some semblance of sense to you.

- Your developer should have code that runs on the main thread and code that runs in the background, and it should be clear, even to you, that at least some code is in each category.

- When in doubt, ask your developer why he or she made something the way it is. You're paying for it, so you deserve to understand its purpose.

11

Pulling the Plug Early

This chapter discusses projects that seem to be heading for failure, what your options are, and how to decide what you should do.

When things aren't going well, remember that your project is on the line. As I've said several times in this book, many software projects fail. Once things get off track, the chance of failure greatly increases. It's much harder to rescue a failing project than to keep a project on track in the first place. If you do nothing to actively manage a project, failure is almost assured. Whatever you're going to do, it's important that you do it decisively. As discussed in Chapter 2, "The App Development Life Cycle," the later in the process a decision is made, the more expensive it is. In that chapter, we were talking about design decisions, but the statement holds equally true of staffing and contract decisions.

App creators really hate to switch developers. It takes time to find and interview and select a developer in the first place, and then it takes time to bring the person up to speed and get him or her to understand enough of what you're trying to do for the developer to be productive at all. Once you've done all that, you don't want to throw it all away and start over with another developer.

But it's more than that. App creators, like most other entrepreneurs and a lot of other humans, hate to admit when they're wrong. It's a perfectly normal desire. It's called the *sunk cost fallacy* or *throwing good money after bad* (see http://www.skorks.com/2010/04/software-development-and-the-sunk-cost-fallacy/). We don't want to believe that we made a mistake, and by hanging on to hope that we didn't, we make our losses worse. And the more money we've already spent, the more we want it not to have been spent in vain.

If there's one consistent message I've heard from the many app creators who have discussed their failed projects with me, it's that they wish they had made the decision to fire their poor developer earlier. In fairness, however, I don't know how many app creators are glad they ended up deciding not to fire their developers; those folks don't end up talking to me about their projects.

I'm going to try to keep the discussion in this chapter as objective as possible. Whether to pull the plug on an app project early is ultimately your decision, and it's not a fun one. Good luck with whatever you decide to do.

So You Missed a Milestone

If you suspect that your project is off track, you need to figure out how far off track it really is.

Typically, you don't find out that a project is off track until your developer misses a milestone deadline. This is sad but true. And it's yet another reason to have frequent milestones. On a project that has deliverables due only at the end of the project, it's far too common for the app creators to be told everything is on schedule right up until the end of the project's schedule, at which point they realize they're nowhere close.

When you know that you're going to miss a milestone, there are two questions you need to ask. The first is "By how much time, effort, and money are we going to miss (or did we miss) the milestone?" and the second is "Why wasn't the milestone hit on time?"

Developers, once confronted with the schedule they've missed, are generally quick to make all kinds of excuses. Do not get into a conversation about why they're late; that's a topic for later reflection. Your priority is to get an answer to the first question. This is going to require another estimation effort; you don't want to authorize a plan to get back onto schedule until you know what you're committing to. But how are you supposed to trust the estimate for the recovery when you obviously couldn't trust the estimate of the milestone?

Stop the Presses! Figure Out Where You Are

First things first: As soon as a milestone is missed, all work should stop. Do not authorize anyone to work further until you have a recovery plan you can live with. If your developer isn't okay with this, then walk away; you're done. Do not let the developer bleed you dry after he or she has already demonstrated not having the project under control.

You should also refuse to discuss any excuses and ask the developer to put together a firm estimate of what it's going to take to get the project back on track for your review. You should not have to pay for this estimate; this planning needs to be on the developer's dime. This is important. You have to make sure the developer understands that the milestones aren't just for show. There should be real consequences for missing milestones and deadlines; one of them is that the developer needs to give you a plan for getting back on track and foot the bill for it.

Make sure the developer understands that there are no second chances for this. If you agree to the recovery plan and the developer misses the date on it, you need to be done with that developer and go with someone else. And if the recovery plan is going to take more than a couple of weeks, then it needs to have intermediate milestones in it, and those can't be missed, either. So if there's uncertainty, the developer needs to guess high and give you an upper bound.

This plan also needs to have one additional section: an explanation of how this estimate was determined and why this estimate isn't going to be just as wrong as the estimate of the milestone the developer just missed. This is how the conversation about what went wrong should start—not with excuses given over the telephone but with an explanation of how the developer plans to do better.

Discussing Failure

I've spent years dealing with Internet connectivity services, hosting providers, developers, consultants, and other vendors, and over time I've come to a guiding principle: "Don't ever yell at the person with the keyboard." If the person who's actually creating the deliverables you need becomes upset with you, then at the very least and regardless of how professional they try to be, you won't get their best work. In the worst case, their emotions can doom your entire project.

Ideally, all discussions about how upset you are or about how badly things might be going should be directed at a manager in the development firm, although depending on the size of the firm, this might not be feasible. But do your best never to upset or blow up at the person whose work you are depending on. You can express displeasure to that person if you must but try to keep it as factual and unemotional as possible. There's no upside for you if the person in the trenches begins to dislike you, and there's lots of downside potential.

Milestone Hit but Bugs Abound

Another scenario is that the developer hits a milestone, but the code produced isn't acceptable. It's buggy or crashes or behaves unacceptably. From the point of view of this chapter, though, it doesn't matter what the particular problem is—just that the code is unacceptable. You need to know how you're going to get back on track and keep it from happening again. (Chapter 12, "Communicating Using Bugs," talks more about bugs.)

The primary thing you need to understand for the purposes of this chapter is whether the bugs were reasonable to expect. Many bugs (like virtually all crashes) are pretty obviously unacceptable and the developer's problem, but not all of them are. Some bugs arise from a difference between the way the developer expected the app to be used and the way the app is actually going to be used. It could be that the app expected one thing from the server and is getting a different thing or that there was a misunderstanding about what your developer thought they were building and what you wanted built (see the "If It Might Have Been Your Fault" section later in this chapter).

Some bugs, however, are indicative of issues with your developer, and you should take them as warning signs.

Regression Failures

Often, the bugs that pop up during a milestone aren't actually related to the milestone at all but are bugs that appeared in portions of the app that previously worked just fine. These are called *regressions*, or *regression bugs*, because they reverse the normal course of progress of the project. Regressions are the first step on the road toward the *whack-a-mole* problem, which is a mostly unrecoverable scenario discussed in Chapter 1, "What Could Possibly Go Wrong?"

Regressions that take noticeable time and effort to fix are not good. They often indicate that your app's infrastructure has been designed badly (not to be confused with the graphic design or interface design). They can indicate that your developer has been cutting corners and doing a poor job of isolating the different pieces of the app from each other, or that the app may be pushing the boundaries of the developer's skills and expertise. In my experience, projects that start experiencing regressions are much less likely to succeed than those that don't. Regressions are a warning sign you should take seriously.

If, after discussing regressions with your developer, you decide to stay with that person, I recommend starting the process of looking around for another developer; you just might end up needing one. And if you have regressions that interfere with a milestone a second time, I recommend that you switch to another developer.

Performance Failures

It's possible for a developer to believe that a milestone has been achieved because the app does what it's supposed to do, but you disagree because the app takes an unacceptably long time to do it.

Device Mismatch

When you and your developer don't see eye to eye on whether a milestone has been reached, you need to figure out what hardware is being used on each side. One cause could be that your developer is only testing on the latest and fastest phone (or a simulator running on a desktop-class machine) and you are using an older or less powerful device. (Chapter 4, "Determining Your App's Components," discusses choosing what devices to support.) It might be time to remind your developer that performance needs to be acceptable on the generation of devices that you selected and presumably agreed upon.

If you catch such a problem early enough, it hopefully won't take your developer too long to get things back on track.

Expectation Mismatch

If your developer insists that performance is fine, but you don't think so, then you have a problem. It's hard to measure objectively what *slow* really means, and it's hard to create a metric that will unambiguously decide which of you is correct. This makes it really hard to write such performance criteria into a contract.

Probably the closest potential metric we use is *frame rate*, which is the number of times an app can redraw the graphics on the screen in a given time period (usually one second). The problem is that we don't use that metric because it's a good one. We use it because it's one of the very few metrics we *can* use. It's easy to calculate and many tools will tell you what that number is, so people tend to gravitate to it. I know of some contracts that have specified acceptable frame rates, but outside of a few specific instances (like real-time games) I haven't found it to be useful, so I don't recommend it. I just wish there were a good metric available.

Recovering from performance problems isn't, unfortunately, a matter of agreeing on a clear-cut requirement so much as having a conversation or discussion with your developer. Pick one or more specific actions or sequences to focus on that feel slow to you (like transitioning from screen A to screen B or scrolling a particular screen). Ideally, you should make a recording of the focus area (as discussed in Chapter 12) so that you are both looking at the same thing. Tell your developer how long it feels to you that it should take (or how much faster you feel it should go) and then ask what would be involved in getting to that level of performance.

If the developer can accept what you are saying, and you can work out a plan to get there, that's great (in which case don't forget to revise the rest of your existing project plan to satisfy the new requirements). If not, then either your developer is saying that your expectations are unreasonable or that implementing them would be too expensive. In that case, you have a choice to make. If your developer is right in saying that, then either you need to adjust your expectations or abandon your project as hopeless. If your developer is wrong about that, then you need to part ways and find another developer.

In general, assuming that you are a regular user of apps on your chosen platform, your instincts are probably correct. If you've seen other apps that can do something similar to what you want your app to do in the amount of time you expect, then it's likely possible. The trick there is that those similar apps might have been far more expensive than yours. If your developer insists that it isn't possible but you've seen it done, then you probably want to move on—and do so sooner rather than later.

Don't Defer Performance Problems

If you get your developer to agree that performance is currently unacceptable, I recommend that you not let feature development continue until the performance issues are fixed. Moving ahead with new features at this point doesn't usually end well. (See the sidebar in the "Leaving the Worst for Last" section of Chapter 1 for one example.) Have your developer fix it as part of the next milestone and then hold the line on performance so that it doesn't get slower over time.

If Your Developer Is Proactive

If your developer comes to you before a milestone is missed and says that something has gone wrong and the milestone isn't going to be hit, you should give the developer some credit for being proactive. But to get credit, the developer has to really be proactive; sending you an email the day before the deadline doesn't count.

So, for example, if you get a communication explaining that something unexpected has just happened—your lead developer has become seriously ill or there was a fire at the developer's office or something—then you can have a conversation. Hopefully, you can just slip the schedule a little bit and try to make up some time later. But you won't be paying for the development while the developer is sick or is recovering from the disaster, so you should still be within your estimate for effort and cost.

This is the kind of working relationship you hope for. Be understanding and realize that things do happen. But if everyone is adult about it, you should be able to get through it just fine.

Remember that by having frequent shorter milestones, you're more sensitive to little delays. That's good because it prevents a series of little delays from adding up to a big delay without your knowledge. But it also means that you need to be reasonable when life happens.

As with any other milestone miss, you still need to get the developer to tell you (preferably in writing) how he or she intends to get back on track. But it's much better to be having this conversation in anticipation of a milestone miss than when the expected date is in the rearview mirror and there's still no deliverable.

If Your Developer Isn't Honest

It is my professional opinion that, if you discover that your developer has hidden things from you or lied to you, you should stop dealing with that person as soon as you can and find someone else. This is especially true if your developer is misrepresenting the progress he or she is making. If the developer says that a milestone has been completed on time, and then you later discover that was not the case, then it's time to walk away. In my experience, a project's chance of success only ever goes downhill from there.

If It Might Have Been Your Fault

There may be times when your developer legitimately believes that a milestone has been hit on time and under budget, and you run the app for yourself and find that it's not what you were expecting at all. This is likely the result of a miscommunication, but it's hard to believe this could possibly be entirely the fault of your developer.

You need to make sure you know what you are supposed to be getting (and paying for), and you need to ensure that you and your developer are on the same page in terms of what the next milestone is and what the app will look and behave like when the milestone is completed. If it turns out that you and your developer can get through a milestone with different ideas about what that milestone was set to accomplish, then something is very wrong with the way you and your developer are communicating.

In the event of such a miscommunication, I recommend that you go back to Chapter 3, "Prototyping and Wireframing Your App," and get an interactive prototype built and/or detailed wireframes to help communicate what your developer is supposed to be building. Get as much down on paper as you can. Then make sure there is agreement about the details involved before development starts again.

The Case of the Unspecified Transition

Once upon a time, I was working on a big project with a large development team, and I was assigned the task of making a particular screen look like the corresponding Photoshop document. It wasn't a tremendously complex screen, but it was complicated by the designer's desire to have the screen be somewhat transparent (or at least translucent) so that another screen was partially visible underneath it.

The screen already existed in the app, so I went about doing the styling, which involved juxtaposing the current screen and the underlying screen in a time-consuming way. I completed the task after a couple days of trial-and-error work, marked it as done, and went on to the next thing.

Some time later, the designer reviewed my work and told me that that screen wasn't supposed to slide in from the right, the way it was currently coded, but was instead supposed to slide up from the bottom of the screen. This meant the screen needed to be placed in the navigation hierarchy a completely different way.

The misunderstanding was twofold: First, I hadn't created the transition—someone else had already created the screen and the transition to get to it before I even started on the project—and second, nothing in the specification document or the description of the task I had been assigned mentioned the transition at all.

I was able to change the transition style of that screen, but it required throwing out and rewriting a lot of the code I had already completed, taking more time (and more of the client's money) than would have been required if I had understood all the relevant requirements at the outset of the task. Better communication and documentation would have avoided this waste.

Evaluating the Recovery Plan

One step in deciding whether a recovery plan is feasible is to understand why the initial milestone was (or is about to be) missed and how likely that is to happen again. There are basically two ways that a milestone gets missed: Either there was more work to be done than the developer expected or there was less effort available than the developer planned. The easy one of these to understand is the second; we've all gotten sick or had unexpected things come up in our lives.

Developer Availability Issues

Whether it's illness, a computer hardware failure, or a natural disaster, sometimes external events take time away from your project. The good news with these kinds of delays is that they generally don't impact the budget, only the schedule.

As long as the time frame of the missing effort is short, recovery in these cases is quite straightforward. The plans stay more-or-less on track, and either the schedule adjusts somewhat or extra hours of effort are found somewhere. For longer delays, things get more complicated. Sometimes a developer becomes unavailable for a longer time, requiring a shift to a new one (either at the same firm or by starting the developer selection process over again). I talk more about changing developers later in this chapter.

One thing to be wary of is multiple issues with developer unavailability. A fairly common technique of unscrupulous developers is to claim one illness or issue after another. If that starts and is left unchecked, it can even reach the proverbial "my dog ate my homework" level of excuses. Exactly when you should stop accepting these excuses is a judgment call. My advice is that when a developer first seems to be straining credibility, you should give an ultimatum that more delays will be deemed unacceptable and then stick to it: Cut off the developer the next time it happens.

Poorly Estimated Task Issues

If all the developers were available for all the planned hours during work on the milestone, the problem was that the developer underestimated the amount of work involved. This is more problematic than the other scenario.

Risky Items, Identified Early

The best-case scenario is that you are still early in your project and the milestone of concern is one you were told might be especially challenging. Chapter 8, "Interviewing and Selecting a Developer," discusses asking your developer what difficulties he or she envisions might arise during the project. Chapter 9, "Managing to Milestones," discusses moving those challenging sections as early in the project as you can. If you've done these things, then the recovery plan should be to find items that are scheduled to be done later in the project and try to reduce their scope to make up for the additional effort required for the current milestone. The whole point of moving risky items early in the project is to have time to make adjustments.

However, a developer identifying something as difficult isn't a "get out of jail free" card. You need the developer to explain to you what he or she is going to do, but to some extent, this is to be expected. Hopefully, the developer has provided you with suggestions on what might be changed to get things back on track and provided a new plan and schedule. Hopefully this new plan seems credible, and you'll be able to continue on your way.

Inability to Stay On Task

Inability to stay on task is probably the most common reason that milestones get missed, although it's generally not phrased exactly this way. Sometimes, developers say that they were using Agile techniques and/or responding to changes you made. Sometimes, they say they were working on tasks later in the project plan. Sometimes they say they were working on tasks that weren't in the plan but needed to get done. Usually, they just act like it's normal and don't say anything at all until you ask.

This is *business as usual* for most developers. We discussed in Chapter 9 that developers need organization, sequencing, and focus to successfully execute a strategy focused on frequent milestones. Most customers don't demand this, and most developers don't bother. It's very common for developers to work on whatever tasks they feel like working on as they go along. This isn't inherently bad, especially from the developer's point of view, but from the app creator's point of view, the scatter-shot nature of task assignment makes it very difficult to see whether things are on track. When this confusion accumulates week after week (or sprint after sprint), it's not unusual for projects to be far off the rails when the deadlines roll around.

If you're setting milestones roughly every week or two, as this book recommends, and if your developers confess to missing a milestone because they were doing off-milestone tasks (and especially if they seem nonchalant about it), it's time for you to put your foot down. If they do that over and over, your project will fail, so you need to make it clear that such behavior is unacceptable and that the next milestone missed will be their last.

If your project has less frequent (say, monthly) milestones, and a developer misses one in this way, I recommend (again) taking the opportunity to insist that milestones going forward should be far more frequent and kept on track.

Unforeseen Platform Bugs or Issues

Sometimes developers might tell you that the milestone was missed because they found bugs in the underlying libraries, frameworks, or platforms they used. This does happen. Famously in 2013, Apple's implementation of Core Data synchronization over Apple's iCloud was buggy and broken, and many projects that relied on it failed, some very publicly. There have also been bugs in numerous third-party frameworks and services, like those from places like Facebook, Twitter, and many analytics and advertising libraries.

Hopefully, they identified this sort of problem as a risk early on, but even if they didn't, you've got a choice to make. If it's true that there is a bug in the underlying platform, then another developer might not be able to do any better than the one you have now. Some limitations are outside the developer's control, no matter who the developer is. On the other hand, it might just be that the developer is using the framework incorrectly, and another developer wouldn't have this problem.

A good path to take here is to ask your developer for independent verification of the bug. For example, a bug report filed with the platform vendor or a question asked on the Internet that indicates that someone else in the world is also having this problem can indicate that this isn't just the incompetence of your developer. (A site called StackOverflow.com is a good place for these kinds of questions, as are vendor-specific developer forums like devforums. apple.com.) If what your developer claims to have seems like a real bug, then you should work with him or her to come up with an alternate strategy. If it seems that it isn't a real bug, then you might want to investigate new developers.

Unforeseen External Dependencies

In rare cases, a milestone gets missed because of something outside the developer's control. Usually this is a planning omission, but sometimes it's something like an unexpected new release of a device or a framework that needs to be incorporated. You should hopefully be able to determine whether it's reasonable for the dependency not to have been realized until the milestone was missed and assign culpability accordingly.

Larger-Than-Expected Overhead

Sometimes, tasks are required that weren't planned and don't involve the creation of artifacts that are part of the project or the project plan. Sometimes, these are small items like conference calls and meetings that don't end up pushing the project too far off track. Other times, these are more complicated and time-consuming tasks like merging together code from multiple developers or bringing new team members up to speed.

When we discussed cost overruns back in Chapter 1, we talked about staffing overhead. In general, it gets worse as the team size grows. This overhead can just be the cost of doing business if you're trying to throw as many developers as possible at a problem to try to get something to market as fast as you can. If, however, you didn't ask for that, it's time to talk to your developer about why so much time is being spent on communication within the team they've put together for you.

Tasks That Weren't Expected to Be Needed

Sometimes a milestone is missed because of tasks that weren't foreseen or estimated but were needed in order to achieve the agreed-upon functionality. This generally means that the person who created the estimate made a mistake and overlooked a necessary requirement. This is problematic.

The question you have to ask yourself is: "If the estimator forgot that something needed to be done once, what's to stop the person from having forgotten something else?" I don't have any foolproof way to answer this question, so you have to make your best guess.

One potential option at this point would be to use this as a negotiation technique to try to get a better price for the rest of the project. If you feel you are paying a premium for an experienced developer, but it turns out the developer isn't as experienced as he or she led you to believe, then asking the developer to reduce the price is not an unreasonable conversation to have (in my opinion). If the developer has proven that the risk to you is higher than you expected, it makes some sense for your costs to be reduced.

Mistakes and Bugs

Sometimes it turns out that the quality of work wasn't as good as planned, and it took extra time to get it up to standard before a milestone's functionality was reached. This isn't good, and it doesn't bode well for the rest of the project, but it isn't necessarily a death knell. Sometimes people make mistakes.

Different kinds of mistakes could have been made, and they have different consequences for the rest of your project.

Wasted or Duplicated Effort

One fairly common mistake that gets made, especially on larger project teams, is for effort to be duplicated or misdirected as a result of poor communication.

For example, in a process where each developer is responsible for grabbing the task that he or she wants to handle next, it occasionally happens that more than one developer grabs the same task. Normally there is some mechanism to prevent this from happening or at least identify when it does (like the *assigned developer* field in the bug-tracking database, discussed in Chapter 12), but sometimes the mechanism isn't used correctly.

One way that effort is wasted or duplicated is that two different developers to each solve the same problem (usually both writing code that does effectively the same thing). Only one of those solutions needs to be kept, so any time spent building the other solution was wasted.

Another way this happens is when information isn't sufficiently captured or specified when a developer is assigned a particular task. Then the developer, working under his or her understanding of the task at hand, expends some amount of effort on a solution. After that, someone with a different understanding explains to the developer what his or her expectations were, and then the developer generally has to expend more effort to change the solution to conform to the new understanding.

This again is wasted development effort. Hopefully, it's not as much of a waste as when two developers do the same thing, but it's still likely demonstrable and enough to cause a milestone date to be missed.

These scenarios indicate a lack of coordination and management of a development team containing multiple developers or designers. If an explicit effort is made to exert sufficient supervision over this team for the rest of the project, then it is possible that a similar issue might be avoided through the rest of your project. It's by no means assured, though, as this shouldn't have happened in the first place. Keep that in mind as you read through the developer's recovery plan and make your own assessment of how likely you think the developer is to have learned a lesson.

Developers Who Failed to Coordinate

Sometimes two (or more) developers can solve related problems in incompatible ways. This causes problems when an attempt is made to combine the disparate solutions, and then someone will have to expend additional effort to resolve the conflict, potentially even having to rewrite one of the solutions in a more compatible way.

As with the previous scenario, this is a result of poor communication, coordination, and/or supervision of the development team. It shouldn't happen (although it does), so talk to your developers about why they let it happen and how they are going to keep this and other communication failures from happening again. If they can't convince you, it's time for a different developer; if they do convince you, keep an extra eye on them anyway.

Bad Estimates

Sometimes tasks that need to be done are tasks that were planned, but they just take longer than the estimator expected. This has happened to me before when I have done an estimate for a project, and the project's development team (with whom I had not worked with before) turned out to be either slower or less experienced than I had anticipated. In some cases, I've created estimates before the developers were even hired. It's easy for any estimator to be pretty far off the mark in such situations.

The good news in this case is that it's fairly correctable; you just multiply the remaining effort in the project by the amount you were off to get the new estimate. The bad news is that it can be a lot more time and effort than you were initially sold.

This is another case where it's worth trying to renegotiate your rate. If the team you got is slower than the team you were promised, it doesn't make much sense for you to be paying the same amount for them.

How Far Gone Are You?

Your project's odds of recovering within your time and budget expectations are largely a function of how close you are to the expected end of your project, as illustrated in Figure 11.1. Consider the case that the milestone whose date your developer just missed was the last milestone in the project. In that event, your project just failed to finish on time, and it's too late to do anything about it.

This is why, back in both Chapter 1 and Chapter 9, we discussed moving the riskier or more uncertain parts of a project as early in the project as possible. By the time you're at the end of the project, hopefully you're dealing with simpler and straightforward tasks and don't have a lot of risk left to face.

If you're late in your project, and the milestone that was just missed is a big one, and your developer doesn't have a way of making it up in a short period of time, then your project has almost certainly failed. You may or may not be able to produce a successful app from it, but even if you can, it's almost certain to cost you more and take you longer than you'd planned.

There's a real problem here: The later you are in your project when something goes badly wrong, the harder it is to switch developers but the more likely you are to need to do so. A bad misunderstanding three weeks into your project is likely recoverable by the same developer, but a bad misunderstanding with three weeks to go means your developer has probably been hiding things from you, and you're far more likely to need to start over.

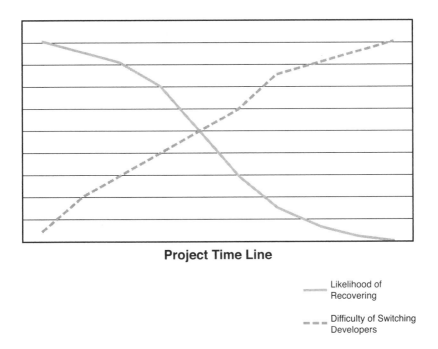

Project Time Line

_____ Likelihood of
Recovering

_ _ _ _ Difficulty of Switching
Developers

Figure 11.1
The further your project progresses, the less likely you are to be able to recover from a problem and the more difficult it will be to switch developers. Therefore, you should try to figure out how well things are going as early as you can, and if you need to switch developers, do it sooner rather than later.

The good news is that if you force your developer to deliver frequent milestones and you get the riskier ones out of the way early, you're far less likely to have a major misunderstanding late in the project.

Trying to Salvage a Project

The normal tendency late in a project is to avoid starting over. This tendency has some real merit. It is almost certainly cheaper, if it's possible, for your existing developer to finish than for a new developer to take over. The downside is that if you have a problem very late in the project, and there isn't a readily available solution, then it's not very likely to be possible.

If there is a big problem with your app, and your budget and schedule are mostly gone, chances are that your big problem is caused by a poor foundation laid much earlier in the project that has gone undetected (or deliberately concealed) until now. A developer who makes a foundational mistake and either didn't notice or actively tried to hide it for much of the duration of a project is unlikely to be qualified to fix it.

If you have any evidence or indication that your developer knew of a problem and actively tried to hide it from you, I strongly recommend that you not waste any more money or time with that person. You may or may not be able to recover any funds already expended, depending on your contract, legal costs, and the laws in your area, but you certainly will not be able to get your time back. Do not throw good money after bad, though. If a developer hid something from you once, he or she will likely do it again. I've talked to app creators who have spent three times more money and time than their initial estimate trying to get their app into a shippable state.

One way to potentially prevent getting sucked dry by a late-project failure is to defer any more payments until the problem is fixed. If the developer is willing and able to assume all the risk of fixing the problem while receiving no more money from you until it's done, then it might be worth letting the developer try. But if the developer requires additional money from you before trying to fix the problem, then it's probably better to walk away.

Fair Compensation

If you decide to change developers, you need to have paid for any code or documentation you take with you from your old developer. If you structured your project with fees based on milestones, then the developer deserves payment for milestones that he or she delivered and you accepted. It's not fair to do otherwise.

If, on the other hand, the developer never managed to produce much of value, then anything you are not planning on paying the developer for should not be used by you or given to the next developer. You may need to retain a copy of your failed developer's work for reference during potential future legal actions, but in no event should you allow any new work to be based on any code or documentation that you didn't pay for. Doing so might be asking for trouble later on, for both legal and supportability reasons.

Transitioning to a New Developer

The hard reality of moving to a new developer is that it means backtracking and wasting money. The new developer must take time to either understand your old developer's code or rewrite it (or both). Given that you already paid your old developer for that as well, you're going to be paying twice. You will have to either come up with more money and time or cut out scope and features (or both). There's just no way around it.

In addition, it's going to be difficult for your new developer to understand or work with your old developer's code, and the risk during this new phase of the project will be greater (see the "Renovation Versus New Construction" section of Chapter 9 for more information). That having been said, it's still better than paying an inadequate developer much more than you planned and still not ending up with an app you can be proud of.

My sincere hope is that by employing some of the techniques in this book, such as frequent milestones and risk-aware sequencing, you can catch a problem with a developer early enough in the project that the duplicate effort won't be devastating.

The process of acquiring a new developer is pretty much the same as that of selecting the first one (see Chapters 7, "Finding a Developer," and 8, "Interviewing and Selecting a Developer"). Hopefully, you will have learned something from your last experience and will be able to pick a better developer the next time around (or, if not, that you'll recognize the warning signs even earlier and cut your losses sooner).

The problem at the moment is that there is more demand for mobile development talent than there is supply. This means that finding a good developer is hard, you might end up paying more than you want, and even the good developers can fail spectacularly if they give in to the temptation to accept more work than they can actually do. But it *is* possible to find and work with a developer who can meet your needs—and tens of thousands of apps that can be offered up as proof.

Wrapping Up

This chapter discusses what to consider when trying to decide whether to keep your problematic developer or to switch to a new one. It also explains what's involved in switching. Here are some key points to take away:

- Most project problems aren't uncovered until a milestone deadline is missed, so make sure milestones occur frequently and pay attention to them.
- Do not let your developer miss a milestone and continue developing and charging you without presenting a plan for corrective action. The developer should provide you that plan free of charge.

- Regression bugs are a big problem and a big warning flag. Don't let them keep happening.

- Deal with performance problems as soon as possible; don't defer them until later.

- Cut off ties with deceptive or dishonest developers as soon as you can. If a developer proactively tells you about an upcoming problem, cut the person some slack and continue working with him or her.

- Legitimate, honest misunderstandings between you and your developer are at least partially your fault and likely indicate that your developer deserves a second chance. (But ensure that you agree on all the details so it doesn't happen again.)

- Understanding the developer's recovery plan and especially how the developer plans not to miss more deadlines the same way is key to deciding whether to keep your developer or get a new one.

- The earlier in your project you discover a problem, the more likely you are to be able to salvage your budget and schedule.

- Switching to a different developer is painful, but sticking with a bad developer is excruciating and potentially fatal to your project.

Communicating Using Bugs

No matter how good your developer is, or how much effort is put into your software, your app isn't going to be perfect. Even the extensively documented Space Shuttle software development process has not been able to produce perfect software, and that has far better quality control than anything your developer is going to approach (see www.fastcompany. com/28121/they-write-right-stuff).

The trick is to find the imperfections and get them fixed, and the best way to do that is to document and track each one of them. These days, the logical place to do this is on the web. This chapter is about using dedicated web applications that serve just that purpose.

Vocabulary

Before I get into the details of working with bugs, I need to deal with some ambiguous terminology. A *bug-tracking tool*, as you might guess from the name, is primarily used to track bugs.

Bug is used in development vernacular to indicate a problem or defect or mistake in a piece of software. As computers have infiltrated everyday life, it's become fairly common term.

Because the tools are called *bug trackers*, people think that all the things these tools track must be bugs. However, bug trackers are also used to track things other than bugs, like documentation errors, tasks, improvements, and features. Because of this, they're sometimes referred to as *issue trackers*, but the term *bug tracker* is more common.

To make things even more confusing, the term *bug* is applied both to an issue with software and to an entry in the bug-tracking tool that refers to that issue. The good news is that most of the time, it doesn't really matter whether a person is referring to the software problem or the corresponding bug tracker entry. For times when it does matter, you should be able to figure it out from the context.

Bug Trackers as Communication Tools

As discussed in Chapter 5, "Finding the Right Tools," a bug-tracking tool is one of the most important pillars of a professional development process. Of the tools that app creators use, the bug tracker is probably the single most useful one—and the most important.

Think of each bug or issue being tracked as a collaborative conversation with your developer (and potentially your testers; see Chapter 13, "Testing"). The bug tracker is a place for expectations to be explained and codified, objections to be raised and answered, and consensus to be reached. In most cases, if used to its maximum potential, a bug tracker is an effective replacement for the specification by the time the project has reached its stride. That's a good thing, because bug trackers are both far more useful and far less likely to become outdated than spec documents.

The other great thing about using a bug tracker is that the data collected in the tool can become a permanent record of how the project progressed over time. If the app becomes successful, this database will be useful long after the project has ended. As a developer, when I'm approaching an existing code base or joining an existing project development team, a well-cultivated bug tracker is invaluable in understanding what's going on.

A bug tracker can collect large amounts of information that users can then easily reference. A bug tracker can provide a URL for the web page for a particular bug, and a developer can use it to get the entire back story on the problem. A bug tracker also allows a developer to cross-reference similar or dependent bugs by including the URL of one bug in the comments field of another. (However, some tools have dedicated mechanisms for linking bugs together.)

In order to live up to its potential, a bug tracker has to be two things: collaborative and comprehensive.

Tracking Bugs Comprehensively

To be comprehensive, a bug tracker needs to contain all the correspondence and information about each particular feature, bug, and issue worked on during a project. The easiest way to make this happen is to make the bug tracker the primary point of communication. When you want to ask a question or get a piece of information about your project, instead of sending an email, add a comment to the relevant bug. After a while, this should become a habit you and your team get into.

It's inevitable that some correspondence will happen outside the bug system. For example, people will certainly send emails to each other. Instead of trying to fight against this tendency, you can simply copy and paste the emails into the comments area of the relevant item(s) in the bug tracker so everything is in the same place. The same goes with meetings and phone calls. When a conversation is over, put a summary of the conversation into the bug tracker. If several issues are discussed during a meeting, update each bug with a summary of what was said. For teams that use chat or instant messaging (IM) systems to discuss things, you can copy and paste chat transcripts into bug comments.

If you use the tracker this way, people will know that they can go to the bug tracker to find out the latest status of an issue, and they can enter any questions or additional information while they're there.

You can encourage this behavior by referring people to the bug tracker. If someone sends you an email asking for clarification about something, you can go the relevant issue in the bug tracker and put your clarification there, and then you can reply to the email with a link to the comment in the bug tracker.

Tracking Bugs Collaboratively

It's important to create a collaborative atmosphere around the bug tracker (as well as elsewhere in the project). This isn't as easy as it might sound. However, your project is far more likely to be successful (not to mention pleasant) if you and your developer see yourselves as being on the same team. If you and your developer see each other as adversaries, you project will be much more difficult to manage.

Bug trackers are, by nature, impersonal. As with email or any other digital communication medium, there are no facial expressions or tones of voice transmitted in a bug report. It's easy for people to take offense or hear accusation in written words when that wasn't intended. By trying to make a bug tracker comprehensive and trying to have it used for communication as much as possible, you encourage the use of a medium that, while good at collecting and retaining facts, is incredibly poor at transmitting human goodwill and understanding. This means you need to be especially careful about the language you use when creating and commenting on bugs to try to reduce the likelihood of someone getting upset.

The best suggestions I can make are:

- Try to use inclusive language; use the words *we* and *us* more than *you*.
- Try to ask questions more than make statements.
- When you make statements (especially about issues you've found with the app being built), be as factual as you can.
- When asking someone to work on a problem (or look at one), *ask* if the person will work on it instead of just assigning the problem to him or her. This doesn't take a lot of effort but goes a long way.
- When in any doubt, say explicitly that you're not blaming anyone or trying to upset anyone and mention your end goal of trying to make an app that everyone can be proud of.

This list might make it sound like all developers are prima donnas or oversensitive crybabies and that you need to walk on eggshells around them. That's not normally the case. But programming can sometimes involve frustrating tasks, and many programmers aren't known for their communication skills. I've seen a few instances of innocuous bug reports coming in as a programmer was fighting with an irritating problem and the programmer ending up with hurt feelings. The problem is that programmers may not be particularly communicative, and they sometimes let resentment build in these sorts of situations, leading to problems later in the project.

Bug Tracker Notifications

In order for a bug tracker to be a useful collaborative tool, it needs to be set up so that it notifies people when bugs are assigned to them or when bugs they are involved with are modified. Virtually all the modern bug-tracking tools have the capability to send emails when bugs are updated, but you do need to make sure that yours is set up correctly.

One Bug per Bug Report, Please

In order for your bug-tracking tool to be effective, you need to make sure that there aren't multiple bugs stuck on the same bug report.

Filling out bug reports can be tedious, and sometimes the temptation to describe several related problems on one bug report can be great, but you should resist that temptation. To help with the tedium, many trackers incorporate a feature that allows you to copy an existing bug and then change only the specific items that are different. See if your tracker has such a feature; if it does, it should help, at least somewhat.

The problem with having multiple bugs in one report is that confusion quickly sets in. When one of the multiple bugs gets fixed, there's no state to represent that. When a developer adds a comment to the bug report explaining what he or she has discovered, it's hard for someone reading the report to know which bug contained in the report the discovery pertains to.

Remember that your bug tracker should be a communication medium, and confusion and ambiguity contribute to poor communication.

Anatomy of a Bug Report

Bug reports vary somewhat, depending on the particular tool you are using, but some elements are common to most of them. However, different bug trackers may use different terms to refer to these elements.

Pretty much all bugs, in any bug-tracking tool, have a *title* or *name*, a short phrase that can be used in conversation so everyone knows which bug is being discussed. That's followed by a longer *description,* which has room for much more detail.

There's always a field (often called *ID* or *number*) that contains the unique identifier for the bug that is used as a reference so the bug can be definitively found. People should use this ID in all correspondence related to the bug so that everyone knows unambiguously what is being discussed. This ID is almost always included as part of a URL that provides a one-click link to the relevant bug. This is a great aid to facilitate communication.

Each bug then has a *type* (or *kind* or *category*) field that contains one selection from a list of words (or short phrases) that indicate what kind of issue it is. *Bug* (sometimes called *defect*) is the most recognized type, and it indicates that the given report is for a specific issue that was discovered in existing code through testing or inspection and that the reporter believes that it should be fixed (although not necessarily before the next release). An *improvement* or *enhancement* is a specific issue that was found either in code or in specification for code that, were it to be fixed or implemented, would make for a better product. A *feature*, by contrast, is a larger issue or piece of functionality that might be made up of several smaller issues. And a *task* is something that someone needs to do that may or may not be related to code at all. (For example, uploading your app to an app store where it will be sold is a *task*, but it's not a bug or enhancement or feature.) There may be others, but these are the most common.

The *priority* field indicates how important a bug is. Sometimes priority is expressed as a number (for example, "Priority 1" or "Priority 5"), sometimes with a quality word (like "Blocker" or "Cosmetic"), and sometimes with a level (like "High" or "Low"). Different teams have different rules for what bugs fall into each of these groups and what process might be used for each.

The *state* field shows what's happening with the bug at the moment. As each bug is worked, it goes through a number of these. See the "Bug States" section, later in this chapter, for more info.

Assigned or *assigned to* shows who is currently responsible for the bug. It might be the programmer currently working on it, the QA person currently testing it, or a project manager who is waiting for a resource to become available.

There's virtually always a way for people to add comments or ask questions, and a *comments* or *history* section of the bug tracker page shows all the comments (timestamped), along with other information, such as the dates the bug moved from one state to another.

There's also a way for people to attach files to a bug. Sometimes this is part of the description or comment field, and sometimes it's separate. Either way, it's a very useful function. Screenshots, videos, log files, and crash dumps can make fixing bugs much easier.

A bug tracker usually has a handful of less-important fields that contain information about when the bug was created and by whom, what other bugs are linked to this one, which users will be notified of changes, what sprint the bug might be attached to, and a number of other things that may vary, depending on the tool's implementation.

The primary purpose of these fields is to make bugs easier to find. When you're looking to see what bugs are being worked on or what is left to be done, being able to filter a bug list by the bug's state is very handy.

Feature Request Versus Bug Fix

The primary purpose of the bug type field is to allow you to search for (or filter by) the kind of issue you want to see right now. However, the terms used in this field can sometimes upset developers.

Some people hear the term *bug* and think that a developer did something wrong, or made a mistake that needs to be fixed. On the other hand, when they hear the term *improvement*, people tend to think that the developer did what he or she was asked to do, and then someone wanted something else. People hear the term *feature* and think that the developer hasn't gotten to something yet (and, if it's not a priority, may never get to it).

It can certainly be difficult to tell which of these terms is appropriate for a given issue, especially if you aren't technical. In theory, if you pick the wrong one, it should be pretty easy for someone to correct the type field and go back to work. In practice, however, it often doesn't work that way.

Developers (especially insecure or inexperienced ones) have a tendency to take things personally when someone opens a bug against code they've written. Eventually, as they get more experience, they realize that there are always going to be bugs, and they'll be grateful for any information that helps to get the bugs resolved and create a better product. This is especially true if the bug reports are well written, as discussed later in this chapter.

The other misconception (especially on fixed-price projects) is that issues marked as *bugs* have to be resolved as part of the existing project, and issues marked as *improvements* require change requests and additional fees. In fact, neither of these is necessarily true. It's perfectly reasonable to decide to live with a particular bug that would cost too much to fix or to roll an improvement that was just conceived into an existing milestone.

The misconceptions and insecurities are prevalent, though, so it behooves you to think about how to deal with them. If you can (not all tools allow it), it might be worth it to create a custom type value that is neutral that might reduce the potential emotional charge. (*To be decided* or *undetermined* would be good potential choices for such a value.) If you can't create a custom type, it might be worth erring on the side of picking *improvement* or *enhancement* over *bug* if there's any question. It should be easy to change the type later—much easier than changing the emotional state of a person who gets offended.

But the type field is only part of it. The first impression someone gets of a bug is usually the title field. This is because it's usually the subject of the notification email. If a bug title sounds accusatory to insecure developers, they're likely to get their hackles up before they even look at the type field or read the longer description.

When choosing a title, you want to be brief and factual but not critical. You want someone who is reading the bug to have an idea of what the issue is, but you don't want to make it sound like anyone's fault. Being politic with the title can be difficult, but practice will help you get there.

One thing I do sometimes is start a bug title with the phrase "[I] Don't understand," like, "Don't understand swipe to delete on History screen." Then I describe what I am seeing and what I expect and then I end the description with a question asking for clarification. Then, once the developer has looked at the issue and we've gotten some clarity on what's going on, we change the title to something more descriptive. (Often I ask the developer working the bug to pick a new, more appropriate title.)

If you're really concerned that someone is going to get upset, try getting someone on your development team on the phone first and talk through the issue before you write it up. They're less likely to get upset with you if they can hear your tone of voice (assuming that you remain calm).

Only after the issue has been investigated and everyone understands what's involved should you make a decision, in conjunction with your developer, about who is responsible for the issue and whether it needs to be addressed. (And if it does, you also need to determine when and whether it requires an extension to the contract.)

Placeholder Issues

Some people like to start off a project by creating one issue for each item in the project plan. I'm not generally a fan of this approach because it's extraordinarily difficult to do it well.

To be useful, an issue report needs to contain enough description and sufficient detail to be useful both to the developer working on the bug and to the QA person who will eventually be testing the issue. It needs to be clear and unambiguous and well written. In short, writing a good issue entry takes effort.

Trying to create one issue for each item over and over, time after time, for each and every line of a project plan is boring and tiring. It's easy to become frustrated and start doing a poor job. After a while, people usually end up copying and pasting the item titles out of the project plan, which is not helpful.

The other thing that happens is that the details of a project change as the project progresses. As lessons are learned early in a project, those lessons are hopefully applied to tasks further down the project plan. If entries have already been created for those later items, they'll have to be updated to reflect the new information. This can happen several times over the course of a project, causing a lot of wasted effort as all those written issue details become irrelevant.

My preference is to wait until an item is scheduled into the next milestone or sprint to fill out an issue entry for that feature.

Bug Trackers as Business Continuity

Using a bug tracker is a good way to capture the state information needed to recover in the event that your developer becomes unavailable (either because something happened to or with him or her or because you needed to make a change).

Personally, I like to update my open bugs as the last item of my workday so I can use them to keep track of what I got done, and so that the next morning I can remember where I left off and therefore where I should start next. But even if your developer doesn't go this far, if your developers keep their bug statuses up to date, they'll make it easier for you to continue on in the event that one or more of them leaves the project.

Bug Trackers Versus Code Comments

When you're documenting the approach to be taken to fix a particular bug or implement a particular feature, there are generally two approaches: Use comments in the source code itself or use the bug-tracking database. I tend to prefer using the bug-tracking database, for several reasons.

First, the bug database is generally available and accessible to a much wider range of project participants than is the source code. It's much easier for the designers and project managers and testers to read the bug web page than to check out and sift through the source code.

Second, the bug database is generally well organized and makes it easy to search for a particular issue or set of details. While bug trackers don't have perfect search capabilities, using them is far better than trying to search through code bases.

Finally, an attempt to solve a problem is current at a particular moment in time, and using a bug report is a better way to capture data in the context of the time that it was conceived than using source code. For example, imagine a developer being hired to work on the third or fourth revision of a particular app. The comments in the code file may have been created by the first developer in the first version of the app, but they were not updated by subsequent developers, so although the code changed for version 2, the comments from version 1 remained. It makes for a confusing situation when you're not sure what comments in the code you can trust. If there has been source control throughout all the revisions, then the developer may be able to figure out when a particular comment was created and then figure out if it's still relevant, but it's a time-consuming process.

Writing Useful Bug Reports

A lot of bug reports are pretty useless. Some even end up wasting development time. This is unfortunate because far more time will be spent with the app by its eventual users (assuming that it's successful) than will be spent during testing, and anything that pops up during the relatively short testing period and is not fixed will almost certainly appear again after release. It's a real shame for a bug to be found but not fixed because it isn't communicated well.

Focus on Symptoms, Not Solutions

The first thing about a good bug report is that it describes the problem, not the solution. Eventually, comments will be added to the bug, explaining what the solution will be, but it's important not to start there.

It's easy, especially for people who know the app well, to jump to a conclusion and miss the issue. I've seen dozens and dozens of hours wasted on implementing solutions that turned out not to address the problem that was actually occurring.

When creating bug reports, try not to write about what you think needs to be fixed, but instead to write about what's not working the way you expect it to and why you think that behavior is wrong. That way, you can make sure everyone understands the problem before you all get started on a solution. It's often helpful to describe the bug in terms of the answers to specific questions like the ones in the next few sections. Collectively, the answers to these questions are sometimes called *reproduction steps*, or *repro steps* for short.

What Screen Were You On?

For context, make sure each bug report contains where in the app you were when the bug occurred (or, for an enhancement, where in the app the change needs to be made). It's easy to assume that your development team will be able to figure out where you meant, but even if it's obvious, you should still clearly write it down for posterity.

Remember that if things go well with the app, at some point you're going to want someone to do a revision of the app. It might not be the same developer, and even if it is, that person might not remember the app process well enough to remember what you meant. By then you might not even remember what you meant, and that reduces the value of the bug history to your future development.

How Did You Get There?

It's often useful to mention what you did in the app before you got to the place where the bug occurred. If the same bug doesn't occur for the developer who is trying to fix the problem, then hopefully your information will help the developer figure out what might have happened.

This kind of information is often relevant. For example, there's a class of bugs that can occur when a developer doesn't clean up code. Say that a screen is created, and then the user taps a button and moves to a new screen, but some element from the old screen was left in memory, and that causes problems. If you describe a problem without explaining which screen you came from, the developer won't realize it was the previous screen that caused the issue.

What State Were You In?

Be sure to add any additional details that might be relevant, such as whether you were logged in and what preferences are set for that app. Also include what device you were using (for example, iPhone 5s or Samsung Galaxy S4), the version of the device platform (the iOS or Android version), and the build version of the app that you were using at the time.

What Did You Do?

Describe what you did right before the bug occurred, ideally in steps so others can be easily reproduce what you did. This is almost always the most useful type of information, so make it as explicit and detailed as you can.

Another thing to put here is whether this happens consistently. If it only happened to you once, you should still write it up, but say that you can't make it happen again. It might later be put together with some other symptom and be the clue that helps the developer understand what's going on there. It's also possible that later, after the app is released, you'll get more information from your users about this problem happening in the field, and this bug report will be helpful in tracking down and fixing that issue.

What Did You Expect?

After you explain what you did immediately before the bug happened, take a minute to describe what you expected. It's possible that it's just a misunderstanding that can be cleared up quickly, and a short conversation can save a lot of wasted effort. On the other hand, without clearly stated expectations, the developer might recognize the problem but fix it in a way that is contrary to your wishes.

What Did It Do Instead?

Next, you need to describe the behavior that you saw from the app that you didn't expect. It might be something as straightforward as an app crash, or it might be much more subtle. Be as explicit as you can about what happened that wasn't what you wanted.

Attaching Files to Bugs

It's a common adage that a picture is worth a thousand words. If that picture is a screenshot of a bug that you're supposed to be fixing, that adage might well be understating its value.

Most modern smartphones and tablets have the built-in ability to take a picture of the screen. On iPhone and iPad, you press the home button and power button at the same time. On Windows Phone 8, it's the Start and Power buttons, and on Android, it's usually Volume Down + Power (but might vary by manufacturer). You should get familiar with how to do this on your device and encourage your testers to do so, as well. (You'll learn more about external testers in Chapter 13.)

When you test your app and see something that indicates a bug, train yourself to take a screenshot as quickly as possible. Sometimes you'll be unable to figure out how to get a bug to happen again. In such a case, a screenshot will give your developer a better chance of figuring out what went wrong.

When you take a screenshot of a bug, attach it to the bug report you create. You might even drop it into a basic image-editing program and draw a circle around or otherwise indicate the part of the screenshot that is relevant (although this isn't required). Again, encourage other testers to do the same. These screenshots will help your developer immensely.

For more complicated bugs, it can be helpful to create a video of the issue you are seeing. You can do this by pointing a camera at your phone and recording it or through some software mechanism. The process I use most often involves Apple's AirPlay on iOS and a Mac app called Reflector to mirror my iPhone or iPad screen onto my Mac and then use the ScreenFlow screen-casting software to record my Mac's screen. It's kind of Rube-Goldberg-like, but so are all the other ways I know of to get a video of what happens on your screen.

But if you have a bug that's hard to understand, getting the right video can save many, many hours and might even be the difference between getting the bug fixed and not getting it fixed.

Likewise, it might be useful to attach console logs or crash report files or other information to your bug reports. Getting those files in an attachable form can be complicated, so ask your developer for instructions for your platform and project settings.

Data-Specific Bugs

Some bugs happen only when specific pieces of data are present in an app. Often apps expect data to be in a particular format, and when it's not, bugs can result. If there's a bug happening to one of your testers or users that isn't happening to anyone else (at least not often), it might be a data issue.

There's not a generic way to handle data-specific bugs for all apps on any given platform, much less across platforms. You should talk to your developer about getting the data out of that tester's copy of the app and looking into whether it might be causing or contributing to the issue.

Reproduction: There's the Rub

There's a dirty secret about fixing bugs, and it's this: Fixing a bug that can't be reproduced is incredibly difficult, even for very experienced developers. The normal process for fixing bugs is:

1. Force the bug to happen.
2. Watch the bug happen.
3. Fix the bug.
4. Try to force the bug to happen again and make sure it's fixed.

If you can't do steps 1 and 2, then step 3 is very difficult, and if you can't do step 4, then knowing for sure whether you did step 3 correctly is impossible.

The best possible chance that your developer has to fix a bug is to know exactly how to make it happen on demand. So the best way you can contribute to getting a bug fixed is to understand how to make it happen.

Ideally, you would go back to where you were in the app before the bug occurred and do the same thing again so you're sure what triggers it. Once you're confident of the trigger conditions, you can create the bug report and describe those conditions.

If you can't make it happen again, you should create the report anyway and describe what happened as best you can. But understand that without some amount of luck, it might not be feasible to fix that bug.

Bug States

Bugs go through a number of different states as they're being worked. See Figure 12.1 for an example of a typical system.

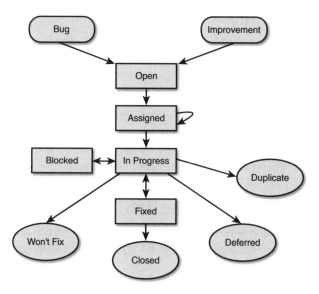

Figure 12.1
A common set of states for a hypothetical bug tool, with arrows showing potential state transitions.

A bug generally starts in the *open* state (sometimes called *new* or *created* or something like that). Later, it gets *assigned* to a person; sometimes this doesn't have its own state value, and you can tell if it's assigned by looking at the assigned field mentioned earlier in this chapter. Bugs can get reassigned, which means the state doesn't change but the responsible team member changes.

Once the responsible party starts working on the bug, the state changes to *in-progress* or something like that; some tools that don't track time on task skip this state and just use *assigned*. While the bug is being worked on, the state can change back and forth between *in-progress* and *blocked*. *Blocked* means that the bug can't be worked because something unavailable is needed (for example, the assigned user is waiting on clarification of a requirement or waiting on a fix from the server team or a platform vendor).

If the assigned user fixes (or thinks he or she has fixed) the bug, that person marks it as *resolved* or *fixed*. At that point, it's typically assigned to a QA resource or the person who originally opened the bug for verification. If that person agrees that the bug has been fixed, it becomes *closed*, and if not, the person sets it back to *in-progress* and reassigns it to the programmer who marked it *resolved*.

Other possibilities include *closed as duplicate*, which means there was more than one bug report opened on the same problem, and this one was not the one chosen to be worked on. *Won't fix* or *as designed* means that the behavior reported as a bug is actually what the designer intended, and no more work will be done. *Deferred* means the bug won't be worked until later, usually the next release.

Other potential states include *in test* and *being verified*, which are in between *fixed* and *closed* and act as *in-progress* states for testers. Some tools also have a *reopened* state, where bugs go if they fail verification.

I'm sure there are others, but this is the majority of them, so you should get the idea. Whatever reporting tool you use should have a list of states documented, and your developer should be able to explain his or her ideas about what process to use.

Reopening Bugs Versus Creating New Ones

One point of contention among development teams is what to do when a bug is closed and then later pops up again. Often this happens with an intermittent bug where it's believed that the bug was fixed because it hasn't happened in a long time, and then it reappears. Some teams at this point reopen the existing bug. That's a valid strategy, but it can cause confusion when later you are trying to understand how long it took to fix the bug. It's especially confusing on tools that have a *reopened* state because when doing a search, it's easy to forget to include that state as a search criterion.

My preference is to open a new bug and link it to the old bug. This is primarily because there were generally code changes associated with the original bug, and there will be new, different code changes associated with the reopened one. It's often the case that there is more than one way for the same symptom to be triggered, and each of these triggers gets fixed in code. In that case, it makes sense to have one bug report for each trigger to be fixed.

Making a new bug also makes it easier to look at the difference in time between when the bug was created and when the programmer got it fixed. This is a useful metric that becomes hard to calculate when a bug gets closed and reopened numerous times.

It's also clearer to me to look at several linked bugs that each have an explanation of what changes the programmer made to try to fix the problem than to look at one long bug that contains explanations of several different attempts at a fix. Your opinion may differ, though.

The Case of the Never-Ending Crashes

Once I was brought in on a project that was well under way. The architecture for the app had long been defined, and there were issues with thread containment.

Certain kinds of components and libraries, in this case Apple's Core Data, are not *thread safe*, which means that the libraries are safe to use only if they're only accessed on one thread at a time. If you need to access these libraries from multiple threads (as you often do for performance), you have to keep your interactions with that component *contained* within a single thread for the length of the interaction. If you have multiple groups of interactions on multiple threads, then it's vitally important that those interactions stay on their own respective threads.

In any case, this app had done a poor job of keeping these interactions separated, and at one point during testing, the app crashed. A bug report was opened, including a crash dump file, and the bug was assigned to me.

I found from the crash dump the line of code where the problem had occurred, and I prevented that sort of issue from happening there again. I resolved the bug and moved on. Soon, though, a similar crash happened at a different place in the code. The previous bug was reopened and assigned back to me. I dissected the crash dump and found that the crash was in a different place. I found the common issue between the two pieces of code and discovered that it was a widespread problem. I suggested that we needed to restructure part of our Core Data interactions, but the lead developer didn't think it was necessary, and I was instructed just to fix the crash that had happened.

This scenario repeated more than a dozen times. Each time the crash was in a different place, and each time I was told it wasn't a systemic problem.

Looking at the bug database, this problem didn't look like a structural flaw that exhibited itself in many different ways, but rather as a single bug that took an apparently incompetent developer more than a dozen attempts to finally fix. (However, my guess is that there were crashes after the project shipped that were attributable to the same bad design pattern.) By having each of those crashes logged as its own bug, it would have been much clearer to show that a significant percentage of the bugs we had were related to a thread-containment problem.

Splitting Bugs

Sometimes when working a bug, a programmer discovers either two potential causes that both need to be fixed or multiple places in code where the same mistake appears. While all those fixes can be piled on the same bug report, I prefer to make copies of the original bug for each change that needs to be made in code. Each copy should then get comments that explain the particular instance of the problem that the programmer is fixing at that time, and then a fix should be made.

Writing up a report for each bug keeps the mapping between the bug report, the associated comments, and the code changes much cleaner, at least in my mind.

Two Bugs, One Cause

Another potential disagreement arises when considering the issue of what to do with two different symptoms that both have the same cause. If one code change can resolve two different symptoms, should that be one bug report or two?

I'm less confident about my preference here than in other areas related to bugs. There are legitimately two symptoms, so it makes sense to me to report on two bugs. But when correlating a single code change to the bug tracker, it's more comfortable to me to have a one-to-one correlation between that change and a bug. I tend to close one symptom as a duplicate and tie the other to the code change (potentially changing the description to be more general so it can potentially encompass more than one symptom).

Whatever you choose, there's not a *right* answer. It is, however, important that whatever you do, you do consistently throughout the project to avoid confusion when working on the next version of the app.

Saving for Posterity

I recommend archiving the bug-tracker database at the end of each project. Few people do this, but the information contained in the numerous conversations that have taken place within the tracking tool can be invaluable when developing future iterations of the app.

Wrapping Up

This chapter discusses bug trackers and how to best use them. Here are some key points to take away:

- Bug trackers can track not just bugs, but also new features, improvements, and tasks.
- A bug tracker is very valuable as a communication tool between you, your developers, and your testers.
- It's important to maintain as close to a one-to-one relationship between code changes and bug reports as possible.
- Bugs trackers are valuable sources of captured information, but it's important to be cognizant of how those bug reports might be emotionally received by your developers and to take their potential feelings into account.
- To be useful and increase the chance of a bug getting fixed, the bug needs to be clear and to contain enough information for the developer and tester to know how to reproduce the bug.
- Archiving the bug database at the end of a project is a great way to create a knowledge store of what happened. This store is very valuable when creating future releases of the app.

13

Testing

An old friend I've worked with at a few different companies is fond of the phrase, "You get what you test for." The unspoken corollary is "Anything you don't test for, you aren't guaranteed (or likely) to get." Over and over through the years, I've found him to be right on this. Testing is where the rubber meets the road, so to speak. It's really the ultimate place to make sure you get the app that you want (and have paid for).

Types of Testing

There are several different kinds of testing. Chapter 3, "Prototyping and Wireframing Your App," discusses testing user interfaces and getting feedback on visual design. This chapter, on the other hand, focuses on testing functionality.

Even when you're just testing how an app works, there are a number of tools at your disposal:

- *Automated testing*, which is very useful but often ignored in the mobile application space.
- *General testing*, which is using an app as intended in real-world situation and seeing if anything goes wrong.
- *Verification testing*, which is checking a specific feature or workflow to make sure it works as intended (often in response to a bug being fixed or right after a new feature is implemented).

- *Regression testing*, where the tester verifies that the behavior of something that previously worked still works. (As with verification testing, this is done in response to a bug being fixed or right after a new feature is implemented.)

- *Permutation testing* or *state testing*, which involves iterating through and testing different situations (like *logged-in while offline with data cached* followed by *logged-in while online with an empty database*, etc.).

- *Exception testing*, where the app is put in unusual situation (like *Airplane mode*, leap years, daylight savings time, low memory, disk almost full, etc.).

- *White box testing*, where an experienced tester looks at the application architecture, makes intelligent guesses about what could go wrong, and constructs tests to see what does go wrong. (For example, what if transaction records are received out of order? What happens if a tweet from user X is received before the app has seen the user profile of user X?)

Each kind of testing has a role in making sure your app has the quality that your users want and expect. And that's what you're going for here: a quality app.

Failures of Imagination

In his testimony during the aftermath of the *Apollo 1* fire, Astronaut Frank Borman famously blamed the disaster on a "failure of imagination" (see http://en.wikipedia.org/wiki/Failure_of_imagination).

Now please understand that by bringing that up, I am not trying to imply or pretend that building apps is anywhere near as difficult as rocket science, and I am not trying to belittle the extraordinary efforts of the *Apollo* engineers or the sacrifices of the brave men and women who have given their lives in the pursuit of space travel. I'm saying that a "failure of imagination" is a human shortcoming that applies across the spectrum of human endeavors, and whether you are testing spacecraft or software, it's a constant risk.

I've lost count of the number of times in my career that I've seen a developer react to a bug report from a user with some variant of the phrase "I didn't know I was supposed to make [the software] do that."

Examples of these bugs abound and include such cases as these:

- Putting 100 or 1,000 times more data into an app than the developer was expecting

- Trying to perform network operations with a fraction of the bandwidth required

- Trying to load a video into an image-processing app
- Adding strings with unexpected data into an app (like hyphenated names, non-roman characters, and words much longer than expected)
- Dealing with confusing daily time zone changes (for example, living in one time zone but commuting to work in a different one)
- Losing access to an email account
- Using the app in an unusual case or mount while driving or working out
- Needing to use the app for both home and work and needing to keep those two contexts separate
- Trying to use an unexpected workflow the user is familiar with from using a competing app
- Wanting to use the app while on the phone, navigating, or listening to the built-in music player
- Using a Bluetooth keyboard (or custom keyboard on operating systems that support one)
- Using the app while projecting it onto a TV or a wall
- Having an unusually small or large screen resolution
- Needing finer-grained control of preferences or notifications
- Using the app on two different devices simultaneously
- Needing to use the app with only one hand
- Having to enter the same data each time they use the app, when the developer expected the data to usually be different each use
- Entering new data every time, when the developer expected the users to normally pick from a most frequently used list

We developers and app creators often fail to imagine the expectations our users have of our software. The previous list is but a tiny fraction of all the ways an app can be misused.

Of course, some bugs are obvious. And those will be found. Others will be discovered in the course of verifying the functionality of the features your developers have built.

Much of the rest of them, though, are mismatches between what the developers built and what the users expected. Finding those bugs requires either flawless imagination or finding people who have similar expectations to your users. Hopefully, you will be able to find testers with appropriate expectations.

Your Testing Schedule

This book has mentioned several times that the later in the process you do the design, the more expensive it is. So it's hopefully no surprise to you that the later in the process a bug is found, the more expensive it is to fix. And, given that all software has bugs, the trick is to find the bugs as soon as possible. So hopefully, despite the fact that this chapter is at the end of the book, you will set up your test process long before the end of your project.

That said, the last thing that always happens before shipping an app is a final round of testing to make sure you didn't miss anything. As discussed several times before (even as far back as Chapter 1, "What Could Possibly Go Wrong?"), leaving testing for the very end of a project results in low odds of success. This chapter is about how to do that testing, both at the end of a project and throughout.

Push for User-Facing Functionality Early

For your app to be fully testable, you need to have functionality in it that's visible to non-developers running the app on their own devices. Very early in the app development process, there's often nothing to see or test. The longer this continues to be the case, the more risk you run.

So do your best to get one of your earlier milestones to involve user-facing functionality and then try to add more functionality every few milestones (if not every single one, which would be ideal). The more functionality you can get into the hands of your testers and the earlier you can do it, the more time you have for testing and the better your app is likely to be.

Scheduling for Epiphany

Although the use of interactive prototypes (refer to Chapter 3) goes a long way toward minimizing it, once you are able to actively use your app over a period of time, it is common to get ideas about how the app could be improved. The same will likely happen with other users once they have used your app frequently over the course of days or weeks.

There's unfortunately no way to predict when (or even if) such moments of epiphany will occur. Ideally, though, you would like them to happen while there is still room in the budget and schedule to incorporate the newly conceived changes.

So the best strategy for taking advantage of this phenomenon is to set the stage by getting a functional (if unfinished and unpolished) app into the hands of as many caring, conscientious people in your target demographic as you can (including yourself) and baking as much time into the schedule as possible for ideas to pop into all those heads.

You also need to make sure there's an easy way for those ideas to make their way back to you, via some sort of feedback mechanism, whether it's email, a dedicated feedback service, or something your developer has built into the app. Once that is in place, you can only hope that any *eureka!* moments happen before you've shipped your app and that they're captured and brought to your attention so that you can decide whether they're worth pursuing. At the very least, you can try to get them into the next version.

Avoiding Wasted Testing Effort

If you start testing early in your project (and you should), and if you use professional testers (and again, you should), you run the risk of frustrating your testers and wasting their time if you have them test things that aren't ready. It's very annoying to both the tester and the developer when a tester spends a lot of time cataloguing issues with a particular part of the app, only to be told, "Oh, we haven't finished that part yet."

There are actually two problems here: a communication problem and a sequencing problem. We've already discussed a solution to the communication problem: Use a bug-tracking tool (see Chapter 12, "Communicating Using Bugs"). By keeping your bugs sufficiently detailed and up-to-date, you can make it possible for your QA testers to know what's ready to test and what isn't.

The sequencing problem isn't so easily solved. It goes back to the milestones discussed back in Chapter 9, "Managing to Milestones," but it's even harder. Organizing a project along milestones can be difficult, but making sure all those milestones are accessible to your testers complicates things further. Many perfectly valid milestones create necessary internal structure but don't expose any user interface that a tester looking at the app running on a device would find useful.

While it's admittedly difficult, it's certainly not impossible. One strategy I use is to identify the various pieces of functionality that it would be useful to have a tester verify, and then I work backward during the planning phases to figure out what tasks will need to be completed in order for that functionality to be exposed. Once you've identified the different interdependencies of the tasks, you or your developer should be able to figure out a sequence that gives your testers something useful to do reasonably early in the project and keeps them occupied through the end.

Publishing Apps to Testers

For most testing to take place, the development version of your app needs to be installed on the tester's smartphone and/or tablet. If the person to be testing is a developer and has access to the source code, that person should be able to get the app installed without help. Most testers, however, need an easier mechanism for getting an app installed.

The most helpful thing you can do is to create an installation procedure to give to your testers that walks them through installing the app. The additional benefit of providing the testers with such a procedure for your app is that you can make sure that they're testing the version of the app that you want them to test. That's more difficult for you to ensure if they're building and installing the app themselves.

Thankfully, creating such a procedure doesn't have to involve figuring out the installation process yourself. A number of third-party services simplify this process for you, as discussed in the "Beta Testing Distribution" section of Chapter 5, "Finding the Right Tools." In the not-too-distant past, the only good choice for this was a service called TestFlight, but that's not true anymore. TestFlight was purchased by another company, and a handful of alternatives have sprung up. There's no predicting what will be the best fit for your needs by the time you read this, but a web search should turn up a list, and your developer should be able to help you narrow it down. Once you've selected the service you are planning on using, you should be able to take the instructions the developer provides and turn them into a procedure for your own testers to use.

Of course, before testers can download your app from your beta distribution service, the copy of the app for them to test needs to be uploaded to the service. I urge you to figure out a way of automating this because it will be happening quite frequently. Uploading the test version from a *continuous integration* (CI) environment is a good choice for this automation and has additional advantages. As you work on that, it's also worth getting set up to collect crash dumps from your beta apps. This might be the same service or a different one, but the upload process should be similar. When (not if) your test app crashes, having access to the crash dump is likely the only real chance you have of getting the crash fixed. See Chapter 5 for more on continuous integration and crash reporting tools.

Another thing that is worth doing while you're putting together this process is to make sure there's some build number or version number that gets embedded in the app on its way to the beta distribution service and that there's some way for the end user (or tester) to find that number and include it with bug reports. It gets very frustrating when testers are reporting bugs that you think should have been fixed and there's confusion about whether the app in which they are still seeing the bug contains the attempted fix for the relevant bug.

Then, once this process—hopefully with step-by-step instructions—is all put together, you should test it yourself and ideally have one other non-developer test it before you send it out to all your testers.

Approaching Deadlines

As you approach the end of an app project, there's a period of time when all development work should have stopped, and only testing, verification, and bug fixing remain. Sometime before this, design work should have stopped, and only development and testing should remain.

If you have a hard deadline (self-imposed or otherwise) for when the app needs to ship, make sure you plan for these phases by scheduling a date for the end of design work followed by a date for the end of feature development work. Don't try adding features right up until the deadline. As we've been saying all along, the later you make a design decision, the more expensive it will turn out to be, and the last-minute design changes lead to lots of performance and reliability problems that can kill an app's adoption.

There's no hard-and-fast rule for how long these two phases need to last (although I generally guess that they should be on the order of some small number of weeks). Talk to your developer about getting these dates baked into the schedule if you need to work backward from a deadline.

Your Testing Team

Testing is a team effort. It's easy during the app creation process for people who have been designing and developing the app day after day to get tunnel vision—to focus only on the way the app is supposed to be used. This reduces their ability to be ideal testers. They don't use the app the way that normal users would. While there is certainly value in having these people do testing, they should be supplemented with other people.

Professional Testers

It is possible for you to test your app yourself, together with your developers and a small group of test users. Unless your app is trivial, however, you're going to miss things. A professional QA department can find the vast majority of the things you're going to miss. They won't catch everything, but QA and testing are skills that people improve over time. In many instances in my career, good QA testers have found bugs that I don't think I ever would have found.

The Value of a QA Department

A good tester makes a huge difference in the quality of the final software product. The more good testers you have, the better your app will likely be.

From what I've seen, there are two things that affect how good a tester someone is: mindset and experience. Some people are just inherently good at thinking in terms of what could go wrong. I don't know how well that can be taught. But whether you have the mindset or not, the more experience you have with testing apps, the more likely you are to find bugs. Experienced testers recognize the patterns of bugs they've seen before, and the more bugs they've seen, the more patterns they can recognize.

The really good testers are the ones that started with the right mindset and then have years of exercising it under their belts. Those are usually the ones who are making a living at it.

The Case of the Perpetually Fresh Cookie

I once worked on a project that used web cookies to maintain login information. That's not bad in and of itself, but the code that managed it was badly buggy.

The first bug was that the logic of whether to refresh the cookie was reversed, so if the cookie was fresh, the app would go get a new one, and if the cookie was expired, it would attempt to use the existing cookie. That generated a lot of unnecessary server load but wasn't fatal. The second bug was in the code that tried to use the existing cookie, and it crashed the app.

The result of this was that every time the app was run, a new cookie was fetched, unless the app hadn't been run in a long time (long enough for the cookie to expire), in which case it would crash on startup and forever more. This is a nightmare scenario—a very hard-to-find case that causes unrecoverable and catastrophic problems for any user who manages to trigger it.

Those of us who were developing and testing the app were running it frequently enough not to trigger the bug. There's no way I would have ever found it. Bugs like that are found one of three ways: by coincidence, by a professional tester who knows how to look for such things and methodically goes about doing it, or by unsuspecting users who stumble across it after the app has already shipped.

This kind of bug, if it isn't found before release, will be found by users if your app becomes widely available. The same is true for many other kinds of hard-to-find bugs. It's the law of large numbers. Even a rare bug happens frequently if you have enough users for your app to possibly be considered a success.

You don't have to hire a professional QA group (or person) to find those bugs, but if those bugs exist, professionals will likely give you the best shot at finding them before your users do.

Acquiring a QA Department

A development firm may have a dedicated QA department that tests all the apps the firm builds for clients. Alternatively, some companies provide dedicated QA testing as a stand-alone service; some of these just do QA, and some provide development services as well.

In my experience, there hasn't been a lot of difference between using a QA department that belongs to the company that is doing the development and using an external QA department. In theory, you might think there could be a conflict of interest because, if the QA folks and the development folks work for the same company, there might be pressure to make the developers look good by hiding bugs or just not reporting them. I can imagine a scenario where that might be the case, but I've never seen it happen. I can also imagine a scenario where two different firms, one doing contract QA and one doing development, might be adversarial to each other. However, I've never seen that happen, either.

The good news is that a bug is pretty much there or it's not; it's not really subjective. So it doesn't make a difference whether the QA testers you are working with came from the same company that you got your developers from. What does matter a great deal is whether you use professional testers.

Developers as Testers

We've already established that your developers have far too much information about how your app is supposed to work to think like your app's typical users. But that doesn't mean they have no role in testing. Much to the contrary, they have the ability to test your app in ways that no one else can.

Forced-Failure Testing

Things can happen when your app is in the wild that are so rare that you might never see them during testing, but some user is almost certain to run into them at some point. While you and the other testers who are using the app itself on a smartphone or tablet can't effectively test those scenarios, your developer can write code to make them happen. The developers can force the app to a failure state on demand.

For example, you can switch your phone into Airplane mode (or whatever your platform calls the setting where access to the data network is blocked) to see what your app does when no network is available. However, you can't control where in the process of the app's normal operations this happens.

Imagine that your app makes two different but related network requests to the server (this is fairly common), like a Twitter app that makes one request to get the text for the latest tweets in your time line and another request (or more than one) to get thumbnails for the pictures embedded in the tweets. Imagine that the request to get the text of the tweets succeeds, but the network goes down before the thumbnail retrieval has completed. What would the app do then? How would you test that? What are the odds that you could flip the Airplane mode switch at the perfect time to be able to check it yourself?

Your developer can write code to drop your app's access to the network at that critical point in order to test the behavior under those conditions. There's no other way to test a scenario like that reliably. That scenario needs to be tested because it can lead (and has led) to intermittent crashes in the real world on real users' phones. And it's just one of many such cases.

Automated Testing

Automated testing, introduced in Chapter 2, "The App Development Life Cycle," is not the holy grail that some advocates might lead you to believe. It's not particularly effective at testing user interfaces, and the testing tools available in the mobile space lag far behind those in other parts of software engineering. That said, for the things that testing does cover well, it's the single most valuable tool in the toolbox.

What automated testing does cover well is a lot: calculations, computations, processing, storage, retrieval, parsing, sorting, filtering...anything that isn't displaying things to the user. If your app does any of these things, then testing will help. If your app doesn't do anything like that, then I'm not sure why you're bothering to create an app. (Even games have calculations.)

Automated testing is not a substitute for real people testing your app; automated tests are written by developers, and so they have the same blind spots and expectations that the developers have. Many things that your professional and external testers will find are things that didn't occur to the developers to test in the first place. If the developers didn't think to test these things, they certainly wouldn't have thought to write automated tests for them.

What automated testing does is reduce a lot of the regression bugs (and reduce the need for regression testing). Once a feature has been written and a test has been written for it, anything that breaks that feature should show up as soon as the tests are run. This is a good thing because, as discussed earlier, the sooner you find a bug, the cheaper it is to fix.

Some people (including many developers) react to the previous assertion by saying that reducing regression testing isn't a big deal because a good developer can figure out how to keep from breaking the existing functionality. And to some extent, for a period of time, that's true. However, in my professional opinion, it's very shortsighted. A developer can only really avoid breaking functionality that he or she understands. If you don't know how everything works, it's hard to know what, if anything, the code you're changing will affect. It's easy for the person who wrote the code in the first place to know how everything works—at least for a while.

Do you hope that your app will still be running in a year or two? I hope so on your behalf, because if you don't, once again, I'm not sure why you're bothering to create an app. If you hope your app is still running in a couple of years, can you imagine wanting to add new features to it then? If so, do you think your developer is still going to remember how everything in your app works in a year or two, when it's time to add new features (assuming that your current developer is even available then)?

Trust me when I say that, as someone who has taken over many code bases, a good automated test suite will save you thousands or tens of thousands of dollars when you go to build the next version of your app. As a developer unfamiliar with a particular code base (because it's new to me or I haven't looked at it in months), tests save a significant amount of development time. And your developer's time is your money.

But more than that, a good test suite encourages experimentation and confidence while reducing hesitation and fear. If I know that I can easily detect and fix anything I break, I'm much more willing and able to build new features. If I know I can break core pieces of an app without easily realizing it, then I'm going to be scared every time I need to make a change, and I'm going to hesitate to give you estimates for adding features, and I'm going to dread giving you new code for fear that I've missed something.

External Testers

You bring on external testers, also called *beta testers*, later in the process. Unlike your professional testers, your external testers need a functional (although not necessarily complete or polished) app to use and test; they generally lack the patience to work around unfinished portions of the app.

Also, unlike your professional testers (but in a good way this time), your external testers are much better representatives of your app's potential audience. They are far more likely to give you the ideas you want that will be of value to your user base. Any issues they find or confusion they have will also be much more valuable to your understanding of your target audience's experiences.

Finding Beta Testers

You will, of course, try to get your friends to use and help test your app, but they're not the best representation of the cross-section of your eventual users.

To some extent, recruiting beta testers is a lot like getting users; it's largely a marketing effort. Before you can ask them if they want to test your app, you have to find them, and they have to find you. Mailing lists (ideally your own) and online forums are good places to find potential beta testers, as are local meet-ups relevant to your app.

Another great way to find beta testers is from the users of one of your existing apps. This is especially true if you're building a new version of an existing app; users of the first version of your app are a very important beta testing cohort for your second version. In order for you to invite users of one version of your app to beta test another one of your apps, you have to have some way of getting a message to them. This could be done either by messaging them inside the existing app or giving them some mechanism to sign up for a mailing list or some other information channel. If you don't have access to such a mechanism now, consider having your developer add one into the app you're currently building, so that it's available to you when you're ready to test your next app.

When asking for volunteers to test your app, give them some information about what the app is and does. They need to be interested in the app to volunteer, and they need to be even more interested in it if they're going to use it and actually give you good feedback about their experiences with it.

It might not be a bad idea to try out the text you are planning on using for marketing copy in the app store here. If no one responds to your email asking for testers, you can be pretty sure the copy isn't persuasive enough for use in the app store.

However, you probably aren't in a position to require your beta testers to sign a nondisclosure agreement (NDA). They're volunteering their time, and the more effort you require of them, the fewer people will want to sign up. Besides, I think NDAs are largely overused. (Refer to Chapter 8, "Interviewing and Selecting a Developer," for more discussion of NDAs.)

You do want to ask your potential external testers what kind of smartphone(s) or tablet(s) they have, and possibly what other apps they've used that could potentially overlap with yours. You need this information because it's important for you to cover a wide range of users.

Getting a Range of Devices and Experience

The most important attribute to seek out in a group of beta testers is diversity. To understand best what issues your users will have, you need feedback from a representative cross-section of your potential user base. External beta testers provide your only chance of getting such a group and thus getting the understanding you need.

Chapter 4, "Determining Your App's Components," talks about deciding what devices and platform versions you wanted your app to run on. Now you need testers (hopefully several) with each one of those devices. There's no way to know beforehand what potential misbehaviors you might find on different devices. And if there's going to be a problem, you'd much rather find it in testing than after you ship.

You also need a range of user experience levels. I find that when I'm testing other people's apps, I tend to offer certain kinds of feedback. It's valuable feedback (or so I've been told), but it tends to be more about performance and implementation suggestions than about the user experience. After years of writing mobile apps, I just don't get confused about user interfaces the way less experienced users do, and I don't tend to do a lot of comparisons with existing, competing apps because my time is limited, and I don't play with every one of the new popular apps the way I used to. (I'm an app developer, an author, and a father in my mid-40s, which isn't all that common a demographic.) A college freshman is going to give you a very different kind of feedback than I will, and if we're both potential users of your app, you're probably going to have more users like the freshman than like me.

One thing that I see often in corporate environments is choosing beta testers from inside the company who aren't likely to be users of the app in the real world. I don't recommend this. On one app project, pretty much all the beta users chosen by the client used Blackberry phones (since they were issued by the corporate IT department) and few of them had actually spent much time with an iPhone or Android phone. I'll just say that their feedback steered the project in a less-than-optimal direction.

Remember that you need to have at least one tester using every device your app will support. If not, you run the risk of some of your users unwittingly being the very first testers of your app on their model of smartphone (or tablet). You do not want to find yourself in that position—especially since, in my experience, the device those unsuspecting users have will be the oldest and slowest device your app can be installed on. That's a recipe for a segment of your users to give you one-star reviews, complaining about performance and crashes because their device is too slow for your app.

Setting Expectations

When signing up external beta testers, it's important to make sure they know what they're expected to do. Otherwise, they're not likely to do what you need them to do. This means you also need to know what they're expected to do. It's funny how that works.

First, you need to get feedback from your testers; if someone tests your app, but you never hear anything back from him or her about it, neither of you should have bothered. Second, you need to be able to contact them. Next, you need them to understand how the app is supposed to work and how they are supposed to use it. You also need to understand what their use case is for the app, so that you can make sure all your use cases are covered by someone. In addition, you need to understand the testers' demographics so that you can make sure all your expected demographic groups are represented. Finally, they need to follow directions (at least to some extent) and at the very least not waste your time complaining about known issues.

Establish a Feedback Mechanism

You need some way for your testers to send requests, complaints, issues, and bugs to you. The simplest way is just to give them an email address where you want the bugs sent. That will work, but it isn't optimal because it requires more effort from your testers than it has to.

The mechanism that will get you the most feedback is an in-app button or gesture that's available throughout the app that lets the user enter comments, feedback, issues, or bugs and tells you who they are, what screen they're on, recent log messages, and other helpful information so they don't have to enter it.

Obviously, creating such a mechanism requires development time, and there's a spectrum of different ways to build a feedback mechanism into your app (hopefully one that will be useful not just for beta testers but for your eventual users, too). Talk to your developer about it. My recommendation is that you don't try to switch to a different feedback mechanism once testing has started, though. If you want one, build it before you start with your external testers and try not to change their workflow too much so that they don't get frustrated and give up.

Document What You Want Testers to Do

You need to give testers a document that explains how to install the app, how to give you feedback, how to use the app, and so on. You've gone through all the trouble of recruiting them. Now go the extra mile and make sure they understand what you want them to do.

Create Useful Release Notes

Each new app version should have a *release notes* document with *areas of attention* and *known issues* sections. An *area of attention* is what you want your testers to focus on testing for each release—usually the last thing or things implemented or fixed, but not necessarily. *Known issues* are things that you know are broken in that beta version but that you didn't want to hold up external testing. Think of them as the testing equivalent of a "wet floor" or "under construction" sign.

Consider Sending Out Surveys

Before each beta cycle (we'll talk about cycles a few sections from now, so don't worry too much about what that means yet), I like to draw up a list of questions that I'm going to want my testers to answer while testing. I send the testers the list of questions at the beginning of the test cycle and ask them to keep those questions in mind. Then at the end of the cycle, I like to send out a survey to all the testers with those questions (and any others I've thought of in the meantime) to collect their feedback. That way, even if they didn't run into any bugs that they felt the need to call to my attention, I at least get some information from them.

Getting and Incorporating Feedback

Feedback makes testing valuable. Do yourself a favor and make a concerted effort to make it easy for your testers to give you their issues and opinions.

I'm often surprised at the lack of effort and lack of follow-up I see companies put forth when trying to get their apps tested, both when I'm doing development for them and when I'm volunteering as a beta tester for an app I'm interested in. Often a company sends out one email saying, "You've been selected as a tester; here's where to get the beta app." Then there's complete silence until the next beta version is released or the app appears in the store.

If you're using testers, keep in contact with them and get feedback from them to make the testing effort worthwhile.

Feedback Infrastructure

In order to make it easy (or at least easier) to get the information you need, a number of pieces of infrastructure are useful, as described in the following sections. You don't have to have all of these, but the more you have, the more actionable information your tests will produce. For more information on these items, see Chapter 5.

Crash Reporting

Apps crash from time to time, especially early in the development process, and each crash happens at a certain place in the code. You need something to capture crashes and inform your developer where each crash came from; without that information, there may be no way to know how to fix a crash.

Usually, you use a web service for crash testing; TestFlight, HockeyApp, Crashlytics, and Crittercism are popular ones at this writing. Alternatively, you can get crash reports by having users plug their devices into their computers and follow a complicated series of steps to extract the data. Of these choices, using a service is of course much easier. Keep in mind that to get any benefit from it at all, you have to settle on one and configure it as part of your app (and your app development workflow) before distributing the app to your testers.

Analytics

Analytics tells you what features your testers are using (and eventually what your end users are using as well). Depending on what you choose to capture (and there are many choices here), you can either get aggregate information or specific workflows for specific individuals at specific times. Analytics is very valuable but often neglected. There are many, many analytics services available.

Log/Console Uploading

Log/console uploading is really a specific kind of analytics that captures the output that your app normally would make to the console of the device. If you and your developer think this is important (and I recommend you do), either make sure your analytics service supports this or get a dedicated log-capturing service as well.

Bug Tracker

Chapter 12 is devoted to bug trackers. You want one. Your professional testers should almost certainly use your bug tracker directly, but how much access you want your external beta testers to have to your bug tracker is an open question (and depends on how much you want to teach your testers about your bug tracker, your developer's wishes, and the licensing agreement of the tool you chose). If you don't end up giving your external testers bug tracker access, someone will need to move issues back and forth between the bug tracker and the testers (maybe via email or maybe some other way).

End-User Feedback Services

A feedback service (sometimes thought of as a customer service portal) is kind of a combination of an online forum and a stripped-down bug tracker. Some of them even integrate with some of the most popular bug trackers. They can be useful both for your testers and for your eventual users. They can get pricy, though.

One of these services can be the primary mechanism that you can use to get feedback, or you can just have the app send email if you don't want to pay for one of them. Just make sure there's an easy way for your testers to get information to you.

Beta Release Cycles

Over the course of your development, you will likely release several different versions of your app to your testers. Each one should have bugs fixes and/or new features added since the previous beta version. Some of them will contain new bugs since the previous beta version, and that's just life (and why we test). There are a number of steps that happen over the course of these cycles. Figure 13.1 shows one example.

Keep your testers informed when new versions are ready. Give them a quick high-level overview of what's changed since the last release and tell them what you'd like them to focus their testing on (especially if you have added or changed a major feature or addressed a large-scale crash or problem). Also include a more detailed summary of what changes were made (and especially what bugs your testers reported were fixed). Not everyone will want to read the longer version, but some will, and some will read just the parts that interest them (like the status of the bugs they've reported).

As noted earlier, I also like to give my testers a set of questions at the beginning of each version release that I ask them to keep in mind while testing, and then I send them a survey before finalizing the next version to get more feedback from them.

Always make sure there's a way for your testers to know which version of the app they are using at any time; also make sure they add that version number (or that it's added for them) on any complaints or comments they send to you.

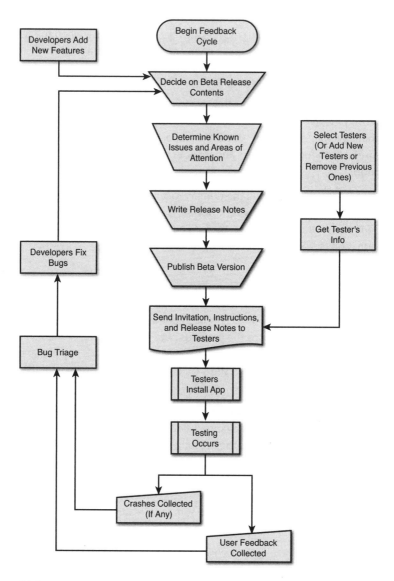

Figure 13.1
An example of the steps that happen during a feedback beta testing cycle.

Bug Triage

Once a bug report comes in from outside the organization (however that happens), one person typically looks at it and decides whether it's a real bug and whether it's a duplicate of a bug that already exists, as well as who should be asked to look at it.

Sometimes this process (called *triage*, after the process used to prioritize battlefield casualties) is done more than once. For example, you might decide it's a development issue and hand it to the lead programmer from your development firm. That lead programmer might then triage the bug himself or herself and decide which programmer on his or her team should fix the bug.

In some instances, the person performing triage is responsible for verifying the priority and severity of the bug, but in other cases that job falls to the developer assigned to fix it. However it happens in your process is fine; just make sure it's consistent and everyone on your team is on the same page about it.

Prioritizing Bugs

All bugs aren't created equal. Some are so important that they have to get worked on as soon as possible. Others can wait until the next version. Some just aren't worth fixing at all.

But although they aren't created equal, many are created from the same cloth. There are a number of common kinds of bugs that are worth pointing out and discussing.

Crash Bugs

Bugs that cause an app to crash are the worst kind of bugs most projects see. The good news about them is that they are so common that there are a lot of crash reporting tools that can help get them resolved reliably.

Between your crash reporting tool; the crash dumps provided by the platform vendor; and the plethora of tutorials, discussions, how-to documents, and vendor guides available, hopefully the crash bugs that occur during your project can be put to rest quickly.

"Roach Motel" Bugs

When I was a kid in the early 1980s, there was a series of commercials on TV with the tag line "Roach Motel: Roaches check in, but they don't check out." The marketing campaign was widely parodied and became part of popular culture.

In mobile development, the phrase "Roach Motel" is sometimes used (in reference to that campaign) to indicate an issue in the navigation controls of the app that allows the user to become stuck on a particular screen, with no way to get out. It happens generally when the programmer fails to cause a button (like the Back button) to appear or fails to program the button to perform the desired function. It normally happens when the programmer is trying to reuse the same screen in multiple places in an app. That reuse requires the screen to be configured differently depending on where in the workflow the screen is currently appearing, and those configurations can get complicated enough that mistakes can occur.

These generally aren't hard bugs to fix once they're found, but they're very frustrating to users, so they deserve a high priority.

Data Loss Bugs

Probably the worst bug is one where the user has data in the app and a bug causes that data to be lost. This is especially true when the data is unrecoverable or would take considerable effort to reproduce. Imagine a camera app that crashes and loses the picture you just took. If you were taking a picture of a landscape or something equally static, it might just be an annoyance; but if you were taking a picture at some event, you might never be able to take that picture of your child's first soccer goal (or whatever) again—and that's inexcusable.

Not all apps include functionality to capture irreproducible data. If yours does, you need to prioritize searching for and fixing of this kind of bug.

Data Consistency Bugs

If your app deals with data, then you might spend a lot of time with data consistency bugs. They include everything from time lines not sorting correctly to the avatar for one user showing up on a post from another user. Any time the data should be filtered or displayed or retrieved or shown one way and for one reason or another it isn't, that's a data consistency bug.

What's most annoying about these bugs is that they are often reproducible only if you have access to the data that was present when the bug was found (not necessarily all the data, but the relevant parts).

Imagine, for example, a screen that sorts users by name but where the developer didn't think about handling the case of two people having the same last name. That bug will never show up until the screen tries to display a list of users that contains two people with the same last name. It's easy to fall into the trap where a tester sees and reports the problem on his or her device, but the developer doesn't see the problem because the developer's data set doesn't contain the data that triggers the bug.

At the very minimum, when this kind of bug appears, you should ask your tester for a screenshot of the bug happening. Hopefully, your developer will be able to figure out the bug from the data being displayed onscreen. However, if your app involves a lot of data manipulations, talk to your developer about creating some mechanism that allows a tester's data to be uploaded or otherwise accessed by the developer. That will help the developer narrow down the source of the issue.

The Case of the Wrong Rollover

I once wrote a piece of server software that, at one point in the code, compared two numbers. But I made a mistake, and I was comparing the two numbers as if they were strings instead of as numbers. As long as the numbers all had the same number of digits, the answer was the same, but once they weren't, the app got the wrong answer. The number 100,000 is sorted after the number 99,999, but the string "100000" is sorted before the string "99999". The program worked fine for more than a year or so, but as soon as the numbers got too big, the bug appeared. That wasn't a bug I could find until it was tested with a data set that contained values with different numbers of digits.

Performance Bugs

Some bugs don't occur because the app doesn't work but because it doesn't work fast enough for the tester's satisfaction. Some of these are unreasonable expectations, and some are real problems.

It's often the case that performance problems are exhibited only on older devices or with certain data sets, which can make them hard to reproduce and fix. It's also often the case that performance bugs can be hard to quantify: The word *slow* means different things to different people.

Whether these bugs are real or imagined, a truly slow app is an app that users won't put up with for long, so you need to treat these bugs seriously. They aren't always the easiest to fix, but there are lots of resources (books, tutorials, and so on) available to you and your developer to help tackle these problems.

Cosmetic Bugs

Sometimes things just don't look right. Whether it's a misspelled word or two fields on the screen whose edges don't line up correctly, apps can generate lots and lots of cosmetic bugs.

Different people (whether they are testers, designers, developers, or app creators) have different thresholds for how important they believe different kinds of cosmetic bugs are. Some people really care about all of them, some care about few, if any, and some are someplace in the middle.

The good news is that each individual cosmetic bug is usually easy (if often tedious) to fix. The bad news is that there can be very many of them. The worse news is that you can waste a lot of time arguing about whether these bugs are worth fixing.

My recommendation is to establish guidelines about what is considered important in your app project's context and try to cut down on the time lost to arguing.

Niche Bugs

Some testers report bugs because they want an app to act in a particular way that they think would be useful for them. To the extent that their suggestions are useful for a large segment of your users, their bugs might be worth working on. I recommend that you avoid implementing every suggestion of every tester, though. Many of them turn out to be a lot of work that benefits only very few users.

However, I believe that it's still worth writing down the testers' suggestions for future reference, even if you don't think they're worth doing now. Over time, you might notice more and more people asking about the same (or similar) things, and you might realize that they're worth doing after all.

Verification of Bugs

Once a developer has resolved a bug, it's customary to inform the tester who reported the bug in the first place and see if the bug is truly resolved to the tester's satisfaction. This makes the tester feel like his or her opinion is valuable and cuts down on the potential misunderstanding between what the tester was trying to report and what the developer thought the tester meant.

It's important, though, to prevent this from turning into an argument between the tester and the developer that takes a lot of time. I've seen bugs reopened dozens of times, and that's just demoralizing on both sides. By (or before) that point, it has become a people problem, not a programming problem, and it needs to be treated as a management issue.

Wrapping Up

This chapter discusses how to test your app. Here are some key points to take away:

- Testing comes in many variations, each with its own focus. To test your app well, you need to perform several different kinds of testing.
- You can test only scenarios that someone thinks of. Try to allow enough time in your schedule for your team to think of them.
- Test early and test often. The last part of your project should be testing, but you shouldn't wait until then to start.
- Professional testers are your best bet for finding really difficult bugs. To find them, look for a good QA department.
- Your developer can also be of help during testing. He or she can write automated tests and force unlikely failure cases that are hard to test otherwise.
- Publishing test versions of your app to external test volunteers is your final line of defense. This works best when your external testers are demographically similar to your target users.
- Getting feedback from your testers is the primary point of testing. Do the extra work and put together the infrastructure to make the most of it.
- Each beta version should come with release notes to facilitate good communication with your testers and keep them updated with the state of the app.
- Bugs should be triaged and prioritized as they come in.
- You should do the testers who reported issues the courtesy of following up with them directly once their bugs have been resolved.

14

Submission and Beyond

So if you've been following along with this book, your idea should have been designed and prototyped; your developer should have been selected, contracted, and managed; and your app should be developed and tested. This means your app project, like this book, should be nearing its end.

Hopefully, you're in pretty good shape at this point, it's been a while since you last tried to add a new feature, and all you've been doing lately is just fixing, testing, and verifying bugs. Hopefully everything has been thoroughly tested. If not, please do another round (or more) of testing and then come back to read the rest of this chapter. Adding features right up until submission day is a recipe for disaster. Just don't do it.

This chapter is about submitting your app to an app store and what to do afterward. While a lot of this chapter (and a lot of this book) applies to many platforms, this chapter gives special attention to the Apple App Store submission process, since it's the most common submission process that requires a review, and getting through the review can be complicated. Google's Play store for Android doesn't require apps to be reviewed before they are published, so that part isn't relevant to apps targeting only targeting that store. Amazon's app store for Android apps and the Windows Store both require app reviews, so some of the review information will be useful for them. Keep in mind that the guidelines change frequently, so some of the specifics may be out of date by the time you read this. Check your app store's relevant guidelines as you near submission time.

Getting Your Marketing Material Together

In order to sell your app (or make it available for free download), you need more than just your app. You also need an entry in the corresponding app store. For that, you need some metadata and information: a title, a description and other marketing copy, an icon (in several different sizes), screenshots, a category, and an age rating. You will probably need other things as well. (I'm not even attempting to make a comprehensive list here because it will be out of date by the time this book goes to print.) Before it's time to submit your app, you'll need to go to your app store of choice and look for its checklist of things you'll need during the submission process. Otherwise, you'll have to stop submission and create the missing pieces and then finish submitting, which may or may not be a big deal, depending on how pressed for time you are. A lot of these items are the same types of things you would traditionally need to launch any app or website commercially; just the avenue for launch and delivery has changed, and the requirements are more explicit.

When creating this metadata, I encourage you to give it some real thought. Many app creators treat this information as an afterthought, and that just isn't helpful.

You may be tempted to feel as though this metadata is just a hurdle between you and getting your app submitted, but it's really critical to your marketing effort. In fact, it's the last piece of the sales funnel when you're getting people to download or buy your app. If your app description or icon isn't enticing, you are giving your potential customer implicit cause to tap Back instead of Buy.

The best resource I know that discusses what's expected of your app store entry is *Pitch Perfect: The Art of Promoting Your App on the Web* by Erica Sadun and Steve Sande (see Figure 14.1).

Another piece of key metadata is the app's category and search keywords. Doing a poor job with these won't just have your potential customer tap Back instead of Buy when on your app's page; it will keep the potential user from ever making it to your app's page in the first place. If they can't find your app, they can't buy it, and if they can't figure out how to search for it, they won't find it. Experiment with running searches in your app store of choice and see if you can figure out what words turn up similar apps and what words users who might want your app would be likely to use. If it doubt, it might be worth looking at popular web search keywords for pages that relate to your app's audience as well.

Figure 14.1
Pitch Perfect contains the best description I've read on what's expected of your app store metadata.

Reviewer Instructions

Something to start thinking about as you get your marketing materials together is whether your app's app store reviewer is going to need any special instructions or access. Remember that the reviewer has never seen your app before and doesn't have all that much time to research it or figure it out. If your app targets a particular population of users, you can't expect that your reviewer is going to be a member of that population.

Your reviewer will read your app's description and category and look at your screenshots, but that's all you can be sure that he or she will know about your app unless you provide more information. An app that's intuitively obvious to all musicians could be very confusing to a reviewer who has never learned how to read music.

When you are filling out the web forms to submit your app, you'll find a section called something like "Reviewer Instructions." This is the place to put extra information that your reviewer might need to know but that your users probably don't. (Write things that both your users and your reviewer need to know in the App Store description field.) Let's now talk through a few potential examples of how this might play out.

Apps That Require Accounts

If your app requires an account, be sure to put the username and password that you want the reviewer to use in the reviewer instructions section. This is true even if an account is required only for certain features; the reviewer might want to test those features, and if you don't give him or her a way to do so, it might be enough to earn you a rejection.

Apps That Require Special Hardware

If your app needs to talk to a special piece of hardware (either one your company sells or one that is generally available [like a Bluetooth Low Energy Heart Rate chest strap] that your app supports), things get a little bit complicated. In some projects I've heard about, Apple has asked for a video showing the app working with the piece of hardware. That's easy enough to provide. Lately, I've heard reports of reviewers requiring the special hardware to be shipped to them. I'm not sure under what circumstances that might be required, but it's something to keep in mind.

Apps That Require Special Locations or Activities

If your app is intended to be used in a specific set of circumstances that don't resemble a reviewer's desk in Silicon Valley, it might be a good idea to include extra instructions and/or a link to a video showing the app in its native environment. For example, if you have a fishing app that's supposed to give you fishing information about the river or lake that your GPS says you are boating over, that's going to be really hard for your reviewer to test. He or she is unlikely to take a fishing trip just to review your app.

There's a useful app for your Mac or a Windows PC called Reflector, from a company called Squirrels (airsquirrels.com). It lets you mirror your recent iPhone or iPad screen onto your desktop or laptop. I use it and screen-recording software to capture a video of what my iOS app is doing (either for reviewers or for marketing to users). There may be other apps that do this as well that you might be able to discover with a quick web search, but Reflector is the only one I've seen to date.

Last-Minute Plea for Sanity

Once you've created all your marketing copy for the app store, uploaded your screenshots, and built your executable, the urge to just push the button and submit your app can be overwhelming. I know. I've been there. It's especially true if you are resubmitting an app that was rejected. (I talk more about this later in the chapter.) Despite that feeling, I strongly recommend that you take a deep breath and go over everything one more time before making the submission. If you make a mistake and your app gets rejected (or, potentially worse, gets through and releases with a fatally obnoxious bug in it), you'll wish you had taken a little more time.

At the very least, you should resist the urge to make any supposedly quick changes right before submitting your app. If you do need to make changes, test them before uploading. I've seen several cases of apps crashing during review because of last-minute changes. I've even been responsible for causing that to happen myself. (In that case I "fixed" what the compiler reported as a potential memory leak right before I submitted, but my change introduced a crash that happened when the reviewer left a screen and then went right back to it.)

Remember that, at least with the Apple App Store, it can take a week or two for your review to start. If you get rejected, you must start the waiting process again. Getting rejected and having to wait an extra week for something trivial that you could or should have caught easily is demoralizing (and can throw off a strategically planned launch date). I've seen it happen several miserable times.

This is the point where the Android developers start to feel smug because they don't have to go through the waiting period. However, that's not always a good thing. Granted, there are times that Apple rejects apps for aesthetic or policy reasons that are arguably not in the developer's best interest, but the majority of the rejections I've seen have been for legitimate bugs that would have caused users real problems. Not having that extra double-checking of your testing effort isn't always a good thing. If those bugs make it out to the wild, they can upset your users, and some of them will never give you a second chance.

The Case of the Fatal Optimization

Back in 2011, there was a bug in Xcode 4.0.1 with LLVM 2.0. The optimizer would generate app packages that crashed immediately on an ARMv6 processor (like the iPhone 3G) but worked fine on an ARMv7 processor (like the iPhone 3GS).

The key word there is *optimizer*. You see, the way Xcode worked at the time (and likely still does) was that apps built for Debugging had optimization turned off, and only apps built for Release ran the optimizer.

And so it was that I built an app for a client and tested it on all the different pieces of hardware I had available to me—but only with Debugging turned on. (After all, if any bugs turned up during that testing, I wanted to be able to figure out what was wrong.) Then I created the Release build to go to the store, and I did one last sanity check with my iPhone 4, but I didn't bother to test it with my old iPhone 3G.

Apple's app reviewers also apparently only checked it with an iPhone 4 (or some other ARMv7 device) because they approved it. And the app got into the store. And all Hell broke loose.

This wasn't a new app; it was an updated version of an existing app that I had written for that client. I had taken an app that worked fine and, in the process of fixing a couple bugs and adding a couple new features, had rendered it utterly unusable for a substantial fraction of the app's existing users. Everyone with older devices who downloaded the update had the app crash immediately when they tried to start it. They couldn't run the app, couldn't see their data, and couldn't get to the feedback address in the app to let us know. So they turned to the App Store review process. In droves.

Within a few minutes of seeing one of the bad reviews, I installed the shipping version of the app onto my iPhone 3G and found the problem. A quick web search told me I wasn't alone, but that was small consolation. I turned off the optimization and resubmitted, but it was days before the new version got through the process, and some users never got over it (although, thankfully, my client eventually did).

It was Apple's bug, and arguably Apple's fault, but the users didn't care. And, ultimately, the decision to release without testing the final version on older hardware was mine, as was the ultimate blame.

I'm now far more careful about pushing the submit button. I've learned the hard way how necessary it is to be absolutely sure before you pull that trigger. I urge you to learn from my past mistakes rather than emulate them. In fact, my normal process now is to do my final testing and get everything into place and then wait overnight before I actually submit, just in case I think of anything else.

Pushing the Button

So you've hopefully done your last-minute testing, made no last-minute changes, and maybe even waited overnight. It's finally time to submit your app.

It's certainly possible for you to have your developer submit the app for you, using your developer credentials. However, I encourage you to do the submission yourself, or at the very least sit with your developer when he or she does it. Your developer (assuming that you contracted him or her for the duration of the project) is likely to leave you soon to go build an app for another client, and you need to know your way around the app submission process in case you need to make changes without that person.

The actual submission process isn't normally very difficult—and it's gotten a lot easier over time. You basically have to go through lots of checklists and follow a lot of prompts and instructions. It is likely to be confusing from time to time. Submission doesn't happen very often, which means the vendors don't get a competitive advantage by having a better app submission process, which in turn means it's not a process they put a lot of effort into making seamless.

If you have a real problem with submission, it's likely to be a code-signing problem, and getting help with that from your developer (or an online tutorial) is perfectly reasonable. Code signing is fundamentally a security measure, and security and convenience are often polar opposites.

I'm not going to walk you through the checklists here. There are plenty of online tutorials that will stay more up to date than the content of this book. Your developer can likely point you toward a good one.

I do want to draw your attention to one part of the process, though. You'll have to answer a question about your app (at least in the Apple ecosystem): Do you want the app to be released as soon as the review is done, or do you want to wait? Waiting gives you the ability to give specific people access to your app to write reviews before your public launch. (See the *Pitch Perfect* book I mentioned previously for more details.)

I often recommend that people who need an app in the store by a hard deadline (to coincide with some external event) submit an early version of their app to Apple to make sure they have something that they can release if they run into review problems; they should have that version held from public view. Then they can submit the more polished version later, knowing that they have a fallback plan if something goes wrong.

Dealing with Rejection

Rejection happens, even to good apps and good people. If it happens to you, try not to take it personally. Some rejections are straightforward and even useful. Some are subjective and less useful. Some (in my experience, not many but definitely some) seem outright unfair. Rejection is a fact of life, and you should try not to get too upset about it if it happens to you.

Rejection Correspondence Often Lacks Specifics

One thing that's annoying and often unhelpful is the way an app may be rejected. In general, when I've gotten a rejection, the rejection has indicated the section of Apple's guidelines that the reviewer believes the app violated and very little information about how, exactly, that violation came about. There's often very little detail. If you get such a rejection, you may end up needing to guess about what exactly needs to be fixed. If you aren't reasonably sure, it's okay to ask; there's a form on the web where you can interact with your reviewer once a rejection has happened. As when you're opening bugs, as discussed in Chapter 12, "Communicating Using Bugs," you should try to word your question in such a way that the reviewer won't take it as an insult. Like developers, most reviewers aren't going to get upset at you, but you never know which ones might, and it's better to be safe than sorry.

Once you understand what has happened with your app during the review process, it's time to figure out what to do about it.

The Case of the Missed Opportunity

A couple years ago, I was lucky enough to get a ticket to Apple's Worldwide Developers Conference (WWDC) before it sold out (although I haven't been so lucky since). At the time, I was working on a Mac app that was a developer tool with a fairly complicated workflow that was in the Mac App Store. I discovered that there are App Store reviewers (and their supervisors) at WWDC, and you can talk to them and ask them about specific issues.

WWDC is a fantastic place to connect with Apple employees and get real answers to your real questions (which I think is why Apple keeps enrollment capped). There are labs where you can get an Apple developer to look at your code and give you advice, and there are lines that can last for hours to talk to developers in specific areas.

Oddly enough, however, I never ended up having to wait to talk to someone on the App Store review team, despite the fact that I went back several times over the course of the week I was there. For some reason, even with as much complaining as you hear about the App Store review process, developers attending the conference didn't take the time to talk to the reviewers.

What I found in those reviewers was a group of conscientious folks who really seemed to care about me, my app, my customers (and potential customers), and the App Store itself. I didn't meet anyone who seemed arbitrary or unreasonable, and I certainly didn't meet anyone deserving of the personal attacks I see on forum threads about apps being rejected.

Think about what the reviewers face. One issue is the sheer volume of apps being submitted for review. It's so huge that it's very difficult for the reviewers to keep up. See Figure 14.2 for an illustration of the number of apps in the store. It's really hard to keep up with this kind of growth. Some people have told me that Apple should just spend more money and hire more people. Those people have never tried to maintain that kind of hiring pace while maintaining consistent and quality work. It's very difficult.

The second problem is that a very large number of the apps that are submitted are just bad. The reviewers couldn't give me percentages or anything (if they even had calculated them), but the impression I got was that a substantial fraction of submissions are unprofessional and of poor quality. That makes their job even harder.

So based on my experience, I stopped thinking of reviewers as capricious and started thinking of them as harried. That did wonders for my attitude when dealing with rejection (and changed my mindset while I prepared for submission, which seems to have cut down on the number of rejections I get). I recommend that you try that perspective and see if it helps.

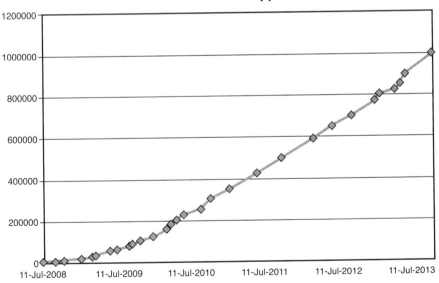

Figure 14.2
Chart of the number of apps available in the Apple iOS App Store (see http://en.wikipedia.org/wiki/App_Store_(iOS)#Number_of_launched_applications). Note that this is the total number of apps approved, not submitted, and it doesn't count updates to existing apps.

Crash/Debugging Rejection

Sometimes the report from a reviewer says that your app crashed or that some other bug was found. You need to treat this kind of problem like a high-priority bug. Get it fixed and resubmitted.

Offline Mode Failure Rejection

Offline mode failure rejection is a fairly straightforward rejection. If your app uses the network but doesn't behave intelligently when the device has no network connection (that is, when in Airplane mode), the app is automatically rejected. Your developer needs to use an Apple library called Reachability to handle this case.

File System Mismanagement Rejection

Apple is picky about where files are allowed to be stored. If you get a file system mismanagement rejection, it should be relatively straightforward to have your developer look up the rules and fix the code and resubmit. The only trick is that Apple reserves the right to delete data that you downloaded from the Internet if the user's disk starts to fill up. Apple does this on the assumption that you can download it again if you have to. You might need to double-check with your developer that the subsequent downloads will be initiated correctly in the event that Apple needs to delete that data.

Copyright Misuse Rejection

Apple is also very picky about what images and names you use. Make sure that you can back up your right to use any graphics or names that you include in your app. Also, if you use graphics that look even somewhat like Apple's built-in graphics, make sure you use them only in the same way that Apple uses those graphics.

The Case of Third Time's a Failure

The third time I submitted one of my apps, it was rejected for containing a silver plus sign in a blue circle. Although I had not used Apple's "add contact" button, I had a button in my app that contained an element that used the same color scheme. I was told to remove the "Apple copyrighted image" and resubmit.

The thing was, the app had already been in the store for months with the offending plus sign, and it had already passed app review twice before. But it turns out that a previous approval is no guarantee of future approval.

It's annoying, but, at least in my opinion, it's not an undue price to pay for access to Apple's customer base. As someone who has tried to make a living selling shareware from my own website in the distant past, it's a bargain I'm willing to make.

And changing the graphic wasn't too much work—at least once I talked myself out of being offended long enough to open my image editor.

Couldn't Verify Claim Rejection

Reviewers seem to want to test at least most of the claims that you put in the app store description when you submitted an app. So if there's something that would be difficult for them to test, think long and hard before you decide to put it in your app's description—especially if it's not likely to be a big draw for new users. It might just not be worth the rejection risk.

When you get to the point where you are submitting updates to your app to the App Store, the same rules apply. Anything that you put in the "what's new" section for the new update that is specific enough for a reviewer to verify becomes one more potential reason for the reviewer to reject your app. That makes the standard, vague "bug fixes and performance improvements" description very safe (if unhelpful) verbiage for your update.

Private API Use Rejection

Apple documents certain APIs that you are allowed to use. Any undocumented Apple API that you find and use will get your app rejected. Sometimes this is a mismatch. Apple tests this by looking at strings, and your developer might have inadvertently picked a method named the same as an Apple secret method, in which case you should just have the developer change the name.

The other time this can pop up is when you are using a third-party library that uses a private API. If that's the case, you need to stop using that library or get a fix from the third party. This is a particularly annoying consequence of using poor-quality third-party code.

Metadata Rejection

You get a metadata rejection when the app you submitted is fine, but the description (or other metadata) you submitted isn't okay with Apple. Usually, this means that you're using a bad word in your description—either profanity, the copyrighted name of a competitor, something under Apple NDA, or the like. This is easy to fix: Just change the wording. Usually, this type of rejection doesn't even slow down the process much.

Resubmission

A lot of people expect to go through a different process to resubmit their app than they went through to submit it the first time. But submitting your fixed app after rejection is pretty much the same process as submitting it the first time. You might need to add additional reviewer instructions to explain what you changed and why, but there isn't a whole different workflow or anything.

Launch

Hopefully after you (re)submit your app, some time will pass and then you'll get an email saying that your app is ready for sale (or ready for you to release it for sale, if you opted for a manual release process). Take some time to celebrate because soon you'll be able to see what the world thinks of your app.

Getting Feedback

No app is perfect, not even yours. Perfect, in fact, isn't possible. One user might think a feature doesn't go far enough, and another user might see it as unnecessary. As long as there are multiple users, there will be multiple opinions. However, not all feedback from users is subject to opinion. Some apps have real bugs that have to be fixed.

But whether the feedback you receive is positive, negative, appreciative, derogatory, a matter of some other opinion, or indicative of a required bug fix on your part, it's your primary source of communication with your user community. How you handle feedback can affect the overall success or failure of your app.

Crash Reports

Once your app ships, at least in Apple's iOS ecosystem, you receive an additional source of crash reports. As users experience crashes in the field, those crash reports are copied up to Apple's servers, where they are aggregated and made available for you to download via your app's dashboard.

In my experience, though, not every crash report shows up in the portal. I don't know whether that's because most users don't opt in to crash reports being uploaded or because normal users rarely sync their phones or because Apple shows you only the common crashes. What I do know is that every time I've had an app in the wild with crash reporting built into it (via a tool, as discussed in Chapter 5, "Finding the Right Tools"), I've seen many more crashes via the reporting tool than via Apple's portal.

So just because you aren't seeing crash reports in Apple's portal doesn't mean they aren't happening, and you might want to consider leaving your crash-reporting tool enabled even after you ship to the app store.

Reviews

Another way you get feedback from users (regardless of where your app is published) is via app reviews. Although good reviews help potential customers decide whether to make a purchasing decision, they aren't ideal from the developer's point of view. Figure 14.3 shows one such review, although it's not one that's actionable.

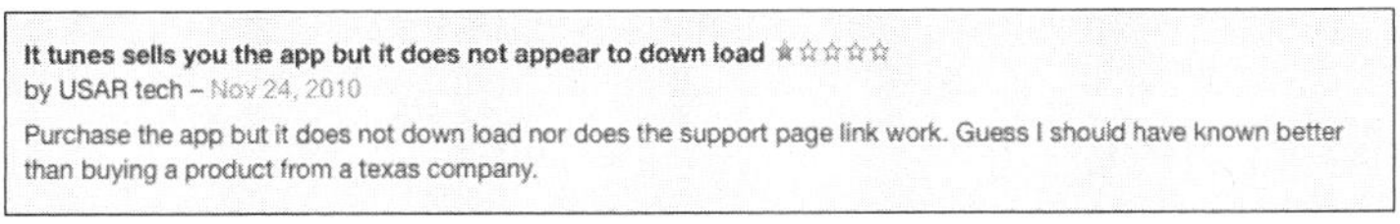

It tunes sells you the app but it does not appear to down load ★ ☆ ☆ ☆ ☆
by USAR tech – Nov 24, 2010
Purchase the app but it does not down load nor does the support page link work. Guess I should have known better than buying a product from a texas company.

Figure 14.3
A less-than-helpful app review. Note that the downloading and installation of the app is outside the app creator's (that is, your) control, so this can't be the app creator's (that is, your) fault. Yet the review is on your app's page. C'est la vie.

Many reviews are like the one in Figure 14.3. The user is upset about something that you can't control or can't reproduce. Such reviews are unpleasant, but your only real recourse is to try not to let them upset you. Remember that you went to all the trouble and effort of creating an app, and all the reviewer did was whine on the Internet. That person's opinion shouldn't be given the same weight as all your months of work. (For the record, the answers to your unspoken questions are "Yes, I really do tell myself that when I get bad reviews" and "No, it doesn't really help that much, and I still get my feelings hurt.")

Some app stores (notably Google Play) allow an app's developer to reply to reviews. I've seen very few instances where replying to negative reviews has made things better, and I've seen quite a few that have made things worse. Your mileage may vary, though, but if that option is available, proceed with caution.

One problem with review systems is that they are an impersonal communication medium that doesn't allow for rapport or a real conversation between people. That makes them often unhelpful to you. So I recommend trying to make it as easy as possible for users with feedback to get it to you outside the review system.

Contact from Users

As discussed in Chapter 13, "Testing," building a feedback infrastructure and making it easy for users to contact you greatly increases the quantity and quality of feedback you get. That's just as true with customers as with testers.

Having a feedback mechanism in place does seem to reduce bad reviews and makes people feel heard (at least in my experience). It can also take a lot of your time and put you in the unpleasant position of telling people that you aren't going to implement their feature requests.

It's up to you do decide if you'd rather let people default to the review system or push them toward another solution.

The Next Release

Just as no app is ever truly perfect, no app is every truly complete. It's not at all unusual to need to push out a new release within a few days of getting into the store in order to fix some bugs that your users have found but your testers didn't.

The problem is that most app creators contract their development team only until the project is done, and when they need to push a bug fix into the app store, the developer has already moved on. I recommend that you have a conversation with your developer about this as the project starts to near completion and see what you can work out. The good news is that a fast follow-on bug fix release doesn't require nearly as many developers or as much development time as the initial programming, so your developer might be able to squeeze you in.

Then there's the next set of features you might want to add. Depending on your budget, your marketing, and how the app has been received, you may or may not be ready to start on the next set of features right away. If you are planning on making your next version soon, you probably want to see if you can keep the same developer (assuming that you were happy with him or her). If not, it's time to head back to Chapter 7, "Finding a Developer," and start your developer search anew.

The Red Queen's Race

In Lewis Carroll's *Through the Looking Glass*, the Red Queen exclaims, "Now, here, you see, it takes all the running you can do, to keep in the same place." Sometimes the app store can give you that feeling. Even if you don't want to add new features, your app that you and your users were satisfied with last month might become a buggy loser. This happens because the app ecosystem itself doesn't sit still.

As platform vendors release new smartphones and new tablets with new operating systems and new features, the things that used to be cool are taken for granted and the things that used to be acceptable become hopelessly outdated.

Screen sizes change, tastes change, performance improves, new capabilities become available, and you can either choose to take advantage of it or not. It's a competitive world out there, and if your app is going to stay competitive, you need to revisit it and tweak it from time to time.

Hopefully, if you did your job well the first time and kept the artifacts like source control and bug-tracker data from your first version, the second go-round won't be too bad.

Wrapping Up

This chapter discusses submission of your app and what to do next. Here are some key points to take away:

- You need to create a lot of metadata—marketing copy, screenshots, and the like—before you can submit your app. Get this stuff together before you sit down to do your submission so you don't get frustrated and have to go back to get them.
- Put some effort into the metadata. Treat it like important marketing material, not an afterthought.
- Don't make last-minute changes before you submit your app.
- Giving your app store reviewer the proper instructions will help reduce your chance of rejection.
- If your app is rejected, don't panic. It's nothing personal, and it happens to the best of us. Just figure out how to fix what needs to be fixed, resubmit the app, and go on with your life.

- As with testing, having a good infrastructure makes getting feedback from users easier. And it can reduce the number of bad reviews you get on app stores.

- It might be worth talking your developer into sticking around long enough to do any needed quick bug fixes soon after launch, but you need to have the conversation about it early in the project.

- Remember that apps need to be updated periodically to stay current as new smartphones, tablets, and mobile operating system updates are released.

Index

Q–R

S

U

CARL BROWN

App
Accomplished

Strategies for App
Development Success

Foreword by Kyle Richter, CEO, MartianCraft

FREE
Online Edition

Your purchase of *App Accomplished* includes access to a free online edition for 45 days through the **Safari Books Online** subscription service. Nearly every Addison-Wesley Professional book is available online through **Safari Books Online**, along with thousands of books and videos from publishers such as Cisco Press, Exam Cram, IBM Press, O'Reilly Media, Prentice Hall, Que, and Sams.

Safari Books Online is a digital library providing searchable, on-demand access to thousands of technology, digital media, and professional development books and videos from leading publishers. With one monthly or yearly subscription price, you get unlimited access to learning tools and information on topics including mobile app and software development, tips and tricks on using your favorite gadgets, networking, project management, graphic design, and much more.

Activate your FREE Online Edition at
informit.com/safarifree

STEP 1: Enter the coupon code: VUDDIWH.

STEP 2: New Safari users, complete the brief registration form.
Safari subscribers, just log in.

If you have difficulty registering on Safari or accessing the online edition,
please e-mail customer-service@safaribooksonline.com